Autism and Spirituality

by the same author

Autism and the Edges of the Known World
Sensitivities, Language and Constructed Reality
ISBN 978 1 84905 042 5
eISBN 978 0 85700 239 6

Sensory Perceptual Issues in Autism and Asperger Syndrome
Different Sensory Experiences – Different Perceptual Worlds
Forewords by Wendy Lawson and Theo Peeters
ISBN 978 1 84310 166 6
eISBN 978 1 84642 410 6

Communication Issues in Autism and Asperger Syndrome
Do we speak the same language?
ISBN 978 1 84310 267 0
eISBN 978 1 84642 002 3

Theory of Mind and the Triad of Perspectives
on Autism and Asperger Syndrome
A View from the Bridge
ISBN 978 1 84310 361 5
eISBN 978 1 84642 251 5

Autism and Spirituality

Psyche, Self and Spirit in People on the Autism Spectrum

Olga Bogdashina

Forewords by Christine Trevett and Larry Culliford
Afterword by Nancy Getty

Jessica Kingsley *Publishers*
London and Philadelphia

First published in 2013
by Jessica Kingsley Publishers
116 Pentonville Road
London N1 9JB, UK
and
400 Market Street, Suite 400
Philadelphia, PA 19106, USA

www.jkp.com

Library of Congress Cataloging in Publication Data
Bogdashina, Olga.
  Autism and spirituality : psyche, self, and spirit in people on the autism spectrum /
Olga Bogdashina ; foreword by Christine Trevett.
    pages cm
  Includes bibliographical references and index.
  ISBN 978-1-84905-285-6 (alk. paper)
  1. People with mental disabilities--Religious life. 2. Autism spectrum disorders--
Religious aspects. I. Title.
  BL625.9.P46B64 2013
  200.87'5--dc23
                              2013003928

British Library Cataloguing in Publication Data
A CIP catalogue record for this book is available from the British Library

ISBN 978 1 84905 285 6
eISBN 978 0 85700 591 5

Printed and bound in Great Britain by Bell & Bain Ltd, Glasgow

To my children, Alyosha and Olesya

Contents

Foreword

There are some words that are 'slippery' as well as much debated. If a list of such words were to be compiled then both 'spirituality' and 'self' might well appear towards the top. In this book the *mysterium tremendum*, with which religion/spirituality is associated, intersects with the perceived 'mysteriousness' of autism. To a great extent autism remains a mystery to the majority 'neurotypical' population.

In our world there is very often a failure to engage with, or to understand, the one who is somewhere 'on the spectrum' of autistic conditions. Individuals, institutions and societies nevertheless attribute meaning to that person and to his or her behaviour and mode of communication (or seeming non-communication). They may tend to pathologise what is not understood and, given autistic 'difference' in areas such as cognition, language development and sensory perception, a further tendency is towards assuming that any learning process must be one way. By contrast, in this book the possibility is raised that there might be things for the rest of us to learn from autistic experience: from people of 'thin boundaries', people who by the nature of their autism may be seeing/hearing/feeling *more* and differently and who may also have a strong sense of justice and of right and wrong. Olga Bogdashina allows this, though the language of feeling and of intuition, she acknowledges, has not been transferred regularly into scientists' analyses nor into a large body of research.

The author has reflected deeply on autism, and on the challenges and insights it offers, in a number of previous publications. In the present book there is a weaving of statements by those who know (i.e. by autistic writers) through chapters concerned with definitions and overviews of thinking about psyche, self and spirituality. The book is not about the spirituality of individual autistic persons but rather Olga

Bogdashina is daring to try to chart a way through big and contested subjects. How has *self* been understood? What has *spirituality* been taken to mean, or *spiritual development?* Where on the spectrum of various theories and interpretations of these things might an autistic person (though not every autistic person) be located? Indeed what is autism like and how might what we learn of autistic understanding and experience shed light on spirituality more generally?

Autism and Spirituality is a work that Olga Bogdashina has had in mind for some time (see Bogdashina 2010, p.13). Its author emerged from the cocoon of Soviet 'scientific atheism' to recognise and acknowledge the importance of spirituality in the lives of others. Through her wide range of professional and personal contact with autistic people and their families she has also come to know that it figures in the lives of many of them also.

Christine Trevett
Emeritus Professor, Cardiff University

Foreword

There are two kinds of knowledge. Science is material knowledge, about the world and the universe. Wisdom is sacred knowledge, about who we truly are, and about how to be and behave for the best. Learning – and teaching each other – how to grow in wisdom, I want to suggest, is a vital aspect of all vocational endeavours. There is more to exemplary medical and nursing practice, for example, than simply gaining scientific knowledge and accomplishment.

When, many years ago, I was training to become a psychiatrist, a wise man (who happened to be a Buddhist monk) gave me some good advice. A few of my patients were causing me concern because their illnesses had not responded to prolonged and extensive treatment. They were simply given accommodation within the mental hospital, where they stayed indefinitely for their own protection and for the safety of others.

I found the plight of one man particularly distressing. Often tearful and crying for help, he seemed to be in almost perpetual torment. When I spoke of him, the monk helped me see that the pain I first had to deal with was my own. He explained that the reason for my discomfort was that I cared. Compassion is innate, he said. It may be dulled. We can try to ignore it, but we have no powers to switch it off altogether.

Compassion means 'suffering with' people; so it must hurt if it is to be genuine. Questioning what could be done in this situation, I was told that, instead of thinking we must always help by giving something, a remedy of some kind, it is better on occasion to think of taking something too, in the sense of letting the person inform you about yourself… About your compassion and the accompanying distress, and about your need to learn how better to manage it. In other words, the wise man said, 'You must let your patients, and those you encounter who suffer, from time to time be your teachers.'

And that is what Olga Bogdashina is also saying to us in this remarkable book. In order to write it, fully cognisant of all the relevant literature on autism, she has similarly let her patients (and her own autistic child) be her principal teachers. Her message is that autistic people experience the world in a way that serves well to remind us of the importance of an often disregarded spiritual dimension in our lives.

She writes, 'Spirituality plays a significant role in the lives of many autistic individuals and their families... [It] can be a powerful element that will help autistic individuals and their families to overcome their difficulties and find meaning in their lives.'

Part of her explanation is that, 'What can be detected by some autistic people would not necessarily be noticed by the majority... Some autistic individuals' senses are very acute...' While admitting that not *every* person with autism displays this degree of hyper-awareness, Bogdashina reports, 'What makes autistic individuals more open to spiritual experiences is their sensitivities: sensory, emotional, cognitive and spiritual – all caused by fundamental differences in their neurobiological development.'

We are told that, most of the time, so-called 'normal' people know only what comes into their reduced awareness (which is further consecrated as genuinely real by concepts and language). In autism, contrariwise, there are no sieves or filters to stop the flooding of information, which then seems to accumulate in a kind of 'preconscious system'. Taking in information with the conscious ego-self 'absent' from the process, and storing it in a pre-conscious reservoir, they sometimes surprise not only those around them, but themselves too, by expressing knowledge they never thought they had. It has the quality of 'unknown knowing', and so is comparable to fruits of the contemplative methodology of many mystical traditions, and the practice in particular of meditation, aimed at the acquisition of wisdom.

Comparing people on the autistic spectrum with children (and even animals), Olga Bogdashina quotes Stillman (2006), who says '[They] often perceive spiritual experiences only because they haven't yet been conditioned *not to*'; helpfully adding, 'The person with autism may simply not be fully cognizant of her very special gift, and may assume *everyone* communicates this way.'

Pioneers like William James, Pierre Teilhard de Chardin, Carl Jung, Aldous Huxley and Evelyn Underhill; and more recent authorities like James Fowler, David Fontana, John Swinton and Victor Schermer; have all pointed towards a new paradigm for psychology that insists on the inclusion of a spiritual dimension if it is to make sense. Organizations like the Spirituality and Psychiatry 'Special Interest Group' of the Royal

College of Psychiatrists, and the British Association for the Study of Spirituality (BASS), have been taking this paradigm forward, beginning not simply to make it work, but to render it increasingly indispensable.

A renewed emphasis is involved on the basic human capacity for what may be called 'spiritual awareness', a faculty common in childhood that does not depend on any type of religious instruction, practices or beliefs. This bold new paradigm depends rather on a kind of holistic vision, one that comprehensively unmasks the illusion of so-called 'objectivity' on which the earlier, scientific paradigm has been constructed.

Objectivity works well for investigating the physical and biological dimensions, but has only partial value where psychology and the social sciences are concerned. It now becomes necessary for people to engage themselves fully – therefore subjectively too – in the processes of discovery. Those who see this, and choose to explore further, soon discover the need to *do the experiment* for themselves, to examine their own personal spirituality and recognise it as involving a kind of journey – sometimes difficult – towards greater maturity and wisdom, opening themselves up, perhaps painfully, to the innate wealth of their compassion.

As dormant powers of spiritual awareness are awakened and kindled, part of that journey will involve the discovery of something greater than ourselves that touches us deeply within, becoming a trusted and valued source of guidance, inner strength, courage and hope, especially in times of adversity.

For people on this journey (and ultimately, of course, this means everyone), autistic people, in contrast to being seen as disabled and burdensome, can be seen rather as offering unique, rare and special learning experiences, not only about themselves and how best to get along with them, but also about ourselves, about aspects of our truer, deeper natures that we may well – individually and collectively – have been neglecting.

Page by page, chapter by chapter, Olga Bogdashina shows us what precious fellow travellers on life's often difficult and perplexing but ultimately rewarding journey people with autism may be. We are truly wise to take them as our teachers.

There are two kinds of knowledge, science and wisdom. This book offers an exemplary synthesis of them both. Giving thanks to the author, I recommend engaging with her gift to us in these pages without delay and as fully as you know how.

Larry Culliford
Author of The Psychology of Spirituality: An Introduction

Acknowledgements

I was encouraged and inspired to write about spirituality and autism as part of the ASPARRG academic network (Autism Spectrum People and Religion Research Group) and I want to thank everyone in it for stimulating my interest in this fascinating subject.

My gratitude goes to the autistic individuals who are willing to share their experiences and ideas in order to educate us all about the diversity of human thinking and ways to perceive the world around us.

I would like to thank the members of an inspirational (online) group of individuals who have shared their unique insight into the capabilities and diversities of autism spectrum disorder (ASD). Feeling that I am a member of this community inspires me to continue to research and discover the different parallels and concepts associated with societal differences. Special thanks go to Mar, Diny, Nancy, Teun and Andrea for their willingness to discuss very unconventional subjects that have enlightened all the participants of these discussions.

The book would not have been written if it were not for my children, Alyosha and Olesya, and my closest friends Lucy and Peter, whose support (and patience) has helped me to complete this book.

And of course, I'd love to thank my publisher, Jessica Kingsley, and all the staff at JKP who were very supportive of this project. This book benefited greatly from the skills of my production editor, Victoria Peters, and copyeditor, Helen Kemp. However, the shortcomings, whatever they may be, remain my responsibility.

Introduction

From the very beginning of human history, at the centre of human life was Man himself. While attempting to understand the world around him, to survive and adapt to it, the meaning of life has always been at the top of the agenda. In whichever era humans may live, some representatives of *Homo sapiens* whom we would call today 'highly intelligent people' (not necessarily possessing paper qualifications, but rather those who are seeking enlightenment and educating themselves in the process) look for answers to very important questions. Sometimes they have to answer them several times in the course of their life, as their circumstances change and they have to adjust their lives to new conditions, making important choices. The first question is: How can I survive, and help my family survive? When the question of survival has been answered, other (more difficult) questions emerge: How shall I live in this world with others (both human and non-human)? And how shall I live with myself (my Self)? Every five to seven years, each and every one of us experiences a crisis, so we have to change our worldview and at the same time relocate and re-evaluate our place in the world (What do I want from this life? Where is my place in this life?).

For example, a baby growing into a toddler can feel as if she were the centre of the universe, with all the people around her admiring her every movement, word and smile, meeting all her needs and fulfilling every wish. Then she goes to school and, what a surprise, there are 30 or 40 centres of the universe in one classroom! The child has to adapt, change the worldview and find her place in this new 'cosmos' where many other 'stars' are choosing their orbits. When at school, our basic needs are met by our parents and other adults, but after the final year exams more adaptations are expected from us, and the decision 'now what?' must be made. Still more adaptations and re-evaluations come with career choices and starting families. And so on and so forth.

While some are too busy building their cosy nests and restructuring their lives aiming to get 'to the top' (whatever they think the 'top' represents), there are others who keep looking for answers to questions like What am I? Why am I here, on this earth? What is the meaning of life in general, and my life in particular? and a more difficult question: How shall I live my life in this world if there is God? Or an even harder one: How shall I live my life if there isn't?

Many great philosophers and thinkers of the past and present have struggled with the answers but never abandoned the questions. One of my favourite authors is the great Russian writer of the end of the nineteenth century, Fyodor Mikhailovich Dostoevsky. He created a character representing one of the 'highly intelligent people' seeking answers to the most important questions – Prince Lev Nikolaevich Myshkin, whom the author endowed with Christ-like spiritual attributes and a child-like naive and innocent belief in the possibility of achieving heaven on earth. Myshkin can be seen as a Russian 'Holy Fool', hence the title of the novel: *The Idiot*. (Interestingly, many characteristics of Prince Myshkin correspond to the 'symptoms' of ASD.)[1] The majority of critics in the West consider this novel as one of Dostoevsky's weakest works, some complaining that the 'good' prince makes everyone's life harder and achieves nothing. For me, *The Idiot* is a masterpiece, along with Dostoevsky's other novels, such as *The Brothers Karamazov, Demons* and *Crime and Punishment*.[2] What critics do not take into account is that *The Idiot* was never supposed to be a fairy tale with a happy-ever-after ending. It is a tragic story, and the tragedy is not that the character 'achieves nothing', but rather that the world is not ready for him. Here we can see a clear parallel with autism – as Jim Sinclair (1993, p.4) expresses it powerfully in his classic essay 'Don't mourn for us': 'The tragedy is not that we're here, but that your world has no place for us to be.' Prince Myshkin is a tragic figure not because of his intuitive feelings and moral attitudes – allowing him not only to see but actually feel the cruelty people around him inflict on each other, and come to the rescue of those who have been wronged (even if only with comforting words and understanding), but because in a world where belief in God is replaced with 'belief in nil' (for Dostoevsky, atheism is a faith – faith in nothing), amorality flourishes, and Prince Myshkin, with his virtues and principles, living his life of honesty and humility, becomes an 'idiot'.

Another favourite of mine, the French philosopher Henri Bergson, claimed that there are at least two types of purpose of life: practical and spiritual ones. On the one hand, humans have to deal with everyday objects and notions to make their life functional and protected from outside dangers. On the other hand, they have their own self-consciousness and spiritual existence to consider. Bergson urged people not to be satisfied with any purely naturalistic interpretation of mental life but rather to understand the qualities and abilities within themselves, which shifts the focus from interpretations of the impressions of the external world and applying them to satisfy bodily and practical needs to the recognition of the spiritual value of the human nature, of a personality, capable of obtaining the understanding of the life of the spirit, with needs beyond bodily and intellectual satisfaction:

> The man who seeks merely bodily satisfaction lives the life of the animal; even the man who poses as an intellectual finds himself entangled ultimately in relativity, missing the uniqueness of all things – his own life included. An intuitive philosophy introduces us to the spiritual life and makes us conscious, individually and collectively, of our capacities for development.[3]

Recently, the concept of spirituality has attracted a lot of attention from both researchers and lay public, and research papers and books on the spiritual dimension of different groups of people have been published.[4] At long last, there is some recognition of the necessity to understand the spiritual dimension in autism. The first book devoted to spirituality and autism was written by a professional working with autistic individuals (Isanon 2001), followed by a trilogy written by an adult with Asperger syndrome (Stillman 2006, 2008, 2010), and quite a few books written by parents of autistic children, from the perspective of different religious denominations.[5] All the research on spirituality suggests new and more creative ways of helping people (both with disabilities and 'normal') to find their place in this world and live meaningful lives.

Another reason that spirituality and morality are at the top of the research list is that since the last decade of the last century we have witnessed what seems to be a large-scale breakdown of morality and deterioration of social relations, increase of violent crime, riots, feelings of entitlement to everything without contributing to the community, and so on.[6]

We have no explanations for many phenomena related to what lies beyond ourselves, and beyond what we know (one of the reasons contributing to our ignorance is that we are not looking for answers because we do not know what questions to ask). It seems that the best some researchers can do is to ignore everything that does not sound scientific; the worst, to label those who have 'unexplained experiences' and those who try to understand them as 'stupid, crazy, delusional', and so on. And maybe they are but, on the other hand, maybe they are not. These are very real experiences and this book is an attempt, if not to find the answers, at least to ask the questions.

There is an assumption that anything that cannot be examined, measured and reproduced under identical conditions in the laboratory (in a controlled setting) is unscientific. So researching, say, emotions, which are unpredictable and hard to either generate or track in a controlled setting, and are very unlikely to be reproduced under identical conditions, is 'unscientific' (Jawer 2009). Some people are more emotionally sensitive than others – a fact that will make measuring and examination even more difficult. However, as Jawer (2009) notes, superstition can, at least in some cases, contain a grain of truth and there may be some underlying validity, even if not presented in scientific terms. Similarly, scientists dismiss without any further thought so-called healers who claim to feel and be able to manipulate and restore the energy of their patients, despite the patients' (anecdotal) reports that the treatment brought significant improvement in their health. Jawer suggests that one of the difficulties might lie in the language healers use to describe how they work, which is mostly based on *feelings* and *intuitions*, something that is not reflected in the language and the concepts scientists use. Any irrational (from a scientific point of view) explanation is automatically categorised as 'superstition', and laughed at. For example, Bruce Hood (2009) (with great wit) dismisses anything 'supernatural' as 'the prejudiced reasoning we exercise whenever we make judgements that fit with our preconceptions' (p.244) and analyses many superstitions from a 'scientific point of view' as being just that – superstitions, originated by the 'supersense' – 'a natural, intuitive way of reasoning that leads…to supernatural beliefs' (p.6). Throughout his book, Hood attempts to convince the reader that:

> we are naturally inclined towards supernatural beliefs. Many highly educated and intelligent individuals experience a powerful sense that there are patterns, forces, energies, and entities operating in the world that are *denied by science* because they go beyond the boundaries of natural phenomena we *currently* understand. More importantly, such experiences are not substantiated by a body of reliable evidence, which is why they are *super*natural and unscientific. (Hood 2009, p.7; emphasis added)

I wonder what some scholars would have identified as unscientific if they had had their scientific career a few centuries ago when many natural phenomena were thought to be manifestations of supernatural entities. 'Through years of systematic investigation, many of these phenomena are now understood in quite ordinary terms. Thus, it is entirely reasonable to expect that [so-called supernatural or paranormal phenomena] are simply indicators of our present ignorance' (Radin 1998, p.19). One of the most complicated structures in the known universe is the human brain. Arthur C. Clarke, one of the world's foremost science fiction writer, whose imagination seems limitless, humbly admits that many brain powers and potentialities are still largely untapped, and perhaps unguessed at. At the present stage of our ignorance, we manage to glimpse the profounder resources of our mind only once or twice in a lifetime (Clarke 2000).

The attitude and prejudiced reasoning of the scientist is also important. For example, this statement sounds very 'scientific': 'Science cannot categorically prove that the sense of being stared at is not true or will never be true in the future, but the evidence is so weak or nonexistent that it *must* be regarded as unproven' (Hood 2009, p.241; emphasis added). But what about a very real phenomenon of 'distant touching' some people with autism experience: when someone is staring at them they can feel it on their skin (O'Neill 1999)? There are some phenomena that seemed so bizarre when they were first discovered that many researchers refused to accept them.

The problems with researching spirituality are even worse: some scientists are not only uninterested in looking for the answers, they refuse to ask religious questions. The foremost spokesman of humanistic Third Force psychology, Abraham Maslow (1970a, p.11) observes that science, too desperately attempting to be value-free:

> mistakenly conceived of itself as having nothing to say about the ends or ultimate values or spiritual values. This is the same as saying that these ends are entirely outside the range of natural human knowledge, that they can never be known in a confirmable, validated way, in a way that could satisfy intelligent men, as facts satisfy them.

Maslow criticises positivists who reject any inner experiences of *any* kind as 'unscientific' and outside the realm of human knowledge; they insist that such data are not objective and therefore not worthy of study by scientific method.

'This is a kind of "reduction to the concrete", to the tangible, the visible, the audible, to that which can be recorded by a machine.'[7] Maslow warns that such an attitude reduces science to nothing more than technology, amoral and non-ethical. Such a science becomes no more than a collection of methods and techniques, nothing but a tool to be used by any person, good or evil, and for any ends, good or evil:

> like the German 'scientists' who could work with equal zeal for Nazis, for Communists, or for Americans. [We have seen] that science can be dangerous to human ends and that scientists can become monsters as long as science is conceived to be akin to a chess game, an end in itself, with arbitrary rules, whose only purpose is to explore the existent...excluding subjective experience from the realm of the existent or explorable. (Maslow 1970b, p.16)[8]

According to Maslow, science and religion have been too exclusively dichotomised and separated from each other, so they have been considered as two mutually exclusive worlds. Dichotomizing pathologises (and pathology dichotomises). Isolating two interrelated parts of a whole from each other, parts that need each other, parts that are truly 'parts' and not wholes, distorts them both, sickens and contaminates them: 'the dichotomizing of science and religion, of facts (merely and solely) from values (merely and solely) and...a splitting off of mutually exclusive jurisdictions must produce cripple-science and cripple-religion, cripple-facts and cripple-values' (Maslow 1970a, p.17). The exclusion of the transcendent and the sacred from the jurisdiction of science makes impossible in principle the study of, for instance, certain aspects of psychotherapy, naturalistic religious experience, creativity, symbolism, mystical and peak-experiences, and even poetry and art, as they 'all involve an integration of the realm of Being with the realm of concrete' (Maslow 1970a, p.16). A shift in perspective is becoming a necessity.[9] Maslow writes that more intelligent and sophisticated representatives of both science and religion can make changes in the attitude to the naturalistic, humanistic, religious questions:

> Such a science...*does* include much that has been called religious. As a matter of fact, this expanded science includes among its concerns practically everything in religion that can bear naturalistic observation... [What the more sophisticated scientist has to learn] is that though he must disagree with most of the answers to the religious questions which have been given by organized religion,

it is increasingly clear that the…religious quests, the religious yearnings, the religious needs themselves – are perfectly respectable scientifically, that they are rooted deep in human nature, that they can be studied, described, examined in a scientific way, and that the churches were trying to answer perfectly sound human questions. Though the answers were not acceptable, the questions themselves were and are perfectly acceptable, and perfectly legitimate.

As a matter of fact, contemporary existential and humanistic psychologists would probably consider a person sick or abnormal in an existential way if he were *not* concerned with these 'religious' questions. (Maslow 1970b, pp.16, 17, 18)

Although this book covers a wide spectrum of topics, the main theme I intend to explore is the spiritual dimension of autism.[10] Autism has often been described (and perceived) as being 'mysterious' because of the differences in sensory perception, cognition, language development and communication that sometimes seem incomprehensible to 'normal' people. Exploration of the spiritual side of this condition can bring better understanding (or more confusion!) to the way we see ASDs and our role in helping autistic individuals and their families. On the other hand, autism (with its differences in sensory perception, cognition and language development) can bring us closer to understanding the phenomenon of spirituality.

The aim of this book is to examine some of the key issues and insights into the way autistic people experience the world and their spirituality. As a bonus, this exploration will provide us with an opportunity to understand ourselves and increase our own perception and understanding of the diversity in humankind. I will try to approach the subject matter from many different perspectives, drawing on interdisciplinary research findings, including psychology, philosophy, anthropology, linguistics, neuroscience and religion. And, of course, my primary source is writings, presentations and personal communication with individuals on the autism spectrum. I believe narrative methods may be the most effective means of depicting the subjective experiences of people with autism in ways that are faithful to the meaning they give to their lives. These methods (narratives) reflect the emotional dimension of human experience (which is often absent from the objective accounts of those who work with autistic individuals) (Isanon 2001).

There is a problem, however – how can we interpret the narratives of those who cannot speak/write/communicate in any conventional ways?[11] In this case, interpretation and analysis are essential (Isanson

2001). I have attempted to combine research findings from various sciences, clinical observations and narratives which have been chosen to cover as wide a perspective as possible (autistic individuals quoted in the text are from diverse cultural backgrounds: England, Scotland, Ireland, Sweden, the Netherlands, Belgium, Australia, the USA, Canada, India, Russia, Ukraine). As a result, it is another story, describing a different framework to accommodate particular human experiences and behaviours with possible explanations, though limited, flexible enough to change when new data become available or when another interpretation of the subject matter is created.

To fully appreciate the spiritual perspectives of autistic individuals we have to take into account their specific ways of perceiving and processing information about the environment and their own selves. Spirituality plays a significant role in the lives of many autistic individuals and their families. It is time we opened our minds to a diversity of interpretations of human experiences, and, without any acquired bias towards these phenomena, we should respect individuals' ways of perceiving and understanding the world, the meaning of life and, yes, mystery. Those who live and/or work with this population will not only gain new knowledge and understanding of the autistic children and adults they are involved with, but also might find that they have to re-evaluate their own lives, values and their own 'selves'. Spirituality can be a powerful element that will help autistic individuals and their families to overcome their difficulties and find meaning in their lives.

Is this book 'practical'? No and yes. No, if you are looking for bullet points of what to do and what not to do, because it does not provide ready-made recipes to 'fix autistic behaviours'. And yes, if you want to understand how some autistic individuals experience their inner worlds and how these worlds shape the spiritual dimension of their lives. It does provide some explanations of why the connection between autism and spirituality is so strong, and what we can learn from 'autistic spirituality' that will help us understand our own selves.

The book is aimed at professionals, parents and autistic individuals who are interested in spirituality and the unknown. (No, there are no answers and explanations of the unknown – will there ever be? – but there are attempts to approach what we do not yet understand from several different angles, to look at some phenomena from various perspectives.)

The background to this book

Some background information on how this book has come to life is necessary.

I have come to my beliefs and ways of thinking through certain experiences, that is, I have developed into the 'present me' who sees the world, people and science from a very different angle than 25 years ago.

As I was born and brought up in the former USSR, when I was growing up I did not have to contemplate whether God existed or not, or which religious denomination would appeal to me (at the time I didn't even know there were different religions). At school we learned that 'religion is the opium of the people' and, as this was a statement by the founder of Marxism-Leninism, Karl Marx, no one doubted it. (All the subjects on the school curricula were based on this 'scientific' Marxist-Leninist approach. All the textbooks (not only in humanities but *all* subjects) were interspersed with pearls from works by Marx, Engels and Lenin.). I remember our history lessons covering the 'logical' and 'correct decisions' made by the Communist Party of the Soviet Union, starting with the Bolsheviks banning any religion (='opium') after the October 1917 revolution. The ban was lifted only during the Second World War – as the Russian writer V.P. Astafyev observed, 'During the war, non-believers do not exist.' After the war, however, religion was pushed back into the (physical and mental) margins of society. There were very few working churches left – usually outside towns and cities, next to the cemeteries. But to go to a church, to attend a service – even out of curiosity – meant trouble. There were always undercover KGB people inside or outside the church, ready to 'register' those who dared step near it, to say nothing of entering the building. Your name on the 'black list' translated into the end of your career, university study, and so on, and public contempt. However, 'babushki' – old women – were 'mercifully' allowed to 'bang their heads against the floor' and 'burn the candles'.

In my childhood, my attitude to religion was simple – any religion was bad, and those very few religious individuals (typically from the old generation – those who survived the Second World War) were deluded, ill-educated 'poor people' who had no idea how the world worked. So there I was, happily going through the ideological conditioning: from 7 to 10 years old being an 'octyabryonok' ('grandchild of the Great October Revolution'), proudly wearing a small metal star-badge with a portrait of young Voldya Ulyanov (granddad Lenin); from

9 to 14 a young pioneer with a red tie around my neck; and from 14 to 27 a member of Komsomol (All-Union Leninist Communist League), with a membership card and a badge in the shape of a red banner with a portrait of Lenin in the middle.

The day of 'becoming' oktyabryonok/pioneer was one of the main solemn and celebratory events every year in all the schools around the country, with bugles and drums playing, and children taking the oath: 'Be ready!' – 'Always ready!', the right arm bent at the elbow springing up in a 'pioneer salute', and while all children got the status of 'oktyabryonok' and 'pioneer' when they reached the appropriate age, joining the Komsomol organisation required a greater level of dedication and formality (*all* pioneers had to join Komsomol – not to be a Komsomol member meant to be ostracised, excluded from all school activities, losing friends). The ceremony was different and it was held in the Communist Party quarters, with teenagers entering the office of the party official one by one, where three or four Communist Party functionaries were sitting at the table covered with a red tablecloth (specially for the occasion). Their task was to find out whether the would-be Komsomol member was knowledgeable about the Komsomol Statute and the decisions of all the Communist Party Congresses (which was the main worry for me, as there had been more than 20 Congresses by the time I qualified and for the life of me I couldn't remember the difference between the conclusions of, for example, the 21st and 22nd Congresses – they all seemed the same: we were building communism, and our industrial, agricultural, scientific, educational progress was better than that of capitalist societies).

After the age of 27, each person decided for themselves whether to join the Communist Party (and it was not easy: every year all cities, towns and villages received their quota for new members, with numbers that were strictly observed – a typical one was for seven candidates of working class background, one candidate from 'intelligentsia') and have a good career, or remain 'non-party' and rely on your luck (or lack of it).

Out of (my friends said 'stupid') principle, I refused even to contemplate the option of getting a party card as a pass to the top and went to Moscow instead to try my luck (and to prove that it was possible) to achieve something in this life without the 'red book'. And I was lucky – my PhD supervisor at the Moscow linguistic university did not care about my not-being-one-representative-of-intelligentsia-to-seven-working-class-representatives and appreciated me for my abilities in the field of linguistics. During those years we became friends and at our regular consultations talked not only about the historical syntax of the Old English language, but many other things that at the time could be discussed only 'in the kitchen' – the place where some families gathered to listen to Western radio stations, to discuss (in whispers) banned works and personalities (like, for example, Sakharov and Solzhenitsyn), grumble about the incompetence of and ridiculous ideas produced by the party apparatchiks. As soon as someone sounded too critical about the official policies, the rest, with a nervous giggle, would turn their heads around the kitchen and loudly chant in chorus, 'We are just kidding' (a private joke that helped to reduce a perhaps unjustified fear of being 'bugged' with all the unpleasant and dangerous consequences – 'We don't think the apartment is bugged, but what if it is?').

It was in my scientific supervisor's kitchen, at the age of 28, that I held the Bible in my hands for the first time. I didn't become religious but it made me think that 'scientific atheism' might not be the only possible way to interpret our reality.

In 1991, the Soviet Union collapsed (at the time I lived in Ukraine) and, all of a sudden, religion (the Russian Orthodox Church) was welcomed by the very apparatchiks who had banned it many years ago. The party functionaries staged televised performances of burning their 'red books' (the Communist Party member cards) and rushing to the cathedrals to light a candle in honour of Jesus Christ. I remember my outrage when watching on TV long queues to the bonfires of 'red books' with former Communists trying to catch the 'eye' of TV cameras, and becoming ecstatic if they were asked by the reporters to give a short interview; another news channel showed overcrowded cathedrals and churches – with ex-Communists in the first row solemnly staring at their feet to show off their suddenly found humbleness in the house of Jesus. No, I wasn't outraged because belief in God was 'legalised' – any allowed freedom was a welcome development – what infuriated me was the rush to disown the party that had catapulted them to the top. I had an impulse to join the Communist Party at the time – out of (stupid) principle but, fortunately, I didn't, because those who remained true to the Communist ideals and didn't desert the party, though they earned my respect, were still too dogmatic in Marxist-Leninist ideology for me to pretend that I agreed with their views. The majority of born-again, and now legal, churches were so grateful to the government that they preached in its favour, and it couldn't be otherwise because many priests were appointed by the government from the pool of 'new-born non-parties' who had lost their jobs in the party nomenclature.

Though I do not consider myself religious, my children have been baptised, I wear a cross (which I bought in the church of my homeland just before I left) and I have a few icons and church candles at home – this helps me feel grounded and connected to my roots. I don't attend church services but I do visit cathedrals and churches (of any denomination) whenever I have a chance while travelling either on business or on holiday, to feel the peaceful atmosphere and the energy created by the prayers of many generations of church-goers.

So, am I religious? The answer is no, I am not religious but I continue my development from the religion of atheism through agnosticism into 'private religion' (in the terminology of William James).[12]

Notes

1. In a letter to his niece S.I. Ivanova, written in 1868, Dostoevsky described the main idea of *The Idiot* as 'to depict a positively beautiful human being. There is nothing harder under the sun than to do just that, and especially now. All writers – and not only ours but also all the European writers, who have attempted to depict the *positively* beautiful – always gave up. The reason of the failure is, the task is immense: the beautiful is the ideal, and that ideal has not been developed yet – neither in Russia, nor in the civilised Europe' (Dostoevsky 1930).

2. After 1917, the Bolsheviks banned all works by Dostoevsky as they were seen as 'capitalistic' and 'anti-Communist'; Maxim Gorky called him 'our evil genius'. The ban was lifted only after the Second World War, when his *Crime and Punishment* was firmly established in the school curriculum.

3. Cited in Gunn 1920, p.62.

4. See, for example, exploration of children's spirituality: Adams, Hyde and Woolley 2008; Coles 1992; Hay and Nye 2006; Hyde 2008; Nye 2009; women's spirituality: Cole and Ochshorn 1995; spirituality in ageing: Jewell 1998, 2003; developmental disabilities: MacKinlay 2008, 2010; dementia and Alzheimer's: Jewell 2011; Shamy 2003; psychosis: Clarke 2008, 2010.

5. For instance, from the perspective of Christianity, Labosh 2011; Langston 2009.

6. See, for example, Etzioni 1995; Selznick 1992.

7. Maslow points out a paradox: the behavioural sciences are considered worthy of scientific investigation, when, in fact, 'human behaviour is so often a defense *against* motives, emotions, and impulses. That is, it is a way of inhibiting and concealing them as often as it is an expression of everything. Behaviour is often a means of preventing the overt expression of everything…just as spoken language can also be' (Maslow 1970a, p.6).

8. This observation by Maslow is still very relevant to our present time, when some 'scientists' insist that they 'do not do politics', and 'in the name of science' accept funding from organisations they resent.

9.   That is exactly what has happened in our perspective on the nature of our physical reality, for example, from flat earth to earth as centre of the universe, to the sun as centre with the earth rotating around it, to the sun being one of millions of stars in numerous galaxies, etc. The transition/shift from one perspective to a different one is not smooth and fluent – Kuhn (1962) compares it with revolution: the pressure for change builds up over time, with bold individuals daring to confront the conventional views. Kuhn distinguishes between three phases of paradigm shift in science: the first phase, the pre-paradigm phase, is characterised by several incompatible and incomplete frameworks with no consensus on any particular theory but all contributing to increased insights. The second phase begins with solving the puzzles within the context of the dominant worldviews. Over time, progress in science reveals anomalies that cannot be explained by the existing paradigm(s), leading to a crisis. Then science enters the third phase – the phase of revolutionary science – in which the underlying assumptions in the field are re-examined and the new dominant conceptual framework is established. The new paradigm, to be accepted by a scientific community, first 'must seem to resolve some outstanding and generally recognized problem that can be met in no other way. Second, the new paradigm must promise to preserve a relatively large part of the concrete problem solving activity that has accrued to science through its predecessors' (Kuhn 1962, p.168). The change of the worldview brings changes in definitions of concepts, terminology and new questions to be asked.

10.   Issues of religious beliefs of autistic individuals are not discussed in this book.

11.   Though this does not mean that they cannot communicate at all. In fact, they are communicating all the time; often it is 'normal' people who cannot interpret their communication, or even insist that this or that non-verbal person is unable to communicate. See more in Bogdashina 2004.

12.   The Harvard psychologist turned philosopher William James (1842–1910) received his MD degree from Harvard in physiology and anatomy, but always regarded philosophy as his 'vocation'. He started teaching courses in psychology and philosophy in 1876, and was soon offered a position as an assistant professor of philosophy at Harvard. The publication of his first book, *Principles of Psychology*, in 1890 firmly established him as the principal spokesman for the empirical theories of psychology. Other books followed, among them a classic, *The Varieties of Religious Experience: A Study in Human Nature* (1902). James's goals in the book are set forth in a letter, reproduced by his biographer Ralph Barton Perry: 'The problem I have set myself is a hard one: *first*, to defend…"experience" against "philosophy" as being the real backbone of the world's religious life…and *second*, to make…the reader believe, what I myself invincibly do believe, that, although all the special manifestations of religion may have been absurd (I mean its creeds and theories), yet the life of it as a whole is mankind's most important function' and 'the genuinely spiritual ecclesiasticisms which it founds are phenomena of secondary or even tertiary order' (cited in Marty 1985, p.xix).

1

What's in a Word?

In the beginning was the word

St John's Gospel reveals the co-eternity of the Word, citing the first words of Genesis: 'In the beginning was the Word, and the Word was with God, and the Word was God' (John 1:1). Thus, according to the Bible, language is at the very heart of creation. Adam became the master of the world when he gave names to everything around him – he created the 'human world' – the world identifiable by humans. And that is what we have now: we have names for objects, plants, animals, abstract notions (and when new ones appear we provide new labels) – thus drawing boundaries around 'our' world (if something is outside the 'bubble' it goes unnoticed).[1]

With the help of words, humans created the conceptual and linguistic world they would inhabit ('Adam's job' done) and this 'created world' is being passed from generation to generation through cultural traditions. But what happens when some children do not develop verbal language (often the case in autism)? It does not mean they have no language at all, rather that they develop non-verbal languages that 'reconstruct' the world differently. Understanding and learning these non-verbal languages ('languages of experience': comprising visual, tactile, auditory, smell, etc. images) will help not only to communicate with autistic individuals 'speaking' these languages, but also to understand spiritual (especially, mystical) experiences, one of the features of which is their ineffability – the experiences should be 'felt', they cannot be described verbally, but are expressed in non-verbal ('sensed') images.

Talking about talking

When people speak different languages misunderstanding can be quite common if there is no skilful interpreter to help. However, even speaking the same language there is no guarantee that they will 'interpret' some words correctly. There are several factors to account for possible problems.

First, we have to distinguish the *denotative* and *connotative* meanings of the word: *denotation* refers to the literal meaning of a word (i.e. its dictionary definition), while *connotation* refers to the associations that are connected to it (connotative meaning is 'charged' with emotions, usually very similar for all members of a certain culture, but each individual can have a very different 'emotional shade' based on his or her experiences and knowledge).

For example, if you look up the word 'autism' in a medical dictionary, its denotative meaning is 'a pervasive developmental disorder characterised by severe deficits in social interaction and communication, by an extremely limited range of activities and interests, and often by the presence of repetitive, stereotyped behaviours'. But the connotations of this word can be very different for different people, depending on personal situation, knowledge about the condition, support available to the person with autism and their family, and so on. Here are just a few examples of the connotative meanings of this word:

A high-functioning person with autism who has learned to cope with her problems while building on her strengths: 'Autism is a marvellous occurrence of nature, not a tragic example of the human mind gone wrong' (O'Neill 1999, p.14).

Mrs N. (a parent of a child with severe autism): 'Autism is like a death in the family; it has stolen my child.'

The connotative meanings are so different that understanding and interpretation of the situations are sure to be different.[2] It is even more complicated with the word 'spirituality' – there is no agreement on its denotative meaning, and too many connotative 'charges' with a wide range of 'emotional shades' attached to it.

From a private person to a stupid one

Often it is connotation that leads to a change in a denotative meaning of the word. For example, the word 'idiot' (from Greek *idiōtēs*) had a literal meaning of 'a private person', then it was expanded to mean 'layman, one who lacks professional knowledge'; from the end of the thirteenth century it was used to define a 'person so mentally deficient as to be incapable of ordinary reasoning', and at some stage it became a technical term in a diagnostic classification system (no longer in use) to denote 'a person of profound mental retardation having a mental age below three years and generally being unable to learn connected speech or guard against common dangers'. Nowadays, it means a foolish or stupid person and is perceived as offensive.

Recently 'political correctness' has invaded the linguistic world we live in. Some people have started seeing negative connotations in 'neutral words'. It is one thing to ban such offensive (as perceived by the majority) words as, for example, 'retard', but quite another when some individuals are 'offended' by everyday language because they see negativity wherever they look, and instead of fighting their own impulsive negative feelings they impose their own meaning onto the words, changing perceptions and making people see what is not there. These very few individuals see offence in everything and anything, and insist on banning dozens of words because of their 'negative connotations'. Funnily enough, before the ban, very few people could see anything offensive in 'blacklisting' or 'brainstorming'.

Another dangerous trend is to 'capture good words' and *redefine* them in a way that suits one particular group. People react automatically by assuming the original meaning of the words, thus supporting (or rejecting) a course they otherwise would not. As an illustration, Maslow describes what happened when he heard about the attack from a 'so-called patriotic women's organisation' on the Supreme Court's declaration that prayer in public schools was unconstitutional. The women's organisation claimed that this destroyed 'spiritual values'. As Maslow was in favour of a clear separation of church and state, his reaction was automatic – he disagreed with the women's organisation. But then it dawned on him that he, too, was in favour of spiritual values (and that indeed his own research and theoretical investigations demonstrated their reality). Maslow had reacted in an automatic way against the whole statement by the organisation, thus implicitly accepting its erroneous definition and concept of spiritual values:

> I had allowed these intellectual primitives to capture a good word and put *their* peculiar meaning to it... I had let them redefine these words and had then accepted their definitions. And now I want to take them back. I want to demonstrate that spiritual values have naturalistic meaning, that they are not the exclusive possession of organized churches, that they do not need supernatural concepts to validate them, that they are well within the jurisdiction of a suitably enlarged science, and that, therefore, they are the general responsibility of all mankind. (Maslow 1970a, p.4)

Often 'intellectual primitives' contaminate and destroy 'good words' and that is exactly what has happened in the field of autism, where some (very few) individuals police the Internet and dictate which words can, and which ones cannot, be used while discussing autism.

In this book I will try to clearly define the concepts we are going to deal with. It is not uncommon that people talk about the same phenomenon using different terms to label it, or that when we discuss vague ideas we struggle to define what we are talking about. Any of these scenarios can make discussion meaningless. So it is necessary to define the main concepts that will be used throughout the book, that is autism, spirituality, self. And when any other notion is introduced, the definition will be given to avoid any misinterpretation or misunderstanding.

Notes

1. Of relevance here is the Sapir-Whorf hypothesis of language relativity – see the analysis of linguistic relativity and its relevance to autism in Bogdashina 2010.

2. On a personal note: in a way I was 'lucky', when 25 years ago I learned that my son had autism. As it happened, after several misdiagnoses (including 'severe mental retardation' and 'schizophrenia') with a final conclusion 'he's hopeless' and 'there is nothing you can do about it', the day I was told (by a specialist who actually had the knowledge and experience) that my son had 'classic autism' was one of the happiest days in my life. It was not because I thought that autism was something good – at the time I knew *nothing* about the condition – it was because I got the 'name' and could research its (denotative) meaning, finding some solutions in the process. For many years, the word 'autism' has had no connotation for me (neither good nor bad) as it is in the category 'autism: now what?' – that is, something I need to address and make adjustments for.

2

Defining Autism

Autism is traditionally defined as a lifelong complex disability that typically manifests itself during the first three years of life and affects the way a person communicates and relates to people around him or her. Although it is a condition with a wide-ranging degree of severity, all those affected have problems in the areas of social interaction and social communication and restricted, repetitive and stereotyped patterns of behaviour, interests and activities. Though conventional, this definition is not necessarily satisfactory, and more and more researchers emphasise the need to reconsider it. The problem is that the 'diagnostic symptoms' are behaviours that are not reliable, as they may be caused by different factors. Some authors urge for a distinction between 'different autisms' as different causes can lead to the same clinical manifestation of the condition. The 'symptoms' we can see (i.e. behaviours) can be misleading as several other disorders display problems in social interaction, communication and rigidity of thought, and may be easily misdiagnosed as autism, for example, narcissistic personality disorder (NPD). People with NPD often have problems communicating with others because they believe their 'genius' is not recognised; in any interaction they see 'attacks' on their 'integrity' and cannot stop 'me-me-me thinking'.

The term 'autism' covers the whole spectrum of the disorders, so it is important not to generalise when discussing certain aspects of the condition. Though individuals with autism spectrum disorders (ASDs)[1] share certain common features (that allow the diagnosis to be made), they differ from each other in their sensory, perceptual, cognitive, social, communicative, and so on abilities and difficulties. That is why we find different 'unofficial' labels in many texts describing ASDs, for example, low-functioning autism (LFA), high-functioning autism (HFA), autistic savants, and so on.[2]

In this book, autism is seen as 'the intense world syndrome' (Markram, Rinaldi and Markram 2007) − a condition with multiple aetiology (genetic and/or environmental factors) in which all traditional diagnostic criteria (impairments in social interaction, communication and inflexibility of thoughts and behaviours) are rooted in different sensory perceptions, sensory overload and hypersensitivity. Autistic people perceive, feel and remember too much. Faced with a bombarding, confusing, baffling and often painful environment, autistic infants withdraw into their own world by shutting down their sensory systems. This brings unfavourable consequences for their social and linguistic development (while their cognitive and emotional development follows an atypical route). Depending on the strategies and adaptations these children acquire and the support they get, they may experience autism differently at different times − sometimes it may feel comfortable, and at other times it may be very frustrating. In contrast to official definitions of autism as outer behaviours (the more 'bizarre' behaviours the person exhibits, the more severe the autism is seen to be), for autistic people autism is an inner reality and it can appear (on the surface), disappear and reappear in various degrees in different circumstances. Autism as an experience is described as a very complex interplay between identity, personality, environment, experience and the equipment with which to make sense of that experience.[3]

In this book, instead of describing outer behaviours (what it looks like from outside), autism is viewed through inner realities (what it feels like from inside). This will restrict it by excluding those who, though exhibiting outer behaviours of 'social interaction impairments', are 'normal' in their perception and thinking, and it will include those who have developed strategies to appear 'normal', while their inner realities (caused by differences in sensory perception, thinking and language development) are strikingly different from the culturally constructed ones.

Notes

1. At present, there is a tendency to refer to autism spectrum conditions (ASCs) to emphasise the differences in contrast to pathological features. But this is a semantic issue and there is no unanimity in this.

2.   There are no clinical definitions of words such as 'high-functioning', 'low-functioning', 'mild' or 'severe' autism. However, because autism is so wide ranging, professionals may use terms like these to describe where on a continuum they believe an individual may lie. Sometimes, cognitive level and verbal functioning are used as the criteria for distinguishing between HFA and LFA or 'severe autism'.

3.   For example, Donna Williams (1998, p.9) defines autism simply as 'an internal human "normality" with the volume turned up'.

3

Defining Spirituality

Spirituality versus religion

There is no consensus on a definition of spirituality and different scholars interpret spirituality differently (both in religious and secular literature). Traditionally, spirituality has often been associated with religion despite the fact that chronologically spirituality precedes religion (Hay and Nye 2006; O'Murchu 1997; Scott 2006).[1] In the religious context the definition of spirituality often refers to humans' awareness of a relationship with God, aiming at the goal of mystical union with the Godhead (Tanquerey 1923) and some insist that there is a definite link between religion and spirituality.[2] At present, the association between religion and spirituality is very uncomfortable for many people, especially in the West. Recent events, such as, for example, 9/11 in the USA or 22 July 2011 in Norway (which were connected to Islam and Christianity respectively), make some people doubt whether world religions carry a spiritual message and whether fundamentalists promote peace or war. Another reason to distinguish spirituality from religion is that, in modern secularised societies, religion is seen by many as the realm of uneducated, narrow-minded people, who rigidly follow 'meaningless' (from the point of view of 'educated atheists') rituals and boring routines, while spirituality is associated with universal love (independent of any specific religious denominations), mystery and personal involvement with the universe ('whatever is there'). Farmer (1992) sees spirituality as something larger than any religion. Although historically spirituality has been closely connected with religion, it is logically prior to it (Hay and Nye 2006).

Definitions of religion

The anthropologist Fiona Bowie (2006) notes that when we look at various definitions of religion we have to remember that the term does not necessarily have an equivalent in other parts of the world, as it is a category we construct based on European languages, and which Westerners understand and interpret in terms of their experience.

> Statements about a people's religious beliefs must always be treated with greatest caution, for we are then dealing with what neither Europeans nor natives can directly observe, with conceptions, images, words, which require for understanding a thorough knowledge of a people's language and also an awareness of the entire system of ideas of which any particular belief is part, for it may be meaningless when divorced from the set of beliefs and practices to which it belongs. (Evans-Pritchard 1972, p.7)

Religion is defined as (1) the belief in a supernatural controlling power, especially a personal god or gods entitled to obedience and worship; (2) a particular system of faith and worship; (3) a set of beliefs, doctrines and practices held by a community.

Different anthropologists approach the origins of religion from different perspectives. For example, Spencer (1876) saw the root of any religion as ancestor worship. This view comes from the observation that in dreams the self (soul) can leave the body, and after death the soul continues to appear to the living relatives in dreams. The ghosts of deceased ancestors or prominent figures eventually received the status of gods. In his account of the origin of religion, Tylor (1958) followed Spencer's lines with a greater emphasis on the role of the soul (or life force), which is present not only in human beings but also in inanimate objects.[3] This point of view was criticised by others.[4] Tylor (1958, p.8) suggested that any definition of religion contains 'the belief in Spiritual Beings' (in whatever form it is presented) that represents an attempt to make sense of the world in which people live.

In contrast to this intellectual approach, the symbolist approach focuses on what religion represents and looks at different ways in which religious symbols and rituals act as metaphors for social life; for instance, religion is seen as 'an institution consisting of culturally patterned interaction with culturally postulated superhuman beings' (Spiro 1973, p.96). For one of the proponents of the symbolic approach to religion, American anthropologist Clifford Geertz (1973, p.4), religion is:

> (1) a system of symbols which acts to (2) establish powerful, pervasive, and long-lasting moods and motivations in men by (3) formulating

conceptions of a general order of existence and (4) clothing these conceptions with such an aura of factuality that (5) the moods and motivations seem uniquely realistic.

For French sociologist Émile Durkheim (1976), religion was a symbolic projection of the social values of society, with the collective representations as a means of symbolic statements about society. In opposition to this social view of religion is structuralism, one of the founders of which was Claude Lévi-Strauss, who analysed religion in a similar way to structural linguistics (showing limited innate linguistic structures that are reflected in diverse human languages; see Chomsky 1957) seeking to reveal a universal psychology which gives rise to social structures (based on certain innate structures of culture), and cognitive constraints on religion – the limited number of ways humans are able to interpret the world. For example, myths in different cultures reflect a common story, 'clothed' in different linguistic expressions. Lévi-Strauss (1970) argues that there are a limited number of ways in which the motifs in myths can be transformed, so a myth cannot be defined by a single correct version but rather by the sum of its many transformations and variations.

As there are systems of thought which do not positively assume a god, but which we still usually call religions, for example, Buddhism, which 'in strictness…is atheistic', William James (1985, p.34) believed that 'from the experiential point of view [the inner experiences that underlie the expressions of their faith] these godless or quasi-godless creeds' must be called 'religions' and 'accordingly when in our definition of religion we speak of the individual's relation to "what he considers the divine," we must interpret the term "divine" very broadly, as denoting any object that is godlike, whether it be a concrete deity or not.' Lehmann and Myers (1997, p.3) propose to expand the definition of religion 'beyond spiritual and superhuman beings to include the extraordinary, the mysterious, and unexplainable', which will allow 'a more comprehensive view of religious behaviors among the people of the world' and will permit 'the anthropological investigation of phenomena such as magic, sorcery, curses, and other practices that hold meaning for both preliterate and literate societies'.

Outside anthropological studies, there is a dimensional approach to religion (following the phenomenological and comparative traditions, and seeking to find similarity in the world's religions while distinguishing religions that are actually lived by people from what might be representations of religious elites who dictate what their religion ought to be), represented by Ninian Smart's analysis of all religions according to different 'dimensions'. In his *Dimensions of the Sacred* (1996, pp.10–11)

Smart proposes eight dimensions: '1. Ritual or practical. 2. Doctrinal or philosophical. 3. Myths or narrative. 4. Experiential or emotional. 5. Ethical or legal. 6. Organizational or social. 7. Material or artistic. 8. Political and economic.' Different religions may differ in their emphasis on each of these dimensions; for example, for societies without written scriptures myths are more prominent, while Roman Catholicism and Orthodoxy Churches put greater emphasis on liturgy and ritual, as well as material and artistic means (such as, for instance, icons, candles and music).

Christian theologian James Mackey (1996, p.8) suggests there should be a less dogmatic and more fluid approach to definition of religion:

> [P]eople who have somehow pre-defined the nature of divinity, and more particularly those who treat the notes of immanence and transcendence in relation to a divine dimension as contraries instead of what they always are in fact, namely, coordinates, can also appear to specify with great accuracy what is to count as religion, as a truly religious dimension of life and knowledge, and what is not. It is interesting to note that this alleged ability is so often shared by those who are dogmatic about religion and those who, allegedly on scientific grounds, are most dismissive of it.

As Ludwig Feuerbach (1957, p.32) once said, 'what today is atheism tomorrow will be called religion'.

Religion versus spirituality: Where are the boundaries?

It has been noted[5] that in many ways, religion has made strong claims to ownership of spirituality, arguing that spirituality cannot exist outside of the religious context. For example, Thatcher (1999) considers spirituality outside religion meaningless, because it requires religious context for spiritual expression. However, these claims fail to recognise the spirituality of those who are not associated with any religion (Meehan 2002). To combat these views, a clear distinction between spirituality and religion has been drawn.[6] According to Ranson (2002), there are two foundational moments: the 'spiritual' (when a person attends to his or her experiences), and the 'religious' (the way the person interprets his or her spiritual experiences and acts on them) – thus placing the person's spirituality in the context of social and communal reality with shared beliefs and values. Adams *et al.* (2008) summarise the argument:

spirituality is much broader than religion, and more primal; it precedes any type of religion and is an innate quality of all people irrespective of whether they are affiliated with a religious tradition, or whether they express an explicit belief in God.[7] William James (1985, p.30) points out another reason to consider spirituality (which he calls 'personal religion') as more fundamental than either theology or ecclesiasticism:

> Churches, when once established, live at second-hand upon tradition; but the *founders* of every church owed their power originally to the fact of their direct personal communion with the divine. Not only the superhuman founders, the Christ, the Buddha, Mahomet, but all the originators of Christian sects have been in this case; – so personal religion should still seem the primordial thing, even to those who continue to esteem it incomplete.

Historically, religion and spirituality are strongly connected with the language and concepts of individual religions. For example, some speak of Catholic spirituality, referring to the lives of Catholic saints, religious orders and practices of Catholics (Rossiter 2005). So, though being different from religion, spirituality is often expressed through the context of the religious tradition the person has been born into – the 'religious' becomes a means of expression of the person's spirituality – there are no other words to use to refer to subjective experiences. Maslow considers this very regrettable: '[the dictionary will tell you that] the words "sacred", "divine", "holy", "numen", "sin", "prayer", "oblation", "thanksgiving", "worship", "piety", "salvation", "reverence"… refer to a god or a religion in the supernatural sense'. As there are no other words to describe spiritual experiences, non-religious people use them 'in the effort to describe certain happenings in the natural world'. Maslow wants to reclaim these and similar words and use them 'to refer to subjective happenings in human beings without necessarily implying any supernatural reference' and insists that 'it is not necessary to appeal to principles outside of nature and human nature in order to explain these experiences' (Maslow 1970a, p.5):

> [The word 'sacred':] If the sacred becomes the exclusive jurisdiction of a priesthood, and if its supposed validity rests only upon supernatural, then, in effect, it is taken out of the world of nature and of human nature. It is dichotomized sharply from the profane or secular and begins to have nothing to do with them, or even becomes contradictory. It becomes associated with a particular

language, even with a particular musical instrument or certain foods. It does not infuse all of life but becomes compartmentalized. It is not the property then of all men, but only of some. It is no longer ever-present as a possibility in the everyday affairs of men but becomes instead a museum piece without daily usefulness. (Maslow 1970a, p.14)

James describes the division in the religious field, on the one side of which is institutional, and on the other personal, religion. According to James, the essentials of 'the institutional branch' of religion include 'worship and sacrifice, procedures for working on the dispositions of deity, theology and ceremony and ecclesiastical organisation', while in the personal (spiritual) branch of religion 'it is on the contrary the inner dispositions of man himself which form the centre of interest, his conscience, his deserts, his helplessness, his incompleteness'; and although the concept of God 'is still an essential feature...the acts...are personal not ritual acts... The relation goes direct from heart to heart, from soul to soul, between man and his maker.'[8] James shows how much the question of definition turns into a dispute about names and decides to 'accept almost any name for the personal religion' (spirituality): 'Call it conscience or morality if you prefer, and not religion – under either name it will be equally worthy of our study' (James 1985, pp.29, 30). James himself believes that personal religion (spirituality) contains some elements which morality does not contain.

Similarly, Maslow describes a tendency in the history of many religions to develop two extreme wings: the mystical and individual on the one hand, and the organisational on the other. To show this division, like William James, Maslow differentiates religion (calling it 'small r religion' – the subjective and naturalistic religious experience and attitude) from Religion (or 'big R Religion' – the institutionalised, conventional, organised religions). According to Maslow, at the higher levels of personal development, 'small r religion' is compatible with rationality, science and social passion (what we would call today 'spirituality'). 'Big R Religion' is seen by Maslow as 'a set of habits, behaviors, dogmas, forms, which at the extreme becomes entirely legalistic and bureaucratic, conventional, empty, and in the truest meaning of the word, anti-religious' when 'organized Religion, the churches...may become the major enemies of the religious experience and the religious experiencer' with the mystic experiences and the great awakenings being forgotten (Maslow 1970a, p.viii).

Culliford (2007) believes that it is very important to distinguish between spirituality and religion because, in itself, spirituality is not the same as holding any particular faith, or being religiously observant, or belonging to some established faith tradition, but rather one can experience the spiritual dimension without any religious references. Culliford emphasises that, while there are many religions, spirituality is universal, and at the same time it is deeply personal in that it is experienced uniquely by different people. It is 'spiritual dimension of human experience...where the universal and the deeply personal meet.' Spirituality interconnects us all – both believers and atheists (Culliford 2007, p.19). Adams *et al.* (2008) note a trend we are witnessing at present: disillusioned by the Church's failure to nurture their inner lives, people actively search elsewhere for what will provide them with a sense of wholeness, meaning and purpose. Many people who do not consider themselves religious still perceive themselves as spiritual.

The association of spirituality (at least in the West) with the 'New Age' movement makes it difficult to discuss it openly in academic circles – critics are quick to label this approach as 'unscientific', and so 'unworthy of serious discussion'. Let us put aside all the preconceptions and try to look at spirituality from many different perspectives in order to determine what is 'worthy' (or 'unworthy') of our attention. And a good place to start is the definitions of this phenomenon which will help draw the boundaries around it.

Definitions of spirituality

The dictionary definitions of spirituality include:

> *Spirituality* – *n.* the quality of involving deep, often religious feelings and beliefs, rather than the physical parts of life. (Cambridge Dictionaries Online 2013)

The Concise Oxford Dictionary (Thompson 1995) does not define the noun, but provides several definitions of the adjective:

> *Spiritual*: of or concerning the spirit as opposed to matter; concerned with sacred or religious things; holy; divine; inspired; (of the mind etc.) refined, sensitive; not concerned with the material; (of a relationship etc.) concerned with the soul or spirit etc., not with external reality.

We will move from a very broad definition provided by Newberg and Waldman (2010), *spirituality* as a broad range of individual values and personal theologies that are not connected to traditional religious institutions, to investigate specific characteristics of the notion (including the means by which a person becomes 'spiritual'). Following the approach of William James to exploration of the variety of religious (spiritual) experiences one has to admit that 'we may very likely find no one essence, but many characters which may alternately be equally important to religion' (James 1985, p.26). Here it is necessary to note that what James called 'religious experiences' would now be interpreted as 'spiritual experiences'. For instance, in contrast to many of his contemporaries, James defined 'personal religion' (spirituality) as:

> *the feelings, acts, and experiences of individual men in their solitude, so far as they apprehend themselves to stand in relation to whatever they may consider the divine.* Since the relation may be either moral, physical, or ritual, it is evident that out of religion in the sense in which we take it, theologies, philosophies, and ecclesiastical organizations may secondarily grow. (James 1985, p.31)

The most common features included in the definition of spirituality are:

- 'a fundamental human universal': however, there is no consensus here. Some authors emphasise the possibility of spirituality among animals;[9] Hart (2003) shifts the emphasis and finds it preferable to consider people as spiritual beings with human experiences, rather than human beings with spiritual experiences

- 'a natural human predisposition, often overlaid by cultural construction, but nevertheless a biological reality' (Hay and Nye 2006, p.10), an ontological reality with a dynamic quality which all people are born with (O'Murchu 1997)

- being holistic in nature, a deep sense of the whole;[10] a sense of unity, or oneness, with everything (Moffett 1994); connectedness and relationality (Elton-Chalcraft 2002; Fisher 1999)

- themes of transcendence (some prefer the term 'transliminality') are prominent in different definitions of spirituality (Piedmont 1999). *Transliminality* is defined as:

  > a hypersensitivity to psychological material originating in (a) the unconscious, and/or (b) the external environment.

'Psychological material' [covers] ideation, imagery, affect and perception... High transliminality tends to imply (alleged) paranormal experience, mystical experience, creative personality, fleeting manic experience, magical ideation, high absorption, fantasy-proneness, hypersensitivity to sensory stimulation, and positive attitude to dream-interpretation. (Thalbourne and Maltby 2008, p.1618)

Themes of transliminality include:

○ 'an awareness of transcendent/transliminal ("the beyond in our midst"), the awareness of something beyond intellectual knowledge of normal sensory experience...thus concerned with: meaning and purpose in life; interconnectedness and harmony with other people, planet Earth and the Universe; and a right relationship with God/a power or force in the Universe which transcends the present context of reality'[11]

○ the sixth factor of personality; one of many ways to express the innate need for transcendence (Piedmont 1999): Piedmont seems to use spiritual transcendence (which he defines as a fundamental, intrinsic motivation to find a deeper sense of meaning by subjecting one's needs to those of a group or a cause) and spirituality interchangeably

○ a sense of 'transcendent providence', the belief that life events are 'meant to be', a feeling of being in harmony with the universe; a general confidence in the existence of a Higher Power (Hay and Hunt 2002)

○ self-transcendence (i.e. identification with everything conceived as essential and consequential parts of a unified whole) that is based on three components: self-forgetfulness, transpersonal identification and mysticism (Cloninger, Svrakic and Przybeck 1993). In contrast to self-consciousness (materialistic feature), *self-forgetfulness* (spiritual) involves becoming so absorbed in something (e.g. work) that one loses the sense of time, place and self, lacking self-consciousness. *Transpersonal identification* is defined as a sense of connectedness to everything and everybody inanimate and animate: nature, animals and people. *Mysticism* includes teaching and practices that encourage a quest to unite with the source of the sacred

– 'a divine being, divine object, Ultimate Reality, or Ultimate Truth as perceived by the individual' (Hill *et al.* 2000, p.66)

- an awareness that there is something Other, something greater than the course of everyday events (McCreery 1996)
- both the internal experience of life purpose or connectedness to higher power and external component of psychological well-being (Speraw 2006; Thompson 2002)
- for some, the word 'spiritual' refers to an aesthetic awareness of/ sensitivity to art (poetry, music, etc.) or to ethical issues, like, for example, being sensitive to the needs of others.

A person's spirituality can be seen as his or her 'connection with the source of a deep-seated sense of meaning and purpose in life, together with both a sense of belonging and of harmony in the universe' (Culliford 2007, p.19).[12]

To summarise, spirituality is 'something biologically built into the human species, an holistic awareness of reality which is potentially to be found in every human being' (Hay and Nye 2006, p.63); it is reflected in 'a heightened awareness or attentiveness', 'connectedness', 'relational consciousness' (i.e. a holistic awareness of one's relationship with material world, with other humans, with oneself and with God) that constitute 'spiritual awareness'. This definition is actually acceptable to secular, religious and agnostic views, as it has 'the three connotations – religious devotion; being fully aware of one's "species-being"; and being aesthetically or ethically aware – all refer to a heightening of awareness or attentiveness...[all expressing] a fundamental insight' (Hay and Nye 2006, p.21). It is also linked to common practices of religious meditation, including the Buddhist Vipassana meditation[13] and contemplative Christian prayer (Hay and Nye 2006).

Common features in many definitions of spirituality are connectedness with other people and with the non-human world, transcendence/ transliminality and relationship to self (inner self), that is, who one really is, being comfortable with one's self or accepting self.

Biological origin or basis of spirituality

Spirituality is a very real phenomenon which has biological roots.[14] The idea of a natural basis for what were known as religious but are now interpreted as spiritual feelings can be traced to the works of some thinkers during the Renaissance and the Enlightenment periods.[15] The German theologian Friedrich Schleiermacher (1928, 1958) (often referred to as the Father of Christian Liberalism) suggested that religious (spiritual) feeling is natural; it is a feeling of absolute dependence, not just an emotion but rather something like an intuition.[16] In his *Addresses on Religion*, Schleiermacher defined religion (spirituality) as something that is neither a metaphysic, nor a morality, but rather (and essentially) an intuition and a feeling that answers a deep need in man; religion (spirituality) is the miracle of close and direct relationship with the infinite, while the religious dogmas are a reflection of this miracle, not a part of it. Similarly, belief in God and/or immortality of the soul, according to Schleiermacher, are not necessarily a part of religion, and one can see a religion without God, as pure contemplation of the universe, while belief in personal immortality indicates a lack of religion because it assumes the desire to preserve one's self rather than lose one's self in the infinite, as religion implies.

The first scholar to explicitly show the biological origin of spirituality was Alister Hardy (1966, 1979). Though Hardy wrote about the relationship between biology and religion, what he said can also be applied to spirituality, as what Hardy called 'religious experiences' are identical to what we would call 'spiritual experiences' today (heightened awareness). Unlike Freud (1928), who saw religion as a neurosis,[17] Hardy hypothesised that these experiences (representing a different from ordinary form of awareness) are biologically based and have evolved in the process of natural selection because they have a survival value to the species *Homo sapiens*. According to Hardy, many world religions are different cultural responses to a biologically based religious (spiritual) awareness of humans that has emerged as an evolutionary mechanism contributing to chances of survival in the process of natural selection. Indirect evidence supporting this claim comes from the work of anthropologists, who confirm that religion provides individuals with comfort, strength to face obstacles, the joy of serenity and the meaning of life itself (e.g. Durkheim 1976; Marrett 1920).[18] Some, however, argue that spirituality does not contribute to any evolutionary advantage for human beings.[19]

If spirituality is biologically rooted and natural to all humans, it should be reflected in biological markers in all people. In *Why God Won't Go Away* (Newberg *et al.* 2001), neuroscientist Andrew Newberg demonstrated that every human brain is uniquely constructed to perceive and generate spiritual realities.

The fact remains that every human brain, from childhood on, contemplates the possibility that spiritual realms exist. Believers like Isaac Newton, agnostics likes Charles Darwin, and atheists like Richard Dawkins have all given serious consideration to humanity's fascination with God, because the moment God is introduced to the human brain, the neurological concept will not go away. (Newberg and Waldman 2010, pp.5–6)

The brain-scan research by Newberg, d'Aquili and Rause conducted at the University of Pennsylvania (2001) shows that four association areas of the brain (the visual, the orientation, the attention and the verbal conceptual) are involved in producing the mind's spiritual potential.

Numerous research studies on spirituality and the frequency of mystical or spiritual experiences show that spiritual experience has always been very common. The surveys conducted by some professional organisations indicate that religious or spiritual issues are often addressed in psychotherapy. Anderson and Young (1988, p.532) state that 'all clinicians inevitably face the challenge of treating patients with religious troubles and preoccupations'. In the clinical context, in a survey conducted by APA (American Psychological Association) member psychologists, 60 per cent reported that their clients used religious language to express their personal experiences, and one in six of their clients talked about issues dealing with religion or spirituality (Shafranske and Maloney 1990). Lannert (1991) refers to another study of psychologists in which 72 per cent reported that at some time they addressed religious or spiritual issues in the treatment of their clients. A national study of psychologists, psychiatrists, social workers and memory therapists revealed that 29 per cent agree that religious issues are important in the treatment of all or many of their clients (Bergin and Jensen 1990).

The percentage of people in the UK and the USA who have had spiritual or religious experiences has varied between 20 and 44 per cent (Back and Bourque 1970; Glock and Stark 1965). It is interesting that, despite the fall in regular church attendance, the number of people who admitted spiritual experiences increased: from 48 per cent (Hay and Heald 1987) to 76 per cent (Hay and Hunt 2000). Hay and Morisy's research study (1985) suggests that a majority of people have strong spiritual intuitions but want nothing to do with any religious institution. The researchers conclude that many people move away from a religious institution because they find it no longer maintains their spiritual needs and turn towards a privatised belief that let them make sense of their spiritual experience.

Spirituality as a social construct

Anthropologist William Durham (1991) suggests that biological and social evolutions occur together, through the process known as co-evolution; both go through natural selection. In biological evolution the main hereditary units are genes, and in social evolution, memes, elements of a culture or system of behaviour passed from one individual to another by imitation or other non-genetic means.[20] Dawkins (1989, p.143) gives examples of memes as:

> tunes, ideas, catch-phrases, clothes fashions, ways of making pots or building arches. Just as genes propagate themselves in the gene pool by leaping from body to body via sperms or eggs, so memes propagate themselves in the meme pools by leaping from brain to brain via a process which, in the broad sense, can be called imitation.

According to Adams and colleagues (2008), co-evolution can account for the continual emergence of spirituality in human communities, as well as for the possibility that social evolution can have a negative and damaging effect on the survival of human species. The researchers state that there can be instances in which, under external pressure (such as, for example, propaganda, brainwashing), there is a voluntary acceptance of memes that are not helpful to survival. The authors conclude that, though biologically selected, spirituality can be repressed by socially constructed processes. Hay and Nye (2006) illustrate this idea with the example of modern individualist philosophies (as memes), such as focus on material success, having destructive consequences for societies and universal values.[21]

One of the objections to seeing spirituality as the result of social constructs is that it places it in the realm of subjectivity, whereas it is more akin to a perception of an objective reality (Hay and Nye 2006).

Diversity of expression

Spirituality is potentially equally present in religious people, agnostics and atheists, but it has a diverse expression in different cultures (and at different times) through different languages, beliefs and both secular and religious doctrines. For example, in the past in some cultures, 'hearing voices' was seen as communication from a deity (Joan of Arc was instructed by a voice to lead the troops, and won the battle). Shamans are respected for their ability to enter the 'other worlds' and to heal the sick with help from their other world's connections. Till recently, in many cultures epilepsy was considered a sacred disease and experiences during the epileptic fits were seen as mystical, and so on.

A spiritual potentiality is in all of us but the cultural context of it and, hence, the ways we express it are different (Hardy 1965), depending on the language (and cultural concepts) that 'shape' the manifestation of it.[22] This brings us to the role of language in 'shaping' the expression (and experience) of spirituality.

According to one theory, that of the American theologian George Lindbeck (1984), in order to have an experience, we need to have a language − a means for expressing/interpreting that experience. While not disputing this argument, Hay and Nye (2006) argue that the primacy of language for giving expression to someone's imaginative response to their awareness and the role of culture in the construction of the person's identity can lead us away from the biologically embodied nature of what it is to be human. As a biological predisposition, spirituality may be seen as pre-linguistic/non-linguistic experience that is *sensed/felt/perceived*.[23] A very interesting research study designed to avoid the limitation of verbal descriptions that are often inadequate to depict spiritual/religious experiences was conducted by Maria Bindl (1965), who analysed more than 8000 children's drawings on religious and spiritual topics. The children were students from Catholic schools, with ages ranging from 3 to 18. Bindl's method of analysis was both severely criticised (Wulff 1996) and supported (Bach 1990; Furth 1988). (This approach is especially relevant to investigating the experiences of autistic children who display difficulties with verbal language as a means of expression.)

Given that in Europe for hundreds of years spirituality has been discussed in the context of Christianity, the terminology for spiritual experiences has been of religious origin. Only recently have there been attempts to find new means of expression of spiritual themes that will fulfil the same task while being free from religious connotations.[24] Spiritual experience becomes 'shaped' when it is interpreted in whatever language the individual is competent in (whether verbal labels or non-verbal images − visual, tactile, auditory, etc.). Hay provides a convincing argument that though what different cultures have to say about spiritual awareness could be very inconsistent with each other at the logical level, they still refer to the same biological human phenomenon:

On the one hand we are not abstract language machines, free to create any kind of world we can imagine. On the other our biological inheritance permits us the possibility of transcending the limitations of the culture that shapes our personality. We are living animals, adapted through the process of evolution to survive within the constraints of a *real* environment. (Hay and Nye 2006, p.26; emphasis added)[25]

Interestingly, analysis of accounts of experiences in different cultures, with a wide range of different metaphors and interpretations, reveals the common underlying phenomenon. For example, the experiences of Christians engaged in contemplative prayer and practitioners of Zen and Buddhist meditation are recognisably similar though the interpretation is different.[26] Despite different types of practices used to induce the awareness, it seems the experiences are not much different from each other. Lindbeck (1984) calls such experiences the 'experiential-expressive' dimension of religion, which constitute a common core experience that is expressed differently in different world religions.

Being biologically predisposed to spirituality means that all of us can potentially experience it. The main restrictions seem to be our preoccupation with everyday activities, lack of time (or, sometimes, lack of a desire) to open up to these experiences, and/or being socially conditioned/pre-programmed to brush aside anything that has not been 'scientifically' proven and relegate it to the 'New Age stuff'.

However, though a natural human predisposition and not a cultural construct, spirituality cannot be identified outside a cultural context, which can either nurture or suppress it. Long-term research of the state of spirituality in modern societies by Hay and Nye (2006), for example, has shown that the modern Western world is more often than not destructive to the natural spirituality of human beings. Young children (who have not yet been conditioned out of it) are more open to spiritual experience, but as they grow and assimilate popular culture they close off their awareness. And here again we see how different it might be for autism. While autism is not a culture in the strict anthropological sense of the word, it *functions* as a culture, as it affects the ways autistic individuals behave, understand and communicate with the world. As the original experience of the world of autistic children is sensory-based, their original internal language (as a tool of formulation and expressing thought) consists of sensory-perceptual (multidimensional) images. This 'language' becomes central to their intellectual and emotional development (Bogdashina 2004), making it closer to the 'original vision' (in terms of Robinson's [1983] conceptualisation) and thus closer to 'spirituality as pre-linguistic/non-linguistic experience'. 'Autistic languages' of non-verbal autistic individuals are very different from conventional verbal and non-verbal languages; and those who are verbal still use verbal language differently from their non-autistic communicative partners: '[Verbal] language has a different usage for an autistic person than it has for a non-autistic person' (O'Neill 2000).

All humans (and possibly some non-human animals) potentially possess the abilities to experience spiritual awareness, but it can be more 'visible' and developed in different cultures and in different individuals.

'Visibility' in cultures implies 'nurturing' these experiences, where it would be considered abnormal *not* to 'feel', 'see', and so on the spiritual side of life, in contrast to cultures suppressing these experiences, conditioned to see only culturally accepted concepts, and labelling any difference as abnormality.

In Western societies, the conditioning out of spiritual experiences begins very early and intensifies when children start school, where the second (rational) way of thinking becomes dominant (and in many cases is the only one allowed). That is how Tito describes the loss of his imaginary (and spiritual) world:

> He tried to think of the staircase and the wonderful world of silence, which he used to imagine. But he could not concentrate as he used to. This was because of education, which had opened a new world for him. He was frustrated for not being able to be on the imagined staircases. He got angry with mother for educating him. Many a time when he tried to get a feeling of bliss, by imagining fantasies, his knowledge about the subject prevents him to dive into the virtual. It was irritating. He could not 'feel' the virtual as he did before. (Mukhopadhyay 2000, p.28)

Although everyone is predisposed to spirituality, some people (and groups of people) seem to be more spiritually aware or gifted than others:

- Recent research[27] has shown that children are 'more spiritual' because they are not yet restricted with cultural constructs: 'Children and animals, as purest of innocents, often perceive spiritual experiences only because they haven't yet been conditioned *not to*' (Stillman 2006, p.70). Growing up, however, most of them lose or forget their ability.

- At times of personal tragedy (for example, loss of someone they love) or stress, some individuals are more open to these experiences.

- It has been noticed that some people with what was once known as a 'mental deficiency' or mental illness have profound spiritual and religious awareness (Bissonnier 1965); people with temporal lobe epilepsy have strong emotional and déjà vu experiences (Mullan and Penfield 1959); people with psychosis are prone to powerful spiritual (whether positive or negative) experiences (Clarke 2010). Sensky and Fenwick (1982) reported a strong connection between epilepsy and religious experiences. Mysticism has often been linked to schizophrenia (Wapnick 1981).

- Individuals with autism.

Some people (including many professionals) deny even the possibility of spiritual or religious awareness in children with autism. They doubt that so-called low-functioning autistic individuals (especially those whom Lorna Wing (1996) calls 'aloof' and 'passive' individuals, living in their own world, unwilling or unable to start and maintain interaction with others) can be spiritual, because they do not seem to be aware of anything going on around them. Then, those who are high functioning ('active but odd' in Wing's classification) seem to be too rigid and too literal to understand such abstract concepts as 'religion' and 'spirituality'. One of the arguments of those who think that spirituality in autism may be problematic is that people with autism (especially at the low-functioning end of the spectrum) lack relationality and connectedness with others because they are seen as 'not wanting' to relate and to communicate to others; they seem to be content to live in their own world. However, it is a common mistake to interpret what we 'see' as what they feel or experience. In this particular case, the contrary seems to be true. Some individuals with autism are *too* aware of *their* environment[28] (with their perception being so sharp that it is painful); they cannot filter the 'irrelevant' (from the point of view of non-autistic people) information; their connectedness to others does exist but it is of a very different nature. In fact, some can be 'spiritually sensitive' or 'spiritually gifted', though 'normal' people may fail to see it. A research study (Speraw

2006) shows that parents and caregivers often feel that their autistic children are very spiritual. For the most part, their spirituality has been either devalued or completely unrecognised by those outside the family. The key seems to be in differences of their sensory perceptual functioning, and cognitive and language development.

> People think of reality as some sort of guarantee they can rely on. Yet from the earliest age I can remember I found my only dependable security in losing all awareness of the things considered real. In doing this, I was able to lose all sense of self. Yet this is the strategy said to be the highest stage of meditation, indulged in to achieve inner peace and tranquillity. Why should it not be interpreted as such for autistic people? (Williams 1999a, p.178)

Unlike non-autistic people, most of whom are conditioned out of spiritual experiences soon after they start school, for some autistic individuals spiritual reality is always part of their lives.

> Some things hadn't changed much since I was an infant swept up in the perception of swirling air particles, a child lost in the repetition of a pattern of sound, or a teenager staring for hours at coloured billiard balls, trying to grasp the experience of the particular colour I was climbing into. (Williams 1999a, p.19)

> 'My world' was a spiritual body. It had been my home, my self, my life, my entire system of making sense of that bastard place called 'the world'. (Williams 1999c, p.7)

What makes autistic individuals more open to spiritual experiences is their sensitivities: sensory, emotional, cognitive and spiritual – all caused by fundamental differences in their neurobiological development.

Notes

1. James, however, notes that there are other things in a chronology of religion that can be seen as more primordial than personal devoutness in the moral sense (spirituality), for example, fetishism and magic can be regarded as stages of religion. However, if magic and religion are opposed to each other (Frazer 1890; Malinowski 1974), the whole system of thought which leads to magic, fetishism and superstitions may be considered primitive science as well as primitive religion. 'The question thus becomes a verbal one' (James 1985, pp.30, 31).

2. Quite common metaphors to illustrate this link are a tree with roots representing spirituality and leaves representing religion; and a journey (spirituality) with a mode of transport (religion) (Hay and Nye 2006).

3. *Animism* – the attribution of a living soul to plants, inanimate objects, and natural phenomena; the belief in a supernatural power that originates and animates the material universe (from Latin *anima* 'life, soul').

4. See, for example, Evans-Pritchard 1972.

5. For example, O'Murchu 1997; Tacey 2000.

6. See, for example, Erricker 2001; Scott 2006; Tacey 2003.

7. Lancaster (2010, p.22) suggests that the move away from religion to spirituality reflects a changing attitude to authority, and that a turning point marking this shift was the First World War when 'the authority of rulers was effectively bankrupted by their inability to bring wisdom to the situation they faced'. Another reason for the shift was the availability of a wide range of teachings from different religions which challenged the acceptance of traditional religious authority.

8. In his book, James ignores the institutional branch and confines himself to personal religion (spirituality).

9. See, for example, Bekoff 2010; Goodall 2008.

10. Bosacki 2001; Erricker *et al.* 1997; Hay and Nye 2006; Tacey 2003.

11. Accessed at www.oxford.anglican.org/page/2316 on 8 November 2007.

12. What is important in the context of psychiatry 'is the idea that [spirituality] is at the heart of what gives life meaning, offering people both a genuine sense of purpose and a warm sense of belonging. It becomes a source of energy and motivation, the perfect antidote to depression' (Culliford 2007, p.226).

13. The Vipassana practice in Buddhism aims to develop a form of meta-awareness (Lutz, Dunne and Davidson 2007).

14. See, for example, Hay 2001.

15. See, for example, Otto 1950; Wach 1958.

16. It is similar to Bergson's (1944) concept of 'intellectual sympathy'.

17. Freud's interpretation of religious experience as a symptom of neurosis or temporary psychosis has been refuted by the research (Greeley 1975; Hay and Morisy 1978): in fact, the opposite is true – those who have these experiences score more highly than others on psychological well-being.

18. I remember my mother's stories of her childhood during the Second World War, when as a young child she was surprised to see an incredible change in the mood and attitude of her mother after the service in their local church: 'She felt much better about the difficult situation we were in and more optimistic about my father's whereabouts [he was arrested as an "enemy of the people" in the middle of the night just before the war and any attempt to find out what had happened to him was unsuccessful] when she came home.' Despite my dislike of Marxism-Leninism I have to admit that Marx's interpretation of religion as 'opium for the people' – a defence and strategy to cope with hardships – is correct, at least for many Eastern Europeans during the most difficult times of their lives. Conversely, Hay's research (1990, 1994), investigating the spirituality of people in the poorest and most oppressed sectors of Western society, has produced the opposite results: they are less likely to report having religious or spiritual experiences (Hay and Nye 2006). However, the 'poorest' in Western societies would not be considered 'poor' in some Eastern European countries.

19. See, for example, Fontana 2003.

20. Not all scholars agree with this notion.

21.   One of the most terrible memes that have been introduced and nurtured in the twentieth and twenty-first centuries is the ideology of leadership and success by any means; it destroys many people: if you are not at the top, you are considered a failure.

22.   Similarly, religions can be seen as conceptual reflections on, and social institutionalisations of, our experience of God. And when any conceptualisation fails to capture the experience, there is always something lost (Rahner 1974).

23.   The role of emotional feeling in conveying the meaning of what is happening has been highlighted by the research of Damasio (1994, 2000) and more recently by Jawer (2009).

24.   See, for example, research on children's spirituality: Hay and Nye 2006; Adams *et al.* 2008.

25.   However, we will have to consider several questions here: What is a *real* environment? The one we can perceive with our senses and/or special equipment? What if there are some people whose sensory perception is strikingly different from the 'normal' one? Whose 'reality' is more real then?

26.   See Graham 1968; Merton 1968; Suzuki 1957.

27.   See, for example, Coles 1992; Hay and Nye 2006; Hyde 2008.

28.   However, conceptually *their* environment is very different from the 'normal' one.

4

Sensitivities in Autism

Sensitivity can be defined as 'a higher (than "normal"/average) degree of being sensitive to something'. When we hear about sensitivities in connection with ASDs, the first impression that springs to mind is hypersensitivity to sounds, sights, smell, touch, and so on. However, the special abilities of autistic individuals to sense the environment are not limited to hypersensitivity to sensory stimuli. Autistic sensitivities can be (roughly) grouped into four categories:

- sensory sensitivities
- 'cognitive sensitivities'
- emotional sensitivities
- spiritual sensitivities.

Sensory sensitivities

Sensory sensitivities have been identified and reported from the very beginning of official descriptions of autism (Asperger 1944; Kanner 1943). In 1949, based on their own clinical observations, Bergman and Escalona suggested that autistic children start life with a higher degree of sensory sensitivity than normally developing children. The researchers observed children as young as three months old and reported in their article 'Unusual sensitivities in very young children' that these children 'were "sensitive" in both meanings of the word: easily hurt, and easily stimulated... Variations in sensory impression that made no difference to the average child made a great difference to these children' (p.333).

Sensory hypersensitivities are quite common in autism. Traditionally, we consider either five or seven senses (vision, hearing, tactility, olfaction, gustation, proprioception, vestibular). Any of these senses (or a combination of the senses) can be hypersensitive.

- *Hypervision* (seeing 'invisible') means that one can see more than other people, that is, one's vision is too acute. For example:

  Visual sensitivity to fluorescent lights can make them appear like strobe lights to a person with autism... [The eyes of people with this type of sensitivity] vibrate in synchrony with 60 Hz. cycling of fluorescent lighting. (Shore n.d.)

  [Some autistic individuals can see] 'stars' and 'spots' (charged energy particles that fill the air and that most people tune out as irrelevant background information or do not have sensitive enough vision to see). (Williams 1999c, p.186)

- *Hyperhearing* (hearing 'inaudible') means one is able to hear some frequencies that only some animals hear. For example:

  There was an increase in sound sensitivity on some frequencies...[and it was] so odd that I did not recognise it because I felt it as vibrations rather than noise. (Blackman 2001, p.200)

- *Hypertactility* results in experiencing even light touch as painful. For example:

  There are certain things I touch that hurt my hands... [Even] the air brushing past my hands is a source of pain. (McKean 1999)

- *Hyperproprioception* is reflected in odd body posture, difficulty manipulating small objects, and so on, and *vestibular hypersensitivity* brings a very low tolerance for any activity that involves movement or quick change in the position of the body.

- *Hypersmell*: some autistic individuals have olfactory sensitivities comparable to canines, and they can be felt as allergies to certain smells. For example:

  My allergic reaction to her perfume made the inside of my nose feel like it had been walled up with clay up to my eyebrows. Her perfume burned my lungs; my mouth tasted like I had eaten a bunch of sickly smelling flowers. (Williams 1999a, p.57)

- *Hypertaste:* for some, almost all types of food taste too sharp, or they cannot tolerate the texture or the sound of the food in their mouth:

> Many children with autism are finicky and will eat only certain foods... I hated anything that was slimy, like Jell-O or undercooked egg whites. (Grandin 2006, p.71)

For the purpose of our investigation it is appropriate to add more senses. Guy Murchie (1978) considers 32 senses, which he divides into five categories.

The radiation senses

Among the traditionally identified senses, vision is in this category, but it also includes senses of radiation, electricity, magnetism and temperature.

A *sensitivity to radiation* (other than visible light) is the ability to see radiation, for instance, under experimental conditions. During spaceflight it is possible to actually see cosmic rays as points or streaks of light (Gerald 1972). 'Though most humans are unable to consciously perceive most forms of magnetic radiation because the frequencies are beyond those of visible light, [it is possible] at least theoretically...to register electromagnetic radiation that lies *outside* of the normal range' (Jawer 2009, p.170).

Sensitivities to magnetism and electricity are well researched in some animals. There have been reported cases of individuals who can hear radar as buzzes and hisses (Frey and Messenger 1973), and someone who receives radio broadcasts through his teeth (Murchie 1978). It also seems that for some autistic individuals sensitivity to electricity can be an everyday experience.

Clarke's error

Arthur C. Clarke, one of the great predictors of future discoveries, whose non-fiction essays contain analysis of past, present and future human achievements, seems to make an error concerning his analysis of human abilities:

> There are some senses that do not exist, that can probably never be provided by living structures... On this planet, to the best of our knowledge, no creature has ever developed organs that can detect radio waves or radioactivity. Though I would hate to lay

down the law and claim that nowhere in the Universe can there be organic Geiger counters or living TV sets, I think it highly improbable. There some jobs that can be done only by transistors or magnetic fields or electron beams, and are therefore beyond the capacity of purely organic structures. (Clarke 2000, p.200)

However, some humans do possess abilities to detect radio waves. For example, a 50-year-old woman with Asperger syndrome has to unplug all the electrical appliances in her flat before going to bed, otherwise she would be unable to screen out the radio programmes from the switched off transistor and buzzing sounds from a (switched off but plugged in) microwave oven, for example, which at night are very 'audible and annoying' (personal communication). (Her partner jokes, 'If a flea sneezes, she jumps.') Temple Grandin writes about her student, Holly:

who is severely dyslexic, [and who] has such acute auditory perception that she can hear radios that aren't turned on. All appliances that are plugged in continue to draw power, even when they're turned off. Holly can hear the tiny little transmissions a turned-off radio is receiving. She'll say, 'NPR is doing a show on lions,' and we'll turn the radio on and sure enough: NPR is doing a show on lions. Holly can hear it. She can hear the hum of electric wires in the wall. And she's incredible with animals. She can tell what they're feeling from the tiniest variations in their breathing; she can HEAR changes the rest of us can't. (Grandin and Johnson 2005, p.63)

These cases are not that rare. Quite a few individuals report that they can hear radio programmes when the radio is switched off but still plugged in, for example:

If I want to get some more or less decent sleep I have to unplug all the electrical appliances in the house, especially radio and TV. During the day, with lots of noises and sounds in the environment it is relatively inaudible, but at night when everything is quiet, the interferences from the electrical equipment become intolerable: irritating buzzing sound of the microwave, bits and pieces of conversations or music from radio programmes (sometimes called 'for those who're awake' – that is very ironic, because it is these very programmes that keep me awake!). Strangely enough, I don't mind the fridge – it is always loud, anyway, so it seems very normal – a part of my auditory environment that is always here. (T., personal communication, 2010)

The feeling senses

Apart from hearing, this category includes awareness of pressure, sense of weight, sense of balance, awareness of one's proximity to someone or something in their surroundings, and a broad sense of what Murchie calls 'feel' – 'particular touch on the skin…awareness of intra- and intermuscular motion [proprioception], tickling, vibration…cognition of heart beat, blood circulation, breathing, etc.' (Murchie 1978, p.1979).

These 'feeling senses' can also include what is often called 'sixth sense', or 'gut feeling'; 'sensing' (the term suggested by Donna Williams 1998); and the ability to predict human behaviour, relying on 'pattern-recognition skills which occur intuitively' (Schoonmaker 2008).

The chemical senses

These include traditional smell and taste, and appetite, thirst and humidity.

The mental senses

These include pain, sense of danger, sexuality, relaxation and sleep, a sense of humour or playfulness, time sense, territorial sense, an aesthetic sense (appreciation of the arts, etc.) and intuition.

Many autistic individuals have a highly developed aesthetic sense, for example:

> the city lights and reflections playing upon the river…statues, beautiful parks, old wooden cathedrals, and marble sculptures, paintings by Renoir and scenes by Monet, captured me and brought home the beauty of 'the world.' … The frosted trees and icy fields… the beauty moved me so deeply I found myself crying. (Williams 1999c, p.157)

The spiritual senses

These include conscience, the capacity to sacrifice, the ability to experience ecstasy, religious bliss, feeling in unity with the cosmos.

Cognitive sensitivities

Strictly speaking, 'sensitivities' is not the best term to describe cognitive phenomena typical in autism. However, in some way at least, the word does stress both positive ('seeing' unusual connections, extraordinary abilities, etc.) and negative (e.g. difficulty in dealing with verbal abstractions) implications of the autistic modes of thinking. We can say that autistic people perceive, feel and remember too much (Markram *et al.* 2007). We will consider the following features of autistic cognitive processes:

- extraordinary abilities
- 'seeing' unusual connections and unconventional patterns
- (autistic) logical thinking
- subconscious thinking.

Extraordinary abilities

There are many different phenomena we cannot (yet) explain (such as, for example, synaesthesia and savant syndrome), and for now the best researchers can do is to suggest plausible theories and hypotheses that can shed some light and/or inspire more research. No matter how extraordinary these phenomena may seem to us, the majority accept them as real, whether we fully understand them or not.

Savant syndrome is not necessarily about 'spectacular skills'

Savant syndrome is thought to be a rare but extraordinary condition in which individuals with serious mental disabilities have some 'islands of genius' that stand in a marked contrast to things they cannot do. Areas of skills traditionally attributed to savants are musical and artistic ability, an exceptional memory for spelling, mathematical abilities, calendar calculating, geographical ability (reading maps, remembering directions, locating places), mechanical abilities (taking apart and putting together complex mechanical and electric equipment), a remarkable ability to balance objects, spatial skills (estimating the size or distance of objects with great accuracy) and outstanding knowledge in a specific field (such as, for example, history, navigation, statistics).

Individuals with savant skills are often able to perform tasks better than 'normal' people because they have direct access to primary areas of the brain and experience no interference from language (Grandin 2006). Only 10 per cent of people with autism are said to have savant skills. However, if we move away from 'spectacular skills' (like the ability to perform a musical piece after hearing it only once, or outstanding drawing abilities, or calendar calculating), we will see that due to the differences of their sensory perceptual and cognitive processes *all* individuals with autism can do something non-autistic people cannot (Daria 2008), while being helpless at some skills which are considered basic. Donna Williams urges us to realise that 'savant skills' can and do extend beyond art, music and 'calendar memories':

> In my experience, [the savant skills] can extend into mimicry, speed-reading, automatic writing, the acquisition of foreign languages and, in some cases, to the intermittent presence of so-called 'clairvoyance'. Taking into account these wider areas in which 'savant skills' may be found, a larger percentage of so-called 'savants' may be present among the 'autistic' population than is presently realised. (Williams 1996, pp.254–255)

Unlike 'recognised savant skills' (that are spectacular because 'normal' people can achieve them only with a lot of practice and hard work), other skills that only autistic people possess are not recognised because the 'normal' population cannot even imagine that they exist. For example, 'sensing time':

> My autistic son cannot tell the time (I've spent hours teaching him how to 'read' time but did not succeed) but he seems to 'sense' it. Recently he left me baffled when he said, 'My clock is ten minutes slow.' (I have to explain here that we have only one clock and it is in his room, the rest of us use wrist watches. He has no mobile phone or computer to see the 'right' time.) First I thought he was just confused and didn't know what he was talking about, but then I went into his room, looked at his clock (and then at my watch) and found that he was absolutely right – his clock was ten minutes slow! It was time to replace the battery.
>
> There have been other strange cases that I cannot explain. Like, for example, eight years ago (my son was 11 then) when we were in the Lake District on the beach and I asked my partner what time it was, and before he could answer, our son loudly announced 'Quarter past two'. Need I say, that it *was* quarter past two? Of course, the first explanation that sprang in my mind was 'it's just a coincidence,' but there have been so many coincidences since then that it begs a question: Are they coincidences, or is he able to sense the time? (T., personal communication)

'Seeing' unusual connections and unconventional patterns

When thinking we often divide the whole into parts, that is, think about separate 'things', while missing the whole. (It is ironic that we 'accuse' autistic individuals of not seeing the forest behind the trees, while categorizing and classifying 'parts of the forest' in our minds all the time and losing the 'big picture' of our reality.) That is why we are often bewildered:

> whenever things seem to go wrong or awry... Sometimes things *seem* to go wrong when in the bigger picture all remains satisfactory. Things are fine, but we are not yet able to see and appreciate that point. Our emotional reactions get in the way, so this type of situation provides us with an opportunity to adjust our perception and thinking, to learn something, to improve our understanding of things and to grow, to mature a little in wisdom. (Culliford 2007, p.62)

In contrast to the 'verbal thinking' of non-autistic individuals, 'autistic thinking' is mostly sensory-perceptual'.[1] When a non-verbal person thinks, there are no words going through his mind, only sensory impressions such as visual images, sounds, smells, taste and touch sensations. The closest analogy is remembering a dream. Gelernter (2006) writes about the cognitive spectrum that is changing its version every day: the most analytical one is when we are most awake; as we grow less awake, our thinking becomes more concrete, and when we start to fall asleep, we begin to free associate and finally reach 'the wholly nonlogical, high concrete type of thought we call "dreaming"'. In terms of development, we trace out the cognitive spectrum in reverse: babies and children think concretely; as they grow up their thinking becomes more analytical (Gelerner 2006, p.167). Conversely, in autism, the 'quality' of visual thinking may depend on the state the person is in, and even the time of day; for instance, thought images are clearer and most detailed when the person is drifting off to sleep (Grandin 2006).

Being a spatial thinker means that a person represents things in their mind with a multidimensional model. This way of thinking brings both disadvantages and advantages. On the one hand, it is more difficult to do things that are sequential (one-dimensional and in linear progression). On the other hand, it is easier to see certain patterns of the world and infer things from those patterns. Since people with autism think with their subconscious they can see the decision-making process that is not perceived by 'normal' people (Grandin 2006).

Many autistic individuals have their own systems for interpreting their surroundings. For example, Gunilla Gerland (1997) had her own internal colour system which she used to connect information about different places ('worlds'), such as the nursery or the garden. The colours helped her to interpret other people's feelings as well as her own, the atmosphere of different places, and so on. It was the colours generated from the inside that assisted her in detecting connections between the places and people.

(Autistic) logical thinking

It is logical to assume that perceptual thinking gives us an unbiased (less biased?) approach to any problem. People who think perceptually are not restricted by traditional conventions. In contrast to 'normal' *sequential* thinking that involves analysis, the progression from simple to complex, organizing information in linear deductive reasoning, *spatial* thinking involves a synthesis, an intuitive grasp of complex systems (often missing the steps), simultaneous processing of concepts, including reasoning (from the whole to the parts), use of imagination and generation of ideas by combining existing facts in new ways (creative thinking). It is influenced by visualisation and images and awareness of space. Spatial, holistic and synthetic functions are thought to be associated with the right hemisphere of the brain (West 1991).[2]

Logical thinking without interference from emotions also seems to be quite common in autism (especially in Asperger syndrome, AS), for example:

> My thought processes…through good times and bad, have been mathematically logical… I put too high a premium on logic and rationality, giving short shrift to the emotions. (Schneider 1999, p.20)

Subconscious thinking

Temple Grandin (2006) hypothesises that in most people language covers up the primary sensory-based thinking that humans share with animals. Sensory-based thinking is subconscious in most people, while those like Temple Grandin think with the primary sensory-based subconscious areas of the brain. When well developed, this brings certain advantages not available to others. For example, 'normal' people have difficulty in conceptualising multidimensional processes (Johnson-Laird 1989), which can be linked to unconscious processes operating 'in a space of a higher number of dimensions than that of our perceptions and conscious thinking' (Matte-Blanco 1988, p.91).[3]

Types of intelligence

Several types of intelligence can be distinguished, and different tests have been designed to measure it.

Rational intelligence: Thinking with a brain

Cognitive abilities (both verbal and non-verbal) are tested with specially designed tests and the results are reflected in the intelligence quotient (IQ).[4] As in non-autism, cognitive functioning in autism involves both positive (such as, for example, acuteness, perfect memory, detecting patterns, seeing unusual connections) and negative (for instance, inability/difficulty in shifting attention between stimuli of different sensory modality, difficulty in dealing with abstractions) features. As the IQ tests have been designed to test 'normal' features of cognitive development, they turn out to be meaningless in testing autistic cognitive intelligence – thinking with a brain.

> Measuring non-autistic people by [the autistic] type of development would often find them failing miserably and appearing to be thoroughly 'subnormal' by 'autistic' standards. (Williams 1996, p.235)

By distinguishing between subconscious and conscious perceptual processing, we can distinguish between conscious and subconscious types of intelligence, the latter with little conscious awareness ('unknown knowing'). They roughly correspond to Bergson's definitions of intellect and intuition (or 'intellectual sympathy'), with intellect being external, looking on reality as different from life, but in 'intellectual sympathy' 'one places oneself within an object in order to coincide with what is unique in it and consequently inexpressible' (Bergson 1944, p.23). Bergson points out that analysis reduces the object to already known elements that are common to it and all other objects; analysis can be seen as a translation into symbols and expresses a thing as a function of something other than itself. Unlike intellectual sympathy (intuition) that leads to the inwardness of life, intellect 'goes all round life...drawing it into itself instead of entering it' (Bergson 1944, p.194). Bergson's intellectual sympathy can be seen in the phenomenon experienced by some autistic people: 'losing oneself' in stimuli to the extent that one becomes 'resonant' with them (terms introduced by Donna Williams). The person can merge with different sensory stimuli as if they become the stimulus itself. Some autistic individuals are able to be 'in resonance' with their surroundings – colours, sounds, objects, places, plants, animals, people. These are very real experiences that can be called 'spiritual experiences'.

Emotional sensitivities

Before defining 'emotional sensitivities', we have to distinguish between the terms 'feeling' and 'emotion'. Are emotions and feelings the same thing or are they different phenomena? There is no consensus here and different researchers define both 'feelings' and 'emotions' differently. For example, Damasio's definition of 'feelings' corresponds to what others define as 'emotions' and vice versa.

Feelings and emotions

Feelings are physical sensations that can be subdivided into *somatic* and *affective*. *Somatic* experiences are feelings of the body, such as, for example, muscle tension, headache, chest pain, goosebumps, tiredness. *Affective* experiences are feelings of the mind (soul), for example, emptiness, panic, homesickness.

Scherer (1994) defines emotions as complex narrative structures that give shape and meaning to somatic and affective experiences, that is, *emotions* are mental states, interpretations of feelings when the sensory perceptual input of both somatic and affective experiences get cognitive explanation and conscious plan of action. According to Shweder (1994), emotions represent somatic and affective experience not simply as a feeling (such as tiredness or heartache or being sick) but as a perception (for example, being in love, or being betrayed) and a plan (withdrawal, retaliation). Both parts are equally important. Damasio (2000) describes how physical manifestation of fear, for example, such as accelerated heartbeat, actually contributes to the feeling of fear.

To emotionalise one's feelings means to give a 'reading' to (interpret and label) somatic and affective experience. Quite often the somatic feeling may be the same but its affective side is different, for example, you may feel sick but it does not necessarily mean that you have eaten something nasty, it can mean you are in love (Shweder 1994).

Emotions start as feelings and they are closely connected to sensory perception as they start as *sensory* feelings. Jawer (2009, p.19) defines 'feeling' as 'a subset of the sensory perceptions', especially 'those most closely associated with the body and its processing of sensory stimuli', including the ones that are usually distant senses, such as hearing, for example. Jawer argues that hearing should be considered as a feeling sense because the sound is literally a vibration and that is why it is felt either on the ear-drums or even on our skin (for instance, the sounds produced by a bass guitar). Following this logic, it is possible to add vision to the list of 'feelings' because it is possible to 'touch' with your eyes ('distant touching'; Bogdashina 2004). Some autistic individuals can actually *feel* (with actual tactile experience on their skin) if they are looked at directly: 'It can feel creepy to be searched with the eyes' (O'Neill 1999, p.26).

Are emotions uniquely human phenomena?

Jaak Panksepp, who believes that feelings originate in the brain stem, disagrees with the concept of the 'uniqueness of emotional states to primates and humans'. The argument is, because the brain stem has not changed much in the course of human evolution, it could, therefore, be involved in producing feelings not only in humans but also in other species as well, so if it looks like fear in people and rats, it probably feels like fear in both species. Opponents question this belief, insisting that although there is neural and behavioural similarity between humans and rats, for example, we cannot prove that rats and people *feel* the same way when they behave the same way.

It turns out that animals have the same basic emotions as humans. This is true not only for mammals but also for birds and other animals, such as lizards and snakes (Grandin and Johnson 2005). Panksepp (1994) believes that most species possess unique sensory perceptual inputs that lead to emotionality. For example, such 'fearful behaviours' of rats in response to the smell of a cat are not acquired by learning. Rats are born with it (Crepeau and Panksepp 1988).

However, the ability to identify and 'name'/'label' what one is feeling is a different matter. The activity of labelling is arbitrary; it is independent of emotional experience. The choice of words to describe the emotion often depends on the communicator's intentions. For instance, some words appear to emphasise the physiological reaction component ('tired' or 'aroused'), others are quite cognitive ('bewildered', 'curious'), still others focus on specific sociomotivation ('jealous'), or highlight the action tendency ('hostile') (Scherer 1994).

Emotional hypersensitivity

As most autistic individuals' senses work in 'hyper', and feelings start as sensations (either conscious or unconscious), it is no wonder that many people with ASD are emotionally hypersensitive.

Wendy Lawson describes how sensory stimuli can evoke very powerful emotion in her:

> I find colour simply fascinating and it stirs all sorts of feelings in me. The stronger and brighter the colour, the more stirred up I become. My favourite colours are rich in emerald green, royal blue, purple, turquoise and all the in-between shades of these colours. (Lawson 1998, p.3)

She is surprised that other people do not bother to enjoy the bright colours around them: the colour of the door they are about to open, or a sign across their path. Colours and fragrance are so vibrant to Wendy's senses that she can *feel* them. To illustrate the point she gives an example of the emotion evoked by freshly fallen snow:

> I remember one particular morning, when I was coming home after a night shift at the hospital... Fresh snow had fallen during the night and my footprints were the first ones to make any impression on the frozen footpath. I stopped, afraid to move for fear of disturbing perfection in front of me. (Lawson 1998, p.3)

Such experiences can be termed as emotional hypersensitivity and accounted for by the intense world syndrome (Markram *et al.* 2007) which indicates that the amygdala and related emotional areas of the brains of autistic individuals are affected with hyper-reactivity leading to hyper-perception, hyper-attention and hyper-memory.

> All things are heightened for me, so what a regular person would be tickled with pleasure over, I'll be totally ecstatic. Likewise, someone else's small irritation will turn into a catastrophe for me, like 100 nails screeching a blackboard (to use a commonly understood simile). (O'Neill 2000)

> My entire *nervous system* is intensely sensitive such that my emotions and senses 'vibrate' at a frequency different than most. For instance, I was unusually sensitive as a child – extremely emotional. The melancholy lyrics to a song like 'Puff the Magic Dragon' or virtually anything by Peter, Paul and Mary could cause me to become

inconsolable. This was, perhaps, most memorably defined by an emancipating childhood incident. Raised in the Episcopal church, I was once removed from my pew, at age six, because I could not control my weeping. Unbeknownst to anyone, I had been staring at a terrible, glorious stained-glass window of the crucifixion and grieving for the pain Christ must endured. The arresting mosaic of that forlorn image etched itself indelibly upon me. And yet at some point, I became emotionally and empathically detached. (Stillman 2006, pp.3–4)

If many autistic individuals are emotionally hypersensitive, how can we explain their (alleged) lack of empathy?

Empathy in autism (and alleged lack of it)

Empathy and sympathy

Empathy: the ability to identify oneself mentally with somebody else, thus understanding what the person feels.

Sympathy: the state of being simultaneously affected with a feeling to that of another person; the ability to share emotion.

Autistic people are said to be (severely) impaired in their ability to empathise with other people which is reflected in the 'mind-blindness theory' of autism (Baron-Cohen, Leslie and Frith 1985; Frith 2003; Happe 1995).[5]

A few functional imaging studies suggest that these deficits may be caused by a hypo-active amygdala,[6] numerous studies confirm that the role of the amygdala in modulating and regulating emotional responses is of paramount importance[7] and pathology in the amygdala has been proposed to be the cause of the social interaction in autism.[8] However, contrary to the belief of lack of emotional compassion in autism, autistic individuals may experience enhanced emotionality (along with enhanced perception) (Markram *et al.* 2007).

Research has shown that people respond to emotional expressions unconsciously, and emotions seem to be contagious (Hatfield, Cacioppo and Rapson 1994); people involuntary tend to mimic facial expressions of those with whom they interact (Surakka and Hietanen 1998). This can explain empathy, when people 'feel' others' moods

(Sonnby-Borgström 2002). 'Emotional contagion' develops very early in life and is fully established by the age of two (Hay 1994). There is some research evidence that the perception of someone's facial expression activates the neurons that would produce the same expression in the self (Preston and de Waal 2002). For example, when people, in response to seeing someone else's smile, pose their own smile, they begin to experience the emotion that goes with it (Tantam 2009). Tantam proposes that persons with autism do not show this involuntary response, but it does not necessarily mean that they lack empathy – they simply may not recognise the 'conventional expression of emotions'. An alternative explanation is that they may not be consciously aware that they have perceived emotion because they are too busy understanding what someone else is saying and preparing their response; their ability to read the emotions of others seems to increase when they can observe their communicative partners without having to think in language (Kimball 2005). However, there is another explanation as well: 'emotional contagion' normally develops with a very early ability to imitate, and by mimicking their carers' facial expressions and body language normally developing children learn to connect outside expressions of emotions with their physical sensations (activating the same areas in the brain). In contrast, in autism 'emotional contagion' develops through resonance, that is, they actually 'catch' the emotional energy of others, resonating with them, and experiencing the same physical sensations through their bodies. So despite having difficulties identifying 'conventional' emotional cues that are easily 'read' by 'normal' people, some individuals with autism are very hypersensitive to the emotions of others. Some resonate with emotional states of their significant others and experience the same emotion inside themselves; many resonate with animals. For example, Temple Grandin feels sensory empathy with cattle: when they remain calm she feels calm and when they are in pain she feels their pain: 'I tune in to what the actual sensations are like to cattle rather than having the idea of death rile up my emotions' (Grandin 2006, p.94).

Jawer (2009) has introduced the concept of 'emotional energy' that, just like other forms of energy, 'can be stored, focused, drained or liberated. It can radiate out to others, for better or for ill; it can be vividly felt or left to work its own way in our bodies and nervous systems' (p.153), and like other forms of energy, it can be felt by some while being 'invisible' to others. '[This] energy produced by the brain and the heart extends outside the body. It can be measured by devices such as electrocardiographs (ECGs), magnetocardiographs (MCGs) and magnetoencephalographs (MEGs)' (pp.169–170).

Many autistic people can easily pick up the emotions (emotional energy) of others and may be very distressed by the emotional behaviour of those around them (even though they cannot interpret the feelings). Often those who take care of autistic children trigger (by their emotional state) what we call challenging behaviours and then are puzzled as to what caused the outburst or meltdown. Many autistic individuals seem to automatically tune into the mood of their carers' and instantly share their emotions. These hypersensitive individuals seem to amplify their carers' emotions and feed them back. If the emotions are negative, 'difficult behaviours' emerge, which, in fact, are caused by the negative emotional energy that has been 'fed' to the children by those around them.

Research has shown that experiences of feeling someone else's pain are, in fact, very real for some people, and reflected in the activity not only in the emotional centres of the brain (common for the majority of people) but also in a greater activity in somatic brain regions, providing the evidence that some people can experience both emotional and sensory components of pain while observing others' suffering, resulting in a shared pain experience.[9] Other studies show that some individuals find it difficult to distinguish between the touch sensation caused by observation of someone being touched and by physical touch.[10]

Some autistic individuals argue that there are different types of empathy: sensory empathy, emotional (affective) empathy and intellectual empathy. 'Normal' people have emotional empathy but some of them may be very deficient in or lack 'sensory-based empathy', quite common in many autistic people.[11] Donna Williams (1998, p.117) describes sensory-based (not mental) empathy as working 'through resonance in a relationship between sender and receiver in which the receiver loses their own separateness in merging with the sender as part of the mechanism of acquaintance before returning to the unmerged state of its own entity'.

Sensory empathy can be very strong in autism, but weak in 'non-autism':

> For me to have empathy I have to visually put myself in the other person's place. I can really empathize with a laid-off worker because I can visualize his family sitting at the dining room table trying to figure out how the bills will get paid. If the worker fails to pay the

mortgage he will lose his house. I really relate to physical hardship. I have observed that normal people have had bad visual empathy. They are often not able to perceive how another person would see something. (Grandin 2006, p.99)

[Watching news on TV] As I feel my worries for trapped coal miners, I can smell the boiling starch, frothing on the brim of the clay pot, then spilling out with the smell of burning rice. My worries grow as the voice of the newsreader continues to say that the miners are still trapped. I smell burning rice all across the room as more starch spills out. (Mukhopadhyay 2008, p.113)

Even when a young child, Gunilla Gerland (1997, p.48) 'could see and understand terror in others'; she 'could empathise with other people being frightened, feeling small, insulted or exposed, because [she] had felt all that, too'.

Recent research studies show that it is an overgeneralisation to claim that individuals with Asperger syndrome have a 'deficit in empathy'. Rogers and colleagues (2006) administered the Interpersonal Reactivity Index (IRI), a multidimensional measure of empathy, and the Strange Stories Test to 21 adults with Asperger syndrome and 21 matched controls. Their data show that, while the AS group scored lower on cognitive empathy and Theory of Mind, they were no different from the controls on an affective empathy scale of the IRI (empathic concern), and scored higher than the controls on the personal distress test.

Intellectual empathy is quite common in some people with autism – typically, high-functioning individuals whose sensory empathy is not pronounced but who are able to feel and appreciate emotions intellectually – through art, music, literature and other creative and artistic means. This is because, through the arts, emotions are translated into sights, sounds and words. 'They register on the intellectual and aesthetic sensibilities' (Schneider 1999, p.52). These 'intellectually emotional people' can become emotionally moved under the effects of arts, music, literature or films.[12] Paradoxically, art (whether visual or music or literature) is a *felt* experience, even if it is not consciously registered. A very good illustration of this is from the (unpublished) account of Ms T. (a woman with AS) about her childhood experience:

When I was nine years old my father took me to Moscow on holiday for seven days. He kept talking about this trip for several years, since he bought a beautifully illustrated book about the Tretyakovskaya

Gallery.[13] We arrived late at night, had a few hours sleep in the hotel and off we went. We headed straight to the Tretykovskaya Gallery – the Red Square, the GUM and other 'must-see' places would have to wait… And they had to wait for more than 10 years because our last six days my dad was nursing me in our hotel room. It was a mistake to 'take' the Gallery in a day. At the end of the day I was physically overwhelmed: I had to lie down and was afraid to move my head – the headache was unbearable. I thought my brain was going to explode; all the pieces of art seemed to 'engulf' my very body with what seemed like the energy they emitted – it was beautiful and very positive, but I couldn't cope with the intensity of it.

A very important feature of 'intellectual emotionality/empathy' is that it is very logical. People can logically explain and rationalise the feelings they have in different situations.

Never in my life have I ever felt grief, or even a sense of loss… Any sorrow I felt was purely intellectual… I am, though, able to intellectually appreciate the grief of another. At one time, I saw an old man lamenting the recent death of his wife. I thought about how there must be a great deal of love to produce that much grief. Not being able to feel what he felt, I was at a total loss as to what to say to him… The irony of this is that I can get all weepy at the tear-jerker endings of operas such as *La Traviata*, *La Bohème*, or *Madama Butterfly*, or novels such as *Dracula*…[feeling 'emotion' only through art]. (Schneider 1999, pp.51, 52)

Sometimes, people with ASDs' interpretation of emotions differs from the conventional one, but isn't the argument logical?

I define ['teasing'] as holding in someone's view something that person wants a great deal, but purposely withholding it, causing that person to suffer. A synonym is 'tantalize', which comes from the story of Tantalus… The gods thought this a fit punishment for someone who had done an evil thing, yet teasing is often done solely for ego-enhancement. I see this as nothing but gratuitous cruelty. (Schneider 1999, p.41)

Sometimes, people with ASD may empathise with those who do not seem to deserve it (from the conventional point of view). For example, Edgar Schneider's logical analysis of fictional characters is very different from 'ordinary readers':

I often find myself in sympathy with characters that the author, I have to admit, did not intend to portray as sympathetic. In fact, the author, I would imagine, would have wanted the reader to consider them as worthy of being outcasts. They are usually cast as the villains...

In Shakespeare's *King Lear*, I developed an immediate fondness for Edmund, the illegitimate son of the Duke of Gloucester, after hearing, at the beginning, his father's conversation about him with the Earl of Kent. Later in the play, when Edmund has his father's eyes gouged out, I could not, in spite of the gruesomeness of it, get over the feeling that the old man had it coming.

Someone who, it appears, is easy to villainize is a husband who is portrayed as 'cold' and 'distant'. He is, nevertheless, a man who works hard to provide for his wife and is genuinely concerned for her welfare. He does not, though, provide any 'excitement' or 'fulfilment'. She gets involved with a man who does provide those, but for whom she is essentially a toy and who suddenly is no longer available when the situation becomes too complicated for his taste. Conceivably she could return to her husband a sadder but wiser woman...but instead does something totally irrational [Tolstoy's *Anna Karenina*]...

I realise that I have viewed [these] characters...in terms of what their actions should have been had they been logical, but that is the only way I know of how to view the world. (Schneider 1999, pp.39–40)

These (intellectual) emotions are as powerful as sensory emotions are. Temple Grandin gets great emotional satisfaction from her career of designing livestock equipment. She feels happy when a client is pleased with the facility she designed. When her project fails or a client criticises her unfairly, Temple becomes depressed and upset. Her emotional satisfaction from doing something that is of value to society is very real and very powerful:

The happiness I feel when a client likes one of my projects is the same kind of glee I felt as a child when I jumped off the diving board. When one of my scientific papers is accepted for publication, I feel the same happiness I experienced one summer when I ran home to show my mother the message I had found in a bottle on the beach. I feel a deep satisfaction when I make use of my intellect to design a challenging project. It is the kind of satisfied feeling one gets after finishing a difficult crossword puzzle or playing a challenging game of chess or bridge; it's not an emotional experience so much as an intellectual satisfaction. (Grandin 2006, p.90)

[T]he gifts that I have been given have made me, in spite of all disappointments and setbacks, able to enjoy life to an extent that few others seem to have been able to duplicate.

This joy that has filled my life due to my intellectual and aesthetic pursuits has more than made up for any joys that I may have missed from my lack of emotional involvement with people. Without it my life would really have been empty. (Schneider 1999, p.118)

So even if they may lack 'affective empathy' because of difficulty reading (conventional) signals, they compensate for it with 'cognitive/ intellectual empathy'.

Gardner's (1983) plurality of intelligence has brought numerous attempts to apply the concept of intelligence to many different aspects of human development, including emotional intelligence, social intelligence, cultural intelligence, collective intelligence, spiritual intelligence. The most prominent ones (which have attracted both support and criticism) are emotional and spiritual intelligences.

Emotional intelligence: Thinking with a heart

The term *emotional intelligence* (EI) was coined by Goleman (1995) to refer to a person's ability to understand and accurately interpret his or her own emotions, as well as the emotions of others.[14] The concept is intended to complement the traditional view of intelligence by aiming at the emotional, personal and social aspects of intelligent behaviour (Mayer and Salovey 1993). This is known as the mixed model of EI (Bar-On 1997; Goleman 1995) because EI is seen as a mixture of abilities, personality dispositions and traits. Despite lack of research support for EI being a separate intelligence (but rather an aspect of personality) (Davies, Stankov and Roberts 1998), the idea of using EI measurements to distinguish between people who understand their emotions and those who are 'emotionally blind' has raised a lot of interest. Mayer and Salovey (1997) have developed the concept of EI further (the ability model), approaching it as 'thinking with a heart', distinguishing EI from distinct personality characteristics, while recognising that they are important elements of EI:

> Emotional intelligence refers to an ability to recognize the meanings of emotions and their relationships, and to reason and problem-

solve on the basis of them. Emotional intelligence is involved in the capacity to perceive emotions, assimilate emotion-related feelings, understand the information of those emotions, and manage them. (Mayer, Caruso, and Salovey 1999, p.267)

Criticism of EI concerns EI measurement instruments, that, according to Davies *et al.*, generally 'exhibited low reliability and indicated a lack of convergent validity' (1998, p.989).

The Mayer-Salovey-Caruso Emotional Intelligence Test (MSCEIT; Mayer, Salovey and Caruso 2002)[15] is based on self-report.[16] It is an ability-based test designed to measure the four branches of the EI model of Mayer and Salovey:

- *perceiving emotions*: the ability to perceive emotions in oneself and others as well as in objects, art, stories, music and other stimuli

- *facilitating thought*: the ability to generate, use and feel emotion as necessary to communicate feelings or employ them in other cognitive processes

- *understanding emotions*: the ability to understand emotional information, to understand how emotions combine and progress through relationship transitions and to appreciate such emotional meanings

- *managing emotions*: the ability to be open to feelings, and to modulate them in oneself and others so as to promote personal understanding and growth.

These tests have been designed to test 'normal' ways to express and understand emotions; they would not work with many autistic individuals – who are often described as 'heart savants' despite the assumption that they lack emotional maturity and empathy.

It has been noticed that sensory and emotional sensitivities are often associated with certain somatic symptoms. Psychologist Ian Wickramasekera (1998) suggests that physical sensitivity can be transmuted into such physical symptoms as asthma, allergy, chronic pain, fatigue, and so on. Wickramasekera explains that psychological distress leads to somatisation (physical illness): when the person 'is being…made sick by distressing secret perceptions, memories, or moods that [he or she] blocks from consciousness' (p.83). Sharon Heller (2002, p.146) also confirms that highly sensitive individuals (she calls them 'sensory defensive') often suffer from such conditions as chronic fatigue, aching muscles, sleep difficulties, headaches, allergies, irritable bowel syndrome, ulcers and gastrointestinal problems, skin disorders and other problems. She explains that environmental stimuli that would be unnoticed by the majority often cause a chronic stress response in these individuals, and 'eventually the immune system is depleted and the body succumbs and breaks down'.

These symptoms have been reported by persons with ASD (who experience sensory and emotional hypersensitivity), for example:

> All the time I was growing up, I suffered from an almost constant shudder down my spine... I became slightly used to it, but it was a constant torture, most noticeable when it changed in intensity... It was like cold steel down my spine. It was hard and fluid at the same time, with metallic fingers lightly drumming and tickling on the outside... It was like a sound of screeching chalk against a blackboard turned into a silent concentration of feeling, then placed at the back of my neck... From there, so metallic, the feeling rang in my ears, radiated into my arms, clipped itself firmly into my elbows, but never came to an end. (Gerland 1997, pp.56–57)

> I had been on painkillers for rheumatism... The pains...had become excruciating, and I would slam myself side-on into the walls and knock my head against them in an effort to ease pain...
>
> Intolerance to different foods can cause allergic reaction in different parts of the body. In my case my skin was not the 'target organ' for my particular allergic reactions. It was...discovered I was suffering from extreme multiple allergies... (Williams 1999b, pp.60, 140)

Spiritual sensitivities

Schneider cites the Bible (Matthew 18:3) saying that we cannot enter Heaven unless we come as little children. He analyses the meaning of 'child-like' and describes several features that characterise it: trusting and exhibiting:

> an insatiable curiosity, coupled with great joy in learning something new, or finding the answer to a question that has been hanging fire for a while. Even in the days when I would not get involved with the world, I always was like that, and from that high school sophomore year onward, it consumed me. (Schneider 1999, p.60)

Like Schneider, many other autistic individuals seem to retain this child-like curiosity and openness to the world. In contrast, 'normal' people typically lose the ability to wonder. Though having become 'cool', 'these people are missing what could be a very full life. It is almost as if their epitaphs would read: "Died at twenty-five; buried at seventy-five"' (Schneider 1999, p.60).

Contrary to the traditional view that autistic people experience difficulty or inability in understanding spiritual and religious notions, due to their differences in sensory perceptual, cognitive and linguistic development, religious and spiritual experiences seem to come more easily to individuals with autism. Some develop 'spiritual giftedness' and what Stillman (2006) calls 'the God connection'.

In one of the first books to deal with spirituality and autism, *Spirituality and the Autism Spectrum: Of Falling Sparrows* (2001), Abe Isanon defines spirituality as the spirit with which we confront concrete reality, and to accommodate the special character of the autism condition, specifies that 'the spirituality of autism and related conditions is, in essence, a liberatory spirituality, a spirituality that seeks to give meaning not only to the life of the person with autism but also to that of the carer' (p.14). A central theme of the spirituality of liberation is 'living with Spirit', or, as Sobrino (1993) puts it, it is being-human-with-spirit, responding to crisis and bringing promise to concrete reality.

Researching spirituality in autism, Bill Stillman, an adult with Asperger syndrome (2006, p.73), comes to a similar conclusion that children and animals, being 'the purest of innocents, often perceive spiritual experiences only because they haven't yet been conditioned *not to.* ... The person with autism may simply not be fully cognizant of her very special gift, and may assume *everyone* communicates this way.' In his three books devoted to spirituality in autism, Stillman (2006, 2008, 2010) provides numerous anecdotes illustrating such features of autistic spiritual connection or giftedness as the heightened awareness, innate gentleness and 'exquisite sensitivity (a capacity to perceive all things seen and unseen)'; for some, 'these blessings came in the form of 'Gifts of the Spirit'. Examples:

> reportedly range from knowing what someone is thinking before it is said; foretelling future events that come to fruition; and enjoying special, unspoken bonds with animals. Still others are said to have perceived visions of grandparents and other loved ones in Spirit, or even communed with angels – abilities seemingly reserved for Old World saints and prophets. (Stillman 2006, pp.6–7)[17]

We are often blind to 'autistic spirituality' because it is not 'projected' to our culturally constructed reality,[18] so these experiences might go unnoticed by the majority of people. Besides, not *every* person with autism displays these sensitivities. However, it is reasonable to expect that it is more common in the autistic population than in 'normal' people due to their differences in sensory perceptual and cognitive functioning. To give just one example of a spiritual experience, Donna was a very young child when she discovered that:

> the air was full of spots. If you looked into nothingness, there were spots... My attention would be firmly set on my desire to lose myself in the spots, and I'd ignore [everything], looking straight through this obstruction with a calm expression soothed by being lost in the spots... I learned eventually to lose myself in anything I desired – the patterns on the wall paper or the carpet, the sound of something over and over again, the repetitive hollow sound I'd get from tapping my chin. Even people [with their conversations] became no problem. I could look through them until I wasn't there, and then, later, felt that I had lost myself *in them*. (Williams 1999b, p.9)

Spiritual intelligence: Is this a useful concept?

Recently some researchers have argued in favour of another domain of intelligence, similar to rational intelligence and emotional intelligence – spiritual intelligence or *thinking with a soul*. Zohar and Marshall (2000, p.4) state that among other intelligences (rational and emotional intelligences) spiritual intelligence is the highest, as it unifies, integrates and complements both IQ and EQ, serving as a 'foundation for effective functioning of both IQ [mental] and EQ [emotional]'. However, despite claiming theirs to be the first well-developed theory of spiritual intelligence, there are many problems with it, starting from the very beginning – definition of it. For example, recognising the meaning of Q in IQ as the 'intelligent quotient' indicating the degree of intelligence, Zohar proceeds with her description of spiritual intelligence – SQ for short:

> By SQ [Zohar means] the intelligence with which we address and solve problems of meaning and value, the intelligence with which we can place our actions and our lives in a wider, richer, meaning-giving context, the intelligence with which we can assess that one course of action or one life-path is more meaningful than another. SQ is the effective foundation of both IQ [intelligence quotient] and EQ [emotional quotient]. It is our ultimate intelligence. (Zohar and Marshall 2000, pp.4–5)

This unfortunate choice for abbreviation (SQ instead of SI) makes the rest of the argument at best confusing and, at worst, meaningless. For instance, reading Q as a measurement, number or degree makes what the author is saying confusing:

> SQ [spiritual (low or high?) quotient] gives us our ability to discriminate. It gives us our moral sense, an ability to temper rigid rules with understanding and compassion and an equal ability to see when compassion and understanding have their limits... (Zohar and Marshall 2000, p.5)

But would it be true if the SQ (spiritual quotient) is very low? Isn't it more logical to talk about spirituality (present or absent/well developed/ underdeveloped) without introducing a meaningless notion?[19]

The proponents of SI argue that viewing spirituality as intelligence locates it within an existing acceptable psychological framework, which 'has proven to be extremely useful in understanding the common ground between personality and behavior. It allows spirituality to become anchored to rational approaches that emphasize goal attainment and problem solving' (Emmons 1999, p.174).

Apart from Zohar, among the prominent proponents of the concept are Emmons (1999, 2000), Sinetar (2000) and Wolman (2001). Robert Emmons (1999, 2000) (drawing on Gardner's multiple intelligences) defines SI as the degree to which a person has mental and emotional properties that enable the person to see a guiding purpose, mid- and short-term tasks that are connected to the higher purpose and maintain behaviours to fulfil them. Emmons (2000, p.10) suggests that there are at least five core abilities enabling people to solve problems and attain goals in their everyday life that define SI:

1. the capacity to transcend the physical and material

2. the ability to enter into heightened states of consciousness

3. the ability to invest in everyday activities and relationships with a sense of the sacred (i.e. the ability to sanctify everyday experience)

4. the ability to utilise spiritual resources to solve problems in living

5. the capacity to engage in virtuous behaviours or be virtuous (to show forgiveness, to be humble, to express gratitude, to show compassion).[20]

Sinetar (2000) offers her definition of SI as inspired thought which animates people of all ages and in all situations. Exploring spiritual features in children, Sinetar stresses that children's introspective abilities shape their actions and creativity. She calls those children with well-pronounced spiritual gifts (spiritually intelligent) 'early awakeners' and suggests that the spiritual qualities are expressed in:

- acute self-awareness, intuition, the 'I am' power. However, 'acute self-awareness' (a materialistic feature) is in opposition not only to the definition of spirituality (unity with the universe) but also to 'intuition' that is the quality of the subconscious

- a broad worldview (the ability to see self, others and the world as interrelated)

- moral elevation, strong opinion, the ability to live by one's own conventions

- a tendency to experience delight

- a sense of destiny

- 'unappeasable hunger' for selected interests

- fresh, 'weird' notions

- pragmatic, efficient perception of reality.

According to Wolman (2001), spiritual intelligence is the ability to ask ultimate questions about God, the meaning of life and the ability to experience the connections between individuals and the world.[21] Wolman distinguishes seven factors of SI: divinity, mindfulness (alternative or integrative health practices), extrasensory perception, community, intellectuality (a desire to study and discuss spiritual material and/or sacred texts), trauma and childhood spirituality.

More definitions of spiritual intelligence (abbreviated as SQ) are in Zohar and Marshall (2000):

SQ…is an *internal*, innate ability of the human brain and psyche, drawing its deepest resources from the heart of the universe itself. (p.9)

Spiritual intelligence is the souls' intelligence…with which we heal ourselves and with which we make ourselves whole. (p.9)

SQ is the intelligence that rests in that deep part of the self that is connected to wisdom from beyond the ego, or conscious mind, it is the intelligence with which we not only recognize existing values, but with which we creatively discover new values. (p.9)

SQ [is] an ability to reframe or recontextualize our experience, and thus an ability to transform our understanding of it. (p.65)

They also (2000, p.15) delineate ten distinctive features that characterise highly developed SQ:

1. the capacity to be flexible (adaptive)

2. a high degree of self-awareness. However, 'a high degree of self-awareness' (a materialistic feature) corresponds to a very low spiritual awareness, cf. 'a high degree of self-awareness' and the feature of spiritual intelligence, suggested by Cloninger and colleagues (1993), 'self-forgetfulness'

3. a capacity to face and use suffering

4. a capacity to face and transcend pain

5. the quality of being inspired by vision and values

6. a reluctance to cause unnecessary harm

7. a tendency to see the connections between diverse things

8. a marked tendency to ask 'why?' or 'what if?' questions and to seek 'fundamental' answers

9. being 'field-independent' (being able to work against conventions)

10. being responsible for bringing higher vision and value to others (inspire others – being a servant leader).

Several instruments to measure SQ have been developed; for example, Piedmont (1999) has originated a scale of spiritual transcendence (a multidimensional instrument). Cloninger (2004; Cloninger et al. 1993) has developed the Temperament and Character Inventory (TCI), including the self-transcendence scale as a measure of spirituality. The scale comprises three components: self-forgetfulness, transpersonal identification and mysticism. In contrast to self-consciousness (materialistic), self-forgetfulness (spiritual) involves becoming so absorbed in something (for example, work) that one loses the sense of time, place and self, lacking self-consciousness. Transpersonal identification is defined as a sense of connectedness to everything and everybody, inanimate and animate: nature, animals and people. Mysticism refers to a fascination with and open-mindedness to phenomena that cannot be explained.

The concept of SI has not been accepted by many researchers. For example, Gardner (2000) (who at one time considered evidence for spirituality as the ninth intelligence) argues that the 'core' to the intellectual aspect is the capacity to perform certain kinds of computations, and these computations cannot be done on elements that transcend sensory perception. There are other problems with the concept of SI. Mayer (2000) argues, for example, that intelligence must reflect mental performance and not just preferred ways of behaving. Then there is ambiguity or overlap between the definitions of spirituality (or spiritual consciousness) and SI, so, as Mayer remarks, spiritual intelligence could be simply a relabelling of spirituality. Is it necessary to introduce a concept of 'spiritual intelligence' (even if the same meaning is covered by the concept 'spirituality') just for the sake of it? Or should SI replace 'spirituality' altogether, meaning a type of intelligence that could be defined as the ability to draw on the spiritual as a means to solve life problems and seek meaning in life? Emmons (2000) attempts to defend the necessity to distinguish between SI and spirituality, defining SI as the adaptive use of spiritual information to aid everyday problem solving, while describing spirituality as a broader construct with the main focus on a search for the sacred. Thus, SI becomes a positive adaptive construct, while spirituality can be both positive and negative depending on the context and personalities: those who use their SI in a creative manner and those who use it in a destructive way.

Another issue that should be explained is that spiritual capacities are age-related, and they develop over the lifespan. For example, as Zohar and Marshall (2000) state: 'To come into full possession of our spiritual intelligence we have at some time to have seen the face of hell, to have known the possibility of despair, pain, deep suffering and loss, and to have made our peace with these' (pp.14–15). Adams et al. (2008) believe that even very young children display many of the characteristics of spiritual intelligence suggested by Zohar and Marshall (2000) as well as those identified by Emmons (1999). But if some children (who are spiritual while they are young) lose (or are conditioned out of) certain spiritual abilities when they grow up, does it mean that their SI (or Zohar's SQ) drops with age?

It seems that if we apply the word 'intelligence' to whatever we are discussing it will raise the prestige and importance of the topic under discussion but, as Mayer (2000) notes, it may diminish the status of intelligence itself.

Notes

1. It is important to remember that perceptual thinking in autism differs not only from 'normal' thinking, but also from the verbal logic of non-visual persons with Asperger syndrome who create word categories instead of picture (image) categories. Grandin (2006) hypothesises that the one common denominator of all autistic and Asperger thinking is that details are associated to form a concept.

2. For more about intuitive thinking, see Bogdashina 2010.

3. This is reflected in memory: because we 'see' concepts we remember a gist of the situation, 'forgetting' what really happened. Thus 'normal' conscious memory is limited and subjective; it is verbal, explicit and more easily forgotten. In contrast, subconscious memory is sensory-based (visual, auditory, kinaesthetic, tactile, etc.), implicit, procedural and resistant to forgetting (Grandin 2006). Grandin stresses that, though subconscious, her memory is not automatic and she has to push a 'save' button to store a memory in her database.

4. Some scales refer to 'ratio IQ' (original way of calculating IQ) and other scales use more recent 'deviation IQ'. Ratio IQ is based on 'mental age vs. chronological age' and deviation IQ scores show how far someone deviates from the average IQ based on their ranking on a bell curve distribution.

5. For a psychological explanation of alleged empathising deficit in autism, see Bogdashina 2005.

6. See, for example, Baron-Cohen *et al.* 1999; Critchley *et al.* 2000; Pierce *et al.* 2001.

7. Adolphs 2006; Davies and Whalen 2001; LeDoux 2003; McGaugh 2004; Zald 2003.

8. Amaral, Bauman and Schumann 2003; Bachevalier and Loveland 2006; Baron-Cohen *et al.* 2000; Schultz 2005; Sweeten *et al.* 2002.

9. Bufalari *et al.* 2007; Jackson *et al.* 2006; Osborn and Derbyshire 2010.

10. Banissy and Ward 2007; Blakemore *et al.* 2005.

11. However, there is a price to pay for being very (sensorily/affectively) empathic: those with high sensory empathy experience the pain or total sense of chaos caused by their sensory hypersensitivity and sensory-based cognitive process (Grandin 2006).

12. This does not mean that they completely lack 'sensory-based emotions'. Emotions such as fear and anger (in Schneider's terminology, 'survival emotions') are very much present. They are often triggered by uncertainty/unpredictability and/or intrusion into their 'space'.

13. The State Tretyakovskaya Gallery is the national treasury of Russian fine art and one of the greatest museums in the world. It contains a unique collection of Russian art (more than 170,000 works) which includes masterpieces created more than a thousand years ago. The gallery was founded by Russian merchant Pavel Tretyakov, who donated his collection to the city of Moscow in 1892. Nowadays the museum is the premier repository of Russian art, starting with the earliest Orthodox icons, which date from Russia's conversion in the ninth century. It then traces the country's history through the naturalism of the nineteenth century, the Art Nouveau works of Mikhail Vrubel, and the twentieth-century avant-garde works of Malevich and Kandinsky.

14. EI roughly corresponds to Gardner's concepts of intrapersonal and interpersonal intelligences. Some researchers interpret it erroneously, adding to the mix 'body intelligence' that is used by gifted athletes or pianists (Zohar and Marshall 2000), while to follow the logic of multiple intelligences, 'body intelligence' should be classified as 'kinaesthetic/ proprioceptive intelligence'.

15. MSCEIT consists of 141 items and takes 30–45 minutes to complete. MSCEIT provides 15 main scores: total EI score, two area scores, four branch scores and eight task scores. In addition to these 15 scores, there are three supplemental scores (Mayer *et al.* 2002). MSCEIT uses a variety of creative tasks to measure a person's capacity for reasoning with emotional information, for example, a task to view a series of faces and report how much of each of six emotions is present; answering questions about emotional situations (e.g. how much joy one might experience while planning a party); solving emotional problems (e.g. decide what response is appropriate when your friend calls you upset over losing his job).

16. It has been criticised by Roberts, Zeidner and Matthews (2001) – the validity coefficients found for EI may not be maintained if personality and ability are statistically controlled.

17. Stillman's research has been based on autistic individuals' and their families' anecdotes related to heightened awareness, hypersensitivity and 'a capacity to perceive all things seen and unseen' (2006, p.6). Stillman is careful not to suggest that *every* person with autism possesses spiritual gifts, but rather that they are better than those with neurotypical brains in 'connecting to God' and possessing 'gifts of Spirit' that reportedly range from knowing what someone is thinking, premonition, enjoying special bonds with animals, having visions of loved ones in Spirit, or even communing with angels. Stillman further hypothesises that, in fact, individuals with other disabilities may share these abilities as well.

18. Similar observations have been made about children's spirituality by Hay and Nye (2006, p.9): '[Children's spirituality] is hidden because of a culturally constructed forgetfulness which allows us to ignore the obvious.'

19. In some passages, SQ seems to mean spiritual quotient (thus making it hard to see where the author means SI and where SQ): 'being religious doesn't guarantee high SQ. Many humanists and atheists have very high SQ; many actively and vociferously religious people have very low SQ' (p.9). 'We can use SQ to become more spiritually intelligent [how can we use the spiritual quotient to become more spiritually intelligent?] about religion. SQ takes us to the heart of things, to the unity behind difference, to the potential beyond any actual expression. SQ can put us in touch with the meaning and essential spirit behind all great religions. A person *high in SQ* might practise any religion, but without narrowness, exclusiveness, bigotry or prejudice. Equally, a person *high in SQ* could have very spiritual qualities without being religious at all' (p.14; my emphasis). (When the degree [e.g. 'high in SQ'] is not specified, does it mean the 'average or low spiritual quotient' that can take us 'to the heart of things'?)

20. These are common in all major religious traditions (Paloutzin, Emmons and Keortge 2003).

21. Wolman (2001) used the PsychoMatrix Spiritual Inventory (PSI) consisting of 114 items.

5

Different Realities
Constructed Worlds Created
through the Filters

*'Unbelievably I lived in a world (and still do) where the environment of
our Earth, with its consistent gravity, sound waves and refracted light, was
but an invention of fiction writers.'*

Blackman 2001, p.155

What we perceive does not include everything that is 'out there'. We
trust our senses (and the equipment we create) too much, and mistake
our personal reality (what our senses/equipment tell us is 'out there')
for the real physical world. Attempts to correct this view have been
undertaken for centuries. For example, in the eighteenth century German
philosopher Immanuel Kant distinguished between the *phenomenon* (the
form emerging in the mind, caused by our perception) and the *noumenon*
(or 'thing-in-itself', inaccessible to our experience). Kant insisted that
the 'thing-in-itself' is beyond our knowing, while what we think
we know about reality is constructed by the mind which shapes our
experience of the world. Both realities (the unknowable world out there
and the world we construct – our personal reality) are real. Some claim
that the subjective reality we experience is an illusion. However, this
is true only in a sense that it does not coincide with the unknowable
reality; on the other hand, what we experience is very real – it is *our*
reconstruction of the world that determines our behaviour in it. If we
accept that it is not a true reflection of the world, that is, it is a false
perception, it is more logical to see it as a 'delusion' – the concept
corresponding to *maya* in ancient Indian philosophy.

Illusions and delusions

Illusions are defined as misperceptions that are perceived by most people, and are based on a specific stimulus received under certain conditions.[1]

Delusions differ from both illusions and hallucinations in that they are not perceptions but beliefs. Delusions can be found in mentally ill patients; for example, a person may have delusions of grandeur (believing that he or she is a very important person or an unrecognised genius who cannot do wrong: 'I can't deal with these people, I don't want to lower *my* high standards to their level'), or delusions of persecution (believing someone or many people are after them): 'They are all against me, wherever I go they are there.'

We are not only delusional (that is 'normal' for 'our' world), we also distort 'what is out there' in our constructed image of it. Distortions can be of several types, most common 'normal distortions' being: (1) believing that we live in the present; (2) adding more than there is there; (3) missing a lot of what is there. For instance:

1. There is a slight delay between the impact of the environment and our awareness of it, as it takes about one-fifth of a second to process the input.

2. A well-known example is the sound of a falling tree that does not 'sound' if there is no one to hear it: the sound is *heard* only if sound waves apply vibrating pressure on the hearing sense organ, in other words it exists only in the experience of the one experiencing it. If there is no one in the vicinity the sound will remain just a wave and will not be 'heard'.

3. There are many potential experiences that we miss because our sense organs (or even the equipment) cannot detect them. The capacity of our senses limits our experience quite considerably.

So, before going any further, we have to discuss several common dysfunctions, starting with sensory dysfunction.

Sensory dysfunction

I have no statistics based on research but I strongly believe that more than 90 per cent of the population can be regarded as dysfunctional in their sensory perception. Often all sensory modalities are involved.

However, as the majority is affected, this can be considered 'normal sensory dysfunction'. The main characteristics are:

- restricted detection of sensory stimuli
- limited amount of sensory information coming through.

Restricted detection of sensory stimuli

All our sensory systems are limited in their ability to detect sensory stimuli. For example, human eyes are sensitive to light frequency between 430,000 to 750,000 gigahertz – everything outside this range is invisible to a human eye (though for some species their 'normal' visual reality is outside the range, which is impossible for the human even to imagine). At low frequencies (below red) is infrared. At higher frequencies (above violet) – ultraviolet. Similar restrictions can be found in other senses. We are not conscious of our limitations, as we have grown up with them and do not know otherwise. In fact, if we compare the senses of other species sharing the planet with us, we are nearly blind, deaf and dumb, to say nothing of our (very limited) ability to smell. Those who are blind, deaf, etc. do better in this category as the lack of one sense leads to development of acuteness in others. In certain circumstances, some people can develop alternative ways to perceive the world which are relatively similar to those of other species. For instance, some blind people develop echolocation ability (by clicking their tongue they can 'see' their environment).[2]

The ability to hypersense

What can be detected by some autistic people would not necessarily be noticed by the majority. This ability is known as hypersensitivity.[3] Some autistic individuals' senses are very acute and they can see, hear, feel, and so on stimuli to which 'normal' people are blind, deaf, numb, and so on. For instance, some autistic persons have been reported to react to positive ion changes in weather systems (Stillman 2006), others are physically sensitive to small differences in colour (Schneider 1999). Temple Grandin (2006) states that the senses of some people with autism resemble the acute senses of animals.

'Sensory filters' limiting the amount of sensory stimulation coming in

Actually, we are meant to be 'dysfunctional' in both (restricted) detection and the (limited) amount of sensory stimulation that we are conscious of. In order to function successfully we have filters in place to reduce sensitivity, thus reducing the ability to detect certain sensory stimuli and limiting the stimulation coming in. Aldous Huxley summarises Bergson's theory on the protective function of the human brain and the nervous system in his 1954 essay *The Doors of Perception*:

> The function of the brain and nervous system is to protect us from being overwhelmed and confused by this mass of largely useless and irrelevant knowledge, by shutting out most of what we should otherwise perceive or remember at any moment, and leaving only that very small and special selection which is likely to be practically useful. (Huxley 2004a, p.10)

So most of the time 'normal' people know only what comes into their reduced awareness (which is further consecrated as genuinely real by concepts and language). But there are some people who seem to be born with a kind of bypass that circumvents what Huxley (2004a) calls the reducing valve – resulting in unlimited or unrestricted perception. In others, temporary bypasses may be acquired, either spontaneously, or as a result of deliberate 'special exercises', meditation, through hypnosis, or by means of drugs. For instance, psychedelic drugs can produce such enhanced and exaggerated sensitivity that the environment may seem more vivid and real. There is no consensus about the 'realness' of these and similar experiences. Some consider them subjective, but others are certain of their objectivity while recognising the subjective aspect of it. Is it not ironic that 'full functionality in sensory perception' becomes 'dysfunction' in the world constructed by 'normal' people?

In autism there are no filters to stop the flooding – brains have 'no sieve', and all the stimuli are competing for processing:

> I have been jumping between processing the white of the page and the print, the flicker of light and shadow as well as the objects themselves, the sounds of the people moving about in between syllables of words being said at the time, the rustle of clothing and the sound of my own voice. (Williams 1996, p.203)

When I step into a room for the first time I often feel a kind of dizziness with all the bits of information my brain perceives swimming inside my head. Details precede their objects. I see scratches on a table surface before seeing the entire table; the reflection of light on a window before I perceive the whole window; the patterns on a carpet before the whole carpet comes into view. (Tammet 2009, p.177)

Recent research (Markram *et al.* 2007) has shown that, contrary to some neurological studies emphasising underconnectivity and hypoactivity of mental processes in autism, autistic brains are, in fact, overperforming and are very hyper-reactive and hyperplastic.[4] Excessive processing of sensory input leads to exaggerated perception, producing extremely intense images, sounds, smells and so on.

I feel that my autism enables me to experience my surroundings in an intense way, both physically and emotionally. I have finely developed hearing and smell, and I react to tiny changes in weather patterns and atmospheric pressure, much the way an animal would. (O'Neill 2003)

It is to describe autism from this perspective that researchers have coined the term 'intense world syndrome' (Markram *et al.* 2007). In this view, ASDs are 'disorders' of hyper-functionality. Minicolumns, the smallest units of the brain capable of processing information, have a higher than normal capacity for processing information. Excessive processing of the sensory input in the microcircuits leads, in turn, to exaggerated perception, producing extremely intense images, sounds, smells, and so on, and bringing overload that causes autistic children to withdraw and miss the opportunity to develop shared conceptual understanding of a 'normal world' (Bogdashina 2010) while creating their own.

Hallucinations and 'hallucinations'

Hallucinations are said to be false perceptions that occur in the absence of appropriate external stimuli, and are usually seen by only one individual. Most often they are experienced by people with specific kinds of mental illness, or under the influence of drugs or alcohol. However, it is important to distinguish between hallucinations and 'hallucinations'. For instance, analysing reported cases of children's 'hallucinations', Mosse (1958) poses a question: How far in degree and in terms of a child's age can magic thinking go before it can be termed pathological, and when should a dreamy child be diagnosed as pathologically withdrawn? Mosse describes cases of several children she examined who were misdiagnosed with schizophrenia on the basis of 'symptoms' that were, in fact, within normal limits, for example:

> John's diagnosis [of childhood schizophrenia] was based mainly on 'visual hallucinations'. He described the following: 'I just close my eyes and I see elephants. Sometimes when I imagine things I can see it. I have to have my eyes closed. Sometimes I see cowboys. I make myself one of them. They do whatever you want them to do. Sometimes when I cannot sleep I do it. Then I go to sleep. (Mosse 1958, p.793)

It is known that children normally have much more vivid visual and auditory experiences than adults. Especially when they are anxious, and before going to sleep, many children experience visual, auditory, and even tactile experiences which they may feel come from the outside, but they may not be quite certain about whether they are real, and they may provide their own explanations and interpretations, like believing that a shadow is a substance (Mosse 1958). Wertham (1950) stresses that most children have a positive eidetic disposition that has to be taken into consideration when analysing these and similar experiences.

Imagination and fantasy that help to interpret the world

Sensory and emotional sensitivities are often associated with the *fantasy-prone personality*, identified by Wilson and Barber (1983) in women 'who fantasize a large part of the time, who typically "see", "hear", "smell", "touch" and fully experience what they fantasize' (p.340). In these individuals, vivid fantasising start from an early age, when imaginary companions and imaginary worlds are experienced 'as real as real' (p.354). While all children go through the stage of fantasising and having imaginary friends, and eventually grow out of it, highly sensitive persons live with their fantasies practically all their lives. The authors suggest that it is the ability to have vivid sensory experiences and the vivid memories associated with them that are precursors of fantasy-proneness, providing the raw material from which the individuals construct their very lucid fantasies (Wilson and Barber 1983).

Some people with autism have vivid imagination that 'blends' into reality all their life. This does not mean they 'live in their fantasy world' but rather that they interpret reality using vivid imaging metaphors that make this new perspective of seeing things very real:

> From his early childhood, Tito used his imagination a lot and saw a chair as a living lady ready to comfort the tired, the cupboard as a big-mouthed person, ready to eat anything you feed. [His mother didn't understand what made him laugh when] the boy laughed... imagining the letters that formed the word 'goat' were in dispute, each one making its own phonetic sound – a resulting noise that was different from the way 'goat' sounded. So the boy made a new game. He had learnt already how to read. He thought about different words and made the letters argue and talk. He tried to make a resulting sound. (Mukhopadhyay 2000, p.22)

As a child, Gunilla Gerland loved cranes. They were one of her great passions (and a 'safety point' that helped her cope with her environment, especially if she was in a new environment). It made her happy just to look at them. She would accept a new environment if she could see cranes from the window. She was sure that the cranes were alive and was convinced that they moved their heads during the night, imagining that after having worked all day, at night they were free to come to life. Gunilla tried to talk to them, but other people laughed at her 'fantasies'. When she was 24 she got confirmation (from a construction engineer) that cranes do move at night (because they are disengaged in the evening and can move freely in the wind). So she was not imagining things, she just interpreted them differently, and connected to the cranes as if they were alive.

Donna Williams wondered if it was others who were missing out by not seeing things the way she did:

> The chair fell over because I walked into it. Logically this was proof that it had felt me knock it. I sat on a chair... The chair clearly knew how heavy I was. I felt sorry for sitting on a chair sometimes. It was as though I was imposing. My feet made indentations on the carpet as I walked across it. It obviously felt I was there. 'Hi carpet,' I said, glad to be home. My bed was my friend, my coat protected me and kept me inside, things that made noise had their unique voices which said *vroom, ping*, or whatever. Windows looked outside at the day, curtains kept the light from coming inside, trees waved,

the wind blew and whistled, leaves danced, and water ran. I told my shoes where they were going so they would take me there.

A tin came down from the shelf. I laughed. It looked like it was suddenly committing suicide as it jumped from the wall. Things never thought or felt anything complex but they gave me a sense of being in company. I felt secure in being able to be in company in 'the world' even if it were things. (Williams 1999c, pp.60–61)

When Donna was told that things need a nervous system in order to think or feel, and there was no exception, she felt trapped by this new logic her mind could not continue to deny; her emotions could not bear it.

Every time I held on to a curtain, every time I looked at my shoes, a new perception of objects as dead things without knowledge, without feeling, without volition, nagged me. I felt my own aloneness with an intensity I had always been protected from… Everything around me had no awareness that I existed. I was no longer in company…

I wanted to run back into 'my world' but it had been bombed. Blocked, unused inner knowledge and understanding… I hit the floor which had once been aware I was walking on it. The floor I had sprawled my body across, the carpet I had run my fingers through, my special sunny spot in the middle of the room, were all dead and always had been and I hadn't known. I realized I'd lived my life in a world of object corpses. God has a curious sense of humour. (Williams 1999c, pp.62–63)

Donna's friend Olivier enjoyed being lost in his mirror reflection:

I was lost in my reflection today… I was lost in my eyes and by the time I 'woke up' it was several hours later. What was crazy, though, was that I was so far 'asleep' that at first I couldn't tell which side of the mirror I was until I moved. (Williams 1999c, p.169)

Donna explains that one cannot walk into a mirror, of course, but there were:

perceptual boundaries beyond which lay something like a twilight zone. Olivier was sane. He had no hallucinations or delusions and yet he could cross those lines almost at will… They were illusions, not delusions. If you asked him if people could fly, he would have told you straight, no. (Williams 1999c, p.169)

Many are quick to dismiss these and similar 'fantasies', created by the child's mind and not to be taken seriously, but are happy to accept any fantasies (or lies) created by 'normal' grown-ups. The history of humankind is an illustration of the 'delusional worlds' created by people. Take any culture, any country at any time and you can see 'fantasies' and 'hallucinations', for example, the Russia of 1917 – a 'new world' of brotherhood, equality and happiness – resulted in millions killed for the 'brighter future'. It takes a few individuals to 'draw a picture' and the ignorance of the rest (accepting it) to turn a 'fantasy' into a 'reality'. Or take recent events in the West – when people were fed with ideas of threat from a country that was not actually threatening to attack the West, again, hundreds of thousands were killed to 'prove' that someone's fantasy was 'real'. One of the means to achieve this is language – use threatening words ('imminent attack', 'exploitation of the poor by blood-sucking tyrants', etc.) and the public finish the picture themselves. Very few decent people are allowed to the top,[5] and that is why so many suffer from the fantasies and delusions of 'normal' individuals. Why aren't they diagnosed as mad? The majority accept the scenarios they are given with no questions asked, while some autistic individuals have to check what is real and what is part of their imagination, because their reality is so different from the one experienced by the majority. For example:

> My boundary between imagining and experiencing something was a delicate one. Perhaps it still is. So many times I need to cross-check with Mother, or someone who can understand my voice now, whether an incident really happened around my body or presence. (Mukhopadhyay 2008, p.22)

All her life, Kammer has struggled to distinguish between reality and imagination. Almost daily she has had doubts about whether she made up the people and things she encountered or whether they were real; whether what she thought about some things were true or were her own feelings projected onto them, and so on.

Or let us consider cases (1) when someone has synaesthesia and his perceptions and interpretations are very different from what is known as 'normal reality'; (2) when someone's senses are very acute and the person can see/hear/smell stimuli that people with 'normal' senses cannot; (3) if someone's perception fluctuates, creating different 'realities', which are often interpreted as distortions; (4) if while remembering they actually hear, smell, see objects, places, people; (5) when thinking about abstract notions they have to create metaphors (as their sensory-based thinking mode is concrete)[6] and visualise these 'metaphorical images' in order to understand what is going on: does it mean that the person is hallucinating? For example:

1. I heard his [the researcher's] voice fill up the space between the files and dig behind the computer monitors. I saw the voice transform into long apple green strings, searching under the tables for who knows what? Threads like raw silk forming from Claude's voice. Claude read. I watched those strings vibrate with different amplitudes... I heard his voice and saw its vibrations blowing away those silk threads all over the floor. [When asked what Claude was reading] I saw all those strings, snapping all at once around his mouth, making a remarkable effect around his face in yellow and green... [When given a piece of paper and a pencil] I [wrote] about the beauty of the color green, when yellow sunshine melts its way through newly grown leaves... I wanted to be honest in my own way about my experience of that situation, as my perception was interpreting it to me when translated into language. (Mukhopadhyay 2008, p.201)

2. Tito could actually feel the energy and see its pathway:

   The intensity of the energy in [the] room was very strong. I felt like a small raft floating in the midst of [it]. The energy bounced across the room, all around the walls, the pictures reflected them, and the tables diverted them toward the ceiling... I could actually see the pathway of the energy wave, bouncing around with speed. (Mukhopadhyay 2008, p.196)

   [M]y bed was surrounded and totally encased by tiny spots which I called stars, like some kind of mystical glass coffin. I have since learned that they are actually air particles yet my vision was so hypersensitive that they become hypnotic foreground with the rest of 'the world' fading away. (Williams 1999b, p.15)

3. To me the shape of the ground itself was completely disconcerting. I simply saw the strange, bumpy, striped landscape as a collection of shifting shapes. I and my body were adrift in a monochrome world. (Blackman 2001, p.152)

   It was the end of a very noisy class. The room had no windows, and the sound bounced off the walls. I had just come from another classroom where I had been tortured by sharp fluorescent light, which made reflections bounce off everything. It made the room race busily in a constant state of change. Light and shadow dancing on people's faces as they spoke turned the scene into an animated cartoon. Now, in this noisy classroom, I felt I was standing at the meeting point of several long tunnels. Blah-blah-blah echoed, bouncing noise wall to wall. (Williams 1999c, p.68)

4.   I can still sense my body ride one of [the escalators]. I can sense their gentle vibration on my body as I cling to the handle, concentrating on the oblique climb upward or downward, ambitious to climb up once again. (Mukhopadhyay 2008, p.49)

5.   The cobweb of uncertainty remained. Mother kept a heavy bag on my hand to prevent me from further flapping. I saw cobwebs forming around the bag, spreading through the bag, infecting the whole compartment, and then engulfing the train reaching further and further beyond. The world was covered with a cobweb of uncertainty... The cobweb of uncertainty covered all over I went while I tried to see my speculations through the mesh... [As soon as predictability and certainty returned] the cobweb of uncertainty disappeared. (Mukhopadhyay 2000, pp.62, 63)

All these and similar scenarios can be (mis)interpreted as 'hallucinations' by 'normal' people.[7]

'Hallucinations' in relation to perceiving non-physical reality

Should perception of non-physical realities be considered a hallucination? The answer to this question depends on the belief system(s) and explanatory model(s) of the observer. If we start with the assumption that there is no other reality except the one we live in, then the answer is 'yes' and those who can 'see', 'hear', and so on anything outside our material world are diagnosed with mental problems. In Western societies the attitude to those who claim to have 'unusual experiences' or to visit non-physical dimensions is negative, and experiencers are described with psychiatric terminology by professionals (and 'mad', 'crazy' or 'insane' by the general public). In contrast, in some so-called 'primitive' societies, 'unusual' experiences are valid and constitute a significant part of their everyday lives. Their belief systems and explanatory models are different, leading not only to the interpretation of 'unusual' experiences as 'usual' and 'normal', but also encouraging them to *experience* these 'normal' (for a particular culture) phenomena. Is it 'seeing what you expect to see' (i.e. illusions or hallucinations created by the brain of the person experiencing it – images from within, not without)? Not quite. It is more about *accepting* what is 'normal' (and functional) for certain societies. Let me explain. During special rituals *all* the members of the group achieve the state when they have the same spiritual experiences, in accordance with their belief system. There is a plethora of published anthropological accounts, revealing unexplained phenomena, when anthropologists themselves are participants in rituals and actually experience 'spiritual powers'. One of these accounts is by anthropologist Edith Turner, who conducted her fieldwork in Zambia in 1985. During a Ndembu ceremony, the anthropologist actually saw a spiritual manifestation. Turner claims that the 'visions' were 'out there', not 'projected through the mind' (Turner 1992, p.171). The anthropologist Gardner has been fascinated by different worldviews he has learned about in fieldwork, when anthropologists have great opportunities to get glimpses of differing realities, and sometimes also achieve explanations of them that can be accepted scientifically. However, every once in a while, the glimpses the anthropologists get are baffling:

> While the empirical facts of these cases are as clear to me as can be, and while my mind continues to ask for a rational explanation of them, I am obliged to conclude for now that reality is more complex than the scientific side of me has been able to accept. (Gardner 2007, p.35)

So why do we deny the existence of something we do not yet understand? This is just one example of 'unexplained yet' experiences by autistic people. Interestingly, they try to find rational explanations themselves for what they call 'day dreams' (for example, Tito), but in some cases, it does not work.

> That was another daydream that kept him occupied. It was that of a middle-aged gentleman sitting near him. It was very annoying to find that he sat everywhere and anywhere the boy turned. It took him years to find out that nobody else except him saw this man.

There were more things that puzzled him. There was a cloud on the chair and he found it difficult to sit on the chair. Sometimes the same [gentleman] sat on the chair.

I thought about his illusions and came to a satisfactory explanation. Probably in some magazines, or somewhere on the TV, he saw a similar person and thus imagined him anywhere. (Mukhopadhyay 2000, p.8)

Cognitive filters: Different interpretations in different cultural constructs

The process of perception is not a passive process, but an active one, involving the construction of an external world that depends on internal (mental) templates. The raw sensory information is decoded into meaningful perception reflected in active processes at the cortical level 'that are influenced by attention, affect, cultural expectations, context, prior experiences and memory and, most importantly, prior concepts' (Oyebode 2008, p.96). This brings us to differences of cognitive interpretations and the role of language in 'shaping' and 'mapping' the outside world. It is the *cultural filter* that rearranges, regroups, adds or ignores the available concepts in a very specific way, in accordance with cultural traditions. Thanks to these 'cultural filters', worldviews of different cultures vary significantly. For example, during his fieldwork in rural Asia, anthropologist David Abram used his skills as a professional sleight-of-hand magician to alter consciousness in order to better understand the realities of the local sorcerers (shamans).[8] He points out that in tribal cultures it is accepted that there are more forms of consciousness than we are aware of. In order to contact other forms of sensitivity and awareness, the sorcerer, temporarily, is able to alter the common organisation of his senses and shed the accepted perceptual logic of his culture, and enter into relation with other species (animating the local landscape) on their own terms. While living among the indigenous people and learning to decipher the shaman's spoken and unspoken references to the unseen and unheard, Abram experienced the shift of his senses and began to *see* and *hear* in a manner he had not before:

When a magician spoke of a power or 'presence' lingering in the corner of his house, I learned to notice the ray of sunlight that was then pouring through a chink in the roof, illuminating a column of drifting dust, and to realize that the column of light was indeed a power, influencing the air currents by its warmth, and indeed influencing the whole mood in the room; although I had not consciously seen it before, it had been structuring my experience. My ears began to attend in a new way, to the sounds of birds – no longer just a melodic background to human speech, but meaningful speech in its own right, responding to and commenting on events in the surrounding earth. (Abram 1997, p.20)

This newly acquired ability to receive communicated messages through his senses opened a new perceptual world for Abram and gave him an opportunity to have non-verbal conversations with the Other(s) with which his conscious awareness has very little to do. When the researcher returned to a 'civilised' North America, very gradually he began to lose his awareness of Others because different 'templates' were imposed, making him notice what was important in the culture he came back to:

I was indeed reacclimating to my own culture, becoming more attuned to its styles of discourse and interaction, yet my bodily senses seemed to be losing their acuteness, becoming less awake to subtle changes and patterns... My skin quit registering the various changes in the breeze, and smells seemed to have faded from the world almost entirely. (Abram 1997, pp.25–26)

Abram concludes that his Western culture's assumptions (regarding lack of awareness in other species and the land itself) are 'less a product of careful and judicious reasoning than a strange inability to clearly...see, or focus upon, anything other than human speech'; the result being that 'civilised' humanity lost the ability to perceive surroundings in a clear manner, and stifled and starved the senses by the patterns of their culture (Abram 1997, p.27).

This example illustrates how cultural constructs affect the way people view the world – both physical and non-physical. Many fascinating views and perspectives on the same 'world' are provided by anthropologists. In Sri Lanka, for example, discarnate beings are perceived to 'overshadow' living relatives, with possible possession to a lesser or greater degree. In the case of 'bad' possession (when it is unsolicited), the spirit can be exorcised; in the case of a 'good' (solicited) possession, the spirit is honoured as it is transformed into a healer or clairvoyant (Obeyesekere 1981). Reichel-Dolmatoff (1997) describes the South American Tukano beliefs on the connectedness of humans on earth to the cosmos: the physical world and the spiritual reality, two co-existing interconnected worlds. Ill health is seen as the inadequate behaviour of a person who upsets the ecological balance. To restore the balance, shamans access the part of the eco-system that has been disturbed. In the West, if a recently bereaved person reports seeing a discarnate being, it may be considered a hallucination, whereas in some other societies it may be a welcome vision (Tobert 2010). For Westerners, these 'culture-bound' beliefs and concepts (explanations) might sound primitive, naive and unscientific (read 'false') but this is because they fall out of our 'scientific' belief framework, which tends to explain reality using the biological or medical model. We consider 'naive and unscientific' beliefs false because they do not fit in our model, so they must be thrown out of the equation and either ignored (as unworthy of 'scientific attention') or considered non-existent in reality and 'seen' only by mentally ill. Many questions are still unanswered, for instance, what happens to us when we die? Is there anything that is beyond the human ability to understand (the 'unknowable')? But some think that if we are not able to provide 'scientific' answers, what is the point of asking these questions?

Explicit versus implicit perception

The way we perceive the world affects the way we store and utilise information. The conscious mind is not the only way of receiving information. What is more, different neural mechanisms are responsible for producing conscious and unconscious processing (Farah and Feinberg 1997; Gazzaniga 1988). Unconscious processing can occur in the absence of conscious realization, well illustrated by the research on blindsight.[9] This brings us to two ways of perception – explicit/conscious and implicit/subconscious perception.

Subconsciously we are perceiving all the time, but very early in life we learn to ignore anything 'irrelevant': we are conscious only of 'our' world – anything beyond our constructed reality is ignored. Research on preconscious processing (Velmans 1991) shows that conscious states may not accompany unconscious processing and, if they do, they follow it. Whether we are aware of it or not, subconscious processes are there all the time. For example, Davis, Hoffman and Rodriguez (2002) acknowledge the role of low-level inner representations of visual input at a pre-attentive stage. They argue that representations need not faithfully reflect all aspects of the environment; all that is necessary is the gist of the scene in order to get an idea of how to act on it. One does not have to have full and accurate knowledge of *their* (constructed) world in order to successfully function in it. Ronald Rensink (2000) suggests that at an early stage of visual processing there is a 'low-level map-like representation' which most are not consciously aware of. It is only at higher levels of processing, where attention plays a major role, that we 'understand' our environment and events occurring there. Rensink makes the point that, although the sensory information of the whole is processed at the low level, little of it is stored in the conceptual level, and that is why little of it is stored in the (conceptual) memory. However, these low-level representations (categorised only by spatial features and location) still play an important role in accounting for changes in attention and in our knowledge of the environment.

We are limited in our ability to process information consciously. However, subconsciously and/or preconsciously it is possible to take in an infinite amount of unprocessed information which is literal and objective and is received directly, without conscious interpretation. The storing capacity is also unlimited, but the access and retrieval of this information is difficult; it can be triggered but not accessed voluntarily (Williams 1998).

In 'normal' development, conscious perception becomes very strong, but very restricted and subjective, while subconscious perception is often ignored or suppressed. (We are too conscious to be 'psychic'!) In autism, conscious perception is weaker (in comparison with the 'normal' consciousness), while subconscious perception may be very strong, unrestricted and objective. Donna Williams describes the process of receiving knowledge from subconscious to preconscious, where the subconscious mind is a storeroom containing uninterpreted information that is still accumulated within preconsciousness, where it can be processed later, removed from the context of the situation in which it had been received. When it is triggered and is processed consciously, it is like 'listening to oneself'. Some autistic people use the preconscious system to take in information, though they themselves (their conscious selves) are 'absent' from the process. That is, they are not aware of what information they have accumulated. When it is triggered from the outside, they surprise not only those around them, but themselves as well with knowledge they have never thought they have. It is a sort of 'unknown knowing' (Williams 1998).

Automatic perception

'Normal' people function in an extremely limited range of reality; the brain fills in the gaps and predicts the final picture, that is, we 'see', 'hear', and so on from the mental (subjective) 'world' we create in our mind:

> [T]he world we perceive around us is not the physical world. The world we actually know is the world that takes form in our minds; the world is not made of matter, but of mindstuff. Everything we know, perceive and imagine, every color, sound, sensation, thought, and feeling, is a form that consciousness has taken on. (Russell 2002, pp.55–56)

'Normal' perception is automatic: we do not bother to *see*, we 'know' what is out there: we 'see' concepts, not things (or whatever is out there), thus limiting or restricting our perception even more, and at the same time we keep on creating 'our' world (consisting of 'perceptual constancies'). So most of the time 'normal' people function on autopilot. Research on skill acquisition (Shiffrin 1988) reveals that conscious awareness fades as soon as automaticity develops, leaving unconscious mechanisms largely in control. But it is not only about skill acquisition, it is also about becoming a 'citizen' of the world constructed by cultural concepts, which become cognitive and linguistic filters of the information, thus restricting even further what is available for conscious processing.

Linguistic filters

Language is a convention, a model of a culture and of its adjustment to the world (Hill 1958).

> Human beings do not live in the objective world alone but are very much at the mercy of the particular language which has become the medium of expression for the society... The 'real world' is to a large extent unconsciously built up on the language habits of the group. We see and hear and experience very largely as we do because the language habits of our community predispose certain choices of interpretation. (Sapir 1949, p.162)

The way we 'break up the flux of experience' (Whorf 1956) into static objects is different in different languages.[10] The reality we believe really exists depends on how we name things and describe them in language. Language seems to create a linguistically restricted mind with (rigid) conceptual intelligence, in contrast to the fluid intelligence of unrestricted mind. Unlike autistic individuals, those without autism see more from the 'inside', from what has been created in their mind (from what they *think* is out there), than what is actually there, outside their mental world. Temple Grandin (2006) insightfully remarks that autistic people see the details that make up the world, while 'normal' individuals blur all the details together into their general concept of the world (not necessarily a correct one).

Anything that does not exist in language goes unnoticed by the majority. 'Normal' perceptions of the outside world are clouded by the verbal notions and concepts in terms of which people do their thinking. All these abstractions are converted into signs but, by doing this, 'normal' people rob the objects and experiences they label with arbitrary signs of a great deal of their thinghood (Huxley 2004b). As soon as we project the linguistic patterns on the universe, we *see* them there, whether they correspond to reality or not. So first we sort out perceptions (shaping them into concepts) and then label them according to the habit of the culture we are born into. The conceptual representations that develop through learning are arbitrarily related to the perceptual states that activate them (Barsalou 1999). People use language to classify the world in a shared way. The problem starts when we do *not* share the experiences: 'I struggled to use "the world" language to describe a way of thinking and being and experiencing for which this world gives you no words or concepts' (Williams 1999c, p.102). Barsalou (1999) argues that if different intelligent systems have different perceptual systems, the developed conceptual systems also differ. Because their symbols contain different perceptual content, they refer to different structures in the world and that is why they are not functionally equivalent. With all the filters in place, how can we be sure that 'our' reality is more real than the reality of those whose sensory perception and cognitive and linguistic interpretation are very different from the 'normal' ones?

When we consider our 'scientific' explanation of the world, there is a question: which particular world we are scientifically exploring? The (limited) one allowed through all the filters? Or the ones that exist outside our filter-restricted 'reality'? Based on data from scientific studies, we formulate theories aimed at explaining how our created world functions, thus creating the stories (actually, it is the mind that creates the stories using the concepts and cognitive mechanisms available to the 'normal' mind) that fit in the framework that is at the time established as 'scientific'. What does not fit in is filtered out and ignored, thus the 'framework of the day' becomes yet another filter, restricting the field to what is allowed to be researched 'scientifically', until some scientists become brave enough to look at the same phenomena from a different perspective and start noticing the unexplained (unseen by the majority of their colleagues), which that has been there all the time. With a shift in perspective we will be able to change the framework and, consequently, change the story describing the way our world functions. New experiences and new data will bring new stories, because these new data will not fit in the existing framework, and the process is repeated again and again. However, what can those who not only see, hear, feel, and so on very differently from the majority, but also draw different boundaries, developing different (often non-verbal) concepts that do not fit in the framework of the accepted reality do? The answer depends on the culture they happen to be born into: in the West they will be (officially) given a diagnosis (based on the way they behave) and unofficially called by whatever name members of the public think fits them best. However, the religious and spiritual dimensions of culture are among the most important factors that structure human experience, beliefs, values and behaviour (James 1985; Krippner and Welch 1992), and they should be considered to be as real as those that the majority accept as valid. If others are 'dysfunctional' in perceiving these dimensions, it does not necessarily mean that those whose perception of the reality is 'unfiltered' ('fully functional') are wrong. This includes the differences in the perception of our selves.

Donna Williams is passionate about her belief that being sane or intelligent is not:

anymore superior than being insane and retarded. Often the insane person has turned their back on the often alienating normality most people become conditioned to believe is a real and desirable goal. Similarly many retarded people are more in touch as they sometimes experience things in a much more sensual way than 'normal' people. They overlook what are sometimes very corrupting complexities, and rely instead on simple instinctual reaction and response. In this sense I am both insane and retarded...for, although the reality of this is being constantly disproved by what I am able to perceive or express, this was often the way I perceived myself to be and behaved accordingly. (Williams 1999b, p.173)

Notes

1. Experiments with animals have shown that some species of mammals and birds are fooled by illusions in the same way as humans are (Block and Yuker 1989).

2. Daniel Kish, president of World Access to the Blind, has pioneered methods for training blind children to use echolocation to 'see', interpret and successfully function in their environment. Kish has coined the term FlashSonar to describe the method of echolocation he and many other visually impaired people use to orient themselves in the environment and to interpret what is going on around them. By clicking the tongue the person perceives echoes which tell them the location, dimension (height, width and depth) of objects and structures (solid versus sparse, reflective versus absorbent). Using this information, combined with other auditory perceptions as well as touch, they can 'see' the environment (Kish 2011). This is just one example Kish provides to illustrate how this method works:

   > I have been clicking to get around for as long as I can remember… It comes as naturally to me as breathing. I click and turn my head from side to side, scanning the expansive space before me, straining to penetrate the heavy curtain of commotion. The world suddenly seems bigger than anything I've ever encountered, and noisier, too… I step cautiously forward, clicking quickly and loudly to cut through the cacophony. I follow the clear spaces, passing between clusters of bodies, keeping my distance from bouncing projectiles. From time to time, I click back over my shoulder. As long as I hear the building call back to me through the crowd, I know I can find it again… Then, suddenly, something whispers back to me from the open expanse, and I jolt to a stop. 'Hi,' I venture in a bell-like treble. There is no reply. As I scan, clicking more softly, the something quietly tells me about itself – it is taller than I am and too thin to be a person. When I reach out to touch it, I know already that it is a pole… Leaving the pole, I move toward this next thing as it calls to me with a similar voice, telling me that it is also a pole. I detect yet another one, and another – nine poles in a straight line… In time I practiced biking by slaloming rows of trees while clicking madly. (Kish 2011)

3. However, the ability to 'hypersense' can be disabling in some environments. For example, some autistic children cannot concentrate in the classroom because they can hear talking in three other rooms; many autistic individuals can see a 60-cycle flicker of fluorescent lighting that results in seeing a room pulsate on and off; others may have a strong aversion to certain colours or certain patterns that actually hurt their eyes and so on.

4. See also research on sensory gating deficit, for example Adler, Waldo and Freedman 1985; Boutros *et al.* 2004; Freedman *et al.* 2003. These studies have focused their attention on schizophrenia. The major difference to autism is probably that in schizophrenia gating abnormalities are ascribed to the thalamus while, in autism, the abnormality appears to be in the cortex (Casanova, personal communication, 2009). For research on autism and imbalance of cortical excitation and inhibition, see Casanova *et al.* 2002; Rubenstein and Merzenich 2003; and for a psychological explanation of the 'filtering model', see Bogdashina 2010.

5. An old joke goes: If you are good at teaching you become a teacher, if you are good at engineering you become an engineer, if you are good at research you become a researcher, and if you are good at nothing you go to the top to rule them all.

6. Contrary to the assumption that they do not understand metaphors, autistic individuals are very skilful in creating metaphorical images to translate abstract notions into sensory-based inner language (whether visual, tactile, smell, etc.) (Bogdashina 2004).

7. It is no wonder that in the past autism was often misdiagnosed as schizophrenia. Even now, with emphasis on the social impairments (and not taking into account hypersensitivities and other differences in sensory perception, and memory functions), schizophrenia may be one of the diagnoses (misdiagnoses) in some cases.

8. Abram defines a shaman as someone who is able to 'readily slip out of the perceptual boundaries that demarcate his or her particular culture – boundaries reinforced by social customs, taboos, and most importantly, the common speech or language – in order to make contact with, and learn from, the other powers in the land' (Abram 1997, p.9).

9. See, for example, Cowey and Stoerig 1991; Weiskrantz 1996; Weiskrantz *et al.* 1974.

10. See how autistic language development provides a new 'take' on the principle of linguistic relativity in Bogdashina 2010.

6

What Is Self?
Or, What/Who Am 'I'?

The concept of self is central to the phenomenon of spirituality, especially in the understanding of connectedness, relationship with or awareness of God or the force of the universe – connectedness between self and other(s). The same concept is very important in autism. In fact, from the very beginning of the official recognition of autism as a separate medical entity (Kanner 1943), the notion of 'self' has been at the core of the condition, reflected in the name chosen for it: the term 'autism' is derived from the Greek *autos*, meaning 'self'.[1] Both Kanner (1943) and Asperger (1944) chose the term 'autism' to illustrate the extreme self-focus of their patients. However, recently this approach has been turned upside down, with a new theory (in which 'self' – or rather lack of it – is central) – 'absence of self' in autism (Frith 2003). Ramachandran believes that autism 'could be regarded fundamentally as a disorder of self-consciousness' because, despite its tendency to be private and independent:

> the self actually emerges from a reciprocity of interactions with others and with the body it is embedded in. When it withdraws from society and retreats from its own body it barely exists; at least not in the sense of a mature self that defines our existence as human beings. (Ramachandran 2011, p.127)

Theories of self in autism
Uta Frith proposes her theory of an 'absent self' in autism and illustrates the 'absence of self' as a common denominator in autism. She revives

an idea of the homunculus ('a little man residing in the brain' – the last visible self or self-aware self), which has been rejected by both philosophers and psychologists, but which can, the researcher claims, explain the development of self (or failure to develop it) in autism. According to Frith (2003, p.218), the last visible self may be 'asleep or absent in autism'. However, there is a problem with this last visible self as a common denominator in autism, because the self-aware self emerges only gradually in older children and adolescents, while autism is present from or even before birth (though often undetected until later).

Frith (2003, p.209) points out that one can do without this homunculus, but 'this would mean high egocentrism' because '[o]nly this self is aware that other people too have self-aware selves'. Frith proposes that 'pure egocentrism has a type of self in the centre that is not ultimately aware of itself and the selves of others'. Frith and Happe (1999) argue that awareness of self and awareness of others tend to go together. Uta Frith hypothesises that:

> Perhaps there is an awareness that is *all* self and does not include the reflection of the self in other selves. [Frith refers to] this kind of self-awareness as self-knowledge. Could it be that individuals with autism who acquire a conscious theory of mind, first and foremost attain knowledge of their own mind? This would mean that they can possess detailed knowledge about themselves, but not about others. If so, we could explain why the autobiographies of autistic people go into remarkable detail about their own inner states, far more so than most autobiographies, and why they hardly ever speculate about how they may have affected people who play an important role in their lives. (Frith 2003, p.210)

The phenomenon 'all self – no other' is well known in autism, when the person perceives only him or herself but lacks the ability to perceive others. However, it is not because the individual has developed the awareness of their self but not of others; it is a state they enter when overloaded and cannot cope with processing too much information; it is a part of a fluctuating state of 'all self, no other; all other, no self':

> In the state of all self, no other, I could perceive myself as a person and it was totally natural to express this self equally aimed at a tree as at animal, object, person, the wind or nothing at all. In the state of all self, no other, all action is perceived as being from self, to self... the sense of other remained theoretical...not held within the same

simultaneous context as self. So selfhood remained whole but the sense of other was partial. The sense of other can cause a switch to the opposite state, able now to perceive a whole sense of other but robbed of a simultaneous sense of self...as though the approach of other causes the self to disappear. (Williams 1998, p.29)

Frith agrees that autistic writers have 'extensive self-knowledge of autistic people. They tell of inner experiences with great detail', and as they tell no one these things when they are children, it is logical to assume that:

> they did not know that their inner experiences were different from the inner experiences of other people. Normal children get this fundamental insight early and for free, by virtue of their intuitive mentalizing ability. With a late-acquired conscious theory of mind, this insight is hard won. (Frith 2003, p.211)

This conclusion is correct if we look from the perspective of a 'normal' person who assumes that his or her Theory of Mind (ToM) is the only possible (or, at least, the only correct) one. As sensory perceptual experiences (leading to different cognitive interpretations) are very different in autism, they do lack ToM, but they develop Theory of Autistic Mind, which many non-autistic individuals (including some researchers) lack. For example, even when she was a young child, Gunilla Gerland's inner self was developed, but she struggled to understand the 'outside world': 'I thought I had a right to be as I was, that I had a right to have my sense of integrity respected. I thought it was other people who were behaving so incomprehensibly and strangely, not me' (1997, p.23).

What is normal for other people is not necessarily normal for many individuals with autism. Many of them are 'terribly ill-equipped to survive' in the 'normal' world (Sinclair 1992, p.302), but this does not necessarily mean they have no self. Jim Sinclair, an adult with high-functioning autism, states: '[M]y personhood is intact. My selfhood is undamaged. I find great value and meaning in my life' (Sinclair 1992, p.302). The absent self theory presupposes less developed self-awareness in autism, whereas it is rather a differently developed self.

Based on the views of Kanner (1943) and Bosch (1970), the theory of autism as *a disorder of affective and social relations* was developed further by Hobson (1989a, b, 1995). Like Kanner (1943), who suggested that these children's primary deficit is their '*inability to relate themselves* in

the ordinary way to people and situations from the beginning of life'
(p.242), Hobson (1995) sees the primary impairment as an inability to
engage emotionally with others, which leads to an inability to receive
the necessary social experiences to develop cognitive structures for
understanding.

An 'experiencing self' theory does not deny the existence of self in
autism but emphasises the difficulty with experiencing it. It has been
proposed that the development of personal episodic memory is closely
connected with the existence of an 'experiencing self' (Brewer 1986;
Dritschel *et al.* 1992). Powell and Jordan (1993) hypothesise that the
difficulty for autistic children of establishing an 'experiencing self' is
one of the fundamental deficits in autism. This idea arose from the
identification of problems autistic individuals experience in 'personal
episodic memory', where all events are remembered and coded 'from
the outside', not as personal occurrences. Autistic individuals can easily
recall events and things happening to others, but find it extremely hard
to recall an event in which they have participated, if no cues are provided
to trigger it (Jordan and Powell 1992). The researchers admit that the
mechanism for developing this sense of self has not yet been identified
but suggest that it might relate to deficits in emotional perception of
the events.

Some autistic individuals do have problems with 'experiencing
self', when they can easily remember events but not their own selves
participating in these events. There are several possible explanations
provided by autistic authors to account for this difficulty, for instance:

Lack of body awareness

Some autistic people lack body awareness (proprioceptive hyposensitivity)
and have no concept of their body (through the proprioceptive channel,
while having self-awareness through other channels). For example, Tito,
an autistic boy, knew about his body only theoretically – he could
recognise himself in photos, because his mother told him it was him
when they looked at the family album, but he did not *experience* his
body. To check that he did exist he used…his shadow: he flapped his
hands and watched his shadow flapping the hands. It seemed he existed
because of his shadow (Mukhopadhyay 2000). Tito had a memory of
his mother teaching him the action songs, and a memory of *his shadow*
doing the action, but he had no memory of his own self doing it. Some
others also write about 'horrible lack of body awareness which left me

adrift in the outside world, and without measurable boundaries between my body and the molecules beyond' (Blackman 2001, p.123).

Hypotactility

Some people with autism can experience problems with tactile sense perception. For example, having locked himself out of his house, Schneider broke a pane of glass with his bare hand:

> Predictably, a piece of that broken glass sliced everything on my forearm all the way to the bone. To the point, I felt nothing, and did not realize that I'd been injured until I glanced down and saw the open, gaping wound and the blood that had gushed all over the front door. Even then, I felt neither fear nor panic. (Schneider 1999, p.48)

Monoprocessing causing 'self–other' problems

One of the versions of monoprocessing (Williams 1996) is the inability to process simultaneously information about oneself and others, when the person is able:

> to perceive a whole sense of other but robbed of a simultaneous sense of self; it is as though the approach of other causes the self to disappear. Information continues to be accumulated but as though accumulated not by [the] self but by a computer devoid of self. (Williams 1998, p.29)

A 'sense of agency' theory, though connected to the intersubjectivity theories, the theoretical model proposed by Russell (1996) has a cognitive basis. Russell argues that the process of mental development aims at understanding the division between an objective reality and a subjective one, with a sense of agency being a vital component in the process. According to Russell, there are two phases in the development of self: at the first phase there is no true self yet, just subpersonal processing that gives a subjective sense in owning both one's actions and one's perceptions; at the second stage the sense of self capable of reflection (true self – self as an agent) emerges that leads to 'I-thoughts' and 'I-actions', that is, 'experiencing self'. Russell (1994) suggests that one of the basic deficits in autism might be disturbance at the stage of 'efferent copying' (at the first phase of development of self). In normal development the 'efferent copying' gives the sense of one's own agency, that is, the nervous system does not only control movements of the head and eyes to scan the environment or keep track of moving objects, but also records those movements, in order to distinguish the case where the movement is in the person's head and eyes, and the world is still. In autism, the researcher suggests, disturbance at the stage of 'efferent copying' prevents a person having a sense of themselves as an agent. In this case a person would not get dizzy in the normal way from spinning and, moreover, might seek the kinds of sensations that would give movement stimulation free from recording head and eye movements in relation to the world. Russell considers autism a condition where executive function deficiencies lead to difficulties in developing the initial stage of agency, and that is why a subjective (self-aware) self cannot develop, resulting in inability to understand the agency of others, and hence problems with development of Theory of Mind of other people. However, there might be other explanations as well. For example, a child can be aware of himself but have problems with body awareness and body control. Tito interprets these problems through introducing concepts of 'two different selves' (which shows he develops his Theory of Mind):

> One was the complete one – the thinking self – which was filled with learning and feelings. It could feel the sorrows, joys and satisfaction… The other self was the acting self that behaved and had no self-control. It was weird and full of actions. The actions which this self displayed were not symmetrical with his thoughts… He would pick up any object that attracted his physical self, through its colour, smell and appearance… The two selves stayed in their own selves, isolated from each other. (Mukhopadhyay 2000, p.50)

Tito experimented with himself: 'when I ordered my hand to pick up a pencil I could not do it. I remember long back when I had ordered my lips to move I could not do it' (Mukhopadhyay 2000, p.73).

Definitions of self

Many researchers have investigated self-awareness and lack of self-awareness in autism, assuming that the subject of their research is obvious. But is it?

Before we can even approach the question of whether there is egocentric self, or lack of self, in autism, or talk about self-awareness (or lack of it) in autism, we have to clearly define the concept of self. And here we face a problem: when people talk about 'self' they think they know what the word means, but ask them to define it and you will get as many definitions as the people you ask; some will fail to define it verbally and will just move their hands in front of you, shaping them into ambiguous signs, while saying, 'It's like this, you know.'

It is not only lay people who find the concept hard to define. A similar situation can be found in research and academic literature. The concept of self, this elusive 'I', shows 'an alarming tendency to disappear when we try to introspect it' (Blackburn 1994, p.344). It is obvious that researchers and philosophers often mean different things while discussing the concept of self. This is not a new problem: philosophers have struggled with the definition and description of 'self' for many decades.[2] The concept of 'self' has been defined and interpreted differently (depending on the perspective of different scientific disciplines) by phenomenologists (as the essence and feel of a mental state), philosophers of mind (e.g. high order representation theory), neuroscientists (looking for correlation of mental phenomena with brain states and structures), cognitive scientists (constructing models of mind), social scientists (focusing on personality features and roles people have in the society), and so on.[3]

Some definitions are relatively narrow, and can be contradictory, for example, some restrict 'self' to conscious experience and see it as the inner subject of one's conscious experience (Campbell 1957; Harre 1987). Others emphasise the unconscious side: one's self is the unconscious mechanism responsible for the unity of one's consciousness (Brooks 1994). Some draw boundaries around the construction made of sensory experiences: one's self is an aggregate of or construction out of one's sense-experience (Ayer 1946). Others presuppose something ambiguous, 'which views the world through one's eyes' (Nagel 1986, p.55). There are definitions restricting 'self' only to humans and denying its existence in animals: the self is a collection of features shared by all and only human beings in all times and places (Solomon 1988). Some definitions are more descriptive, attempting to embrace several different features of the concept; for instance, Kircher and David (2003, p.2) consider our 'self' as a construction of our minds and a construction of understanding how we perceive, think, feel and decide, central to our understanding of who we are individually:

What we mean by *self*...is as a first approximation the commonly shared experience, that we know we are the same person across time, that we are the author of our thoughts/actions, and that we are distinct from the environment. It is the immediate, pervasive, automatic feeling of being a whole person, different from others, constant over time, with a physical boundary, the centre of all our experience.

In dictionaries, one of the meanings of self is given as 'ego', which reflects a common situation of using these two terms interchangeably.[4] Here we will distinguish between 'self' and 'ego', which will be defined as the part of mind that reacts to reality, has a sense of individuality and a sense of self-esteem.

Soul and spirit

Soul: (1) the spiritual or immaterial part of a human being or animal, often regarded as immoral; (2) the moral, emotional, or intellectual nature of a person (Thompson 1995, p.1328).

Spirit: (1) the vital animating essence of a person or animal; the intelligent non-physical part of a person; (2) a rational or intelligent being without a material body; a supernatural being such as a ghost, fairy, etc. (Thompson 1995, p.1341). Swinton (2001, p.14) defines spirit as 'the essential life-force that undergirds, motivates and vitalizes human existence'.[5]

In some cultures, soul is seen as an essential part of a human being – along with a biological aspect, so a spiritual input is needed to produce a new life. For example, in Sabarl Island, *hinona*, or 'essence of life', is the vital substance that makes the body breathe (Battaglia 1990). In Indonesia the Laboya peoples consider pregnant women to be containers of ancestral breath and spirit, and a newborn is seen as an unidentified being coming 'from foreign realms related to realms of ancestors' (Geirnaert-Martin 1992, p.230). For the Muslim Malay people, all newborns have several energy components: the soul (*ruh*), the breath of life (*nyawa*) and the spirit of life (*semangat*) (Laderman 1993). Soul is seen as a non-physical component of a person that can leave the body, for example, during sleep, or at will if the person knows how to do it.

Reincarnation: Many religions have some concepts of rebirth of souls, indicating the belief that souls are eternal and reborn repeatedly. The main aim of some Eastern religions (e.g. Hinduism and Buddhism) is liberation from human cycles of rebirth (*moksha*) through enduring consequences of behaviour in previous lives – *karma*.

There have been attempts to verify reincarnation. For example, Stevenson (1997) provides an analysis of 225 cases of people born with birthmarks or birth defects who claim that these marks are related to their past lives or the way they died in their past lives. Violent deaths seem to be more remembered. On the basis of these, and similar findings, some researchers speculate that human bodies and consciousness are not limited by space and time and extra-cerebral memories can be transferred from one life to another.[6]

Tobert suggests that there is a plurality of frameworks for understanding human existence, and belief in one model does not necessarily exclude the others from existing. The researcher points out that it would be better if we could take an *emic* rather than an *etic* perspective that acknowledges the beliefs and explanatory models of different cultures about mental problems.[7] 'This would consider the possibility of reincarnation, communication with disincarnate beings and the reality of possession…entailing slipping into a non-physical dimension, picking up material and confusing it with common consensus reality' (Tobert 2010, p.43).

The ambiguity and polysemic character of the word 'self' (with its metaphysical, linguistic and psychological distinctions) is not surprising; the word has many meanings:

> personality, character, an individual's central character traits, the way(s) one carries oneself in the world, the way one represents oneself to oneself and to others, the dynamic integrated system of thoughts, emotions, lived events, and so on, that make up who one is from the God's eye point of view. All these senses are useful. (Flanagan 1996, p.vii)

Without denying the usefulness of all the meanings of the word, it can be confusing when the particular meaning is not specified in a discussion: if one person talks about personality traits, the other about an abstract notion – both using the same word ('self') that has different meaning for them – the discussion becomes meaningless. Because there is no agreed use of the term 'self', some even propose to drop it altogether, as there can be no problems with the self if there is a doubt that it even exists (Olson 1998). However, the concept of self is too important to lose and we will define it in the context of this discussion.

For William James (1950), self is one half of the universe, with the division between self ('me') and 'not me'. Some find it useful to distinguish between the *physical* or *somatic* self, the bearer of subjective experience (Hall 1897) and the *psychological* self, the contents of that subjective experience (Pillsbury 1908).[8] In his *Treatise on Human Nature*, David Hume (1978) introduced the bundle theory of self where self is an aggregate of mental states – a bundle or collection of different perceptions which succeed each other with an inconceivable rapidity, being in a perpetual flux and movement.

So what is self? Does it exist at all? There surely must be something that is connected to *my* body and that thinks and directs *my* actions; in short, there must be *me*. Can we at least identify any characteristic features of a self even if we cannot provide a precise and universally accepted definition of it?

Characteristics of self

Originally, Ramachandran (2003) identified five defining characteristics of self, and later (2011) added two more.[9]

1. Continuity: we have a sense of time (past, present and future) that runs through the mind.

2. Unity, or coherence of self: despite the diversity of sensory experiences, memories, beliefs and thoughts each individual experiences oneself as one person, as a unity.

3. The sense of embodiment or ownership: each individual feels anchored in his or her body.

4. A sense of agency: what we call free will, the sense of being in charge of our own actions, our own destiny.

5. Capability of reflection: being aware of oneself.

There are also five characteristics of self-awareness (roughly similar to the five Ramachandran categories) that are distinguished in the modern psychiatric literature.[10]

As any or all of these different aspects of self can be differentially disturbed in brain disease, Ramachandran believes that the self is actually not one thing but many. The researcher suggests that the solution to the problem of self may not be a straightforward one but rather a radical shift in perspective, and points out curious parallels between this idea and the Hindu philosophical view that there is no essential difference between self and others or that the self is an illusion (Ramachandran

2003). Conversely, some of what are considered mental problems or brain diseases in psychiatry (if one or a combination of these aspects is 'disturbed') can correspond to 'spiritual experiences' that 'normal' people may spend years learning how to achieve.

Here we briefly consider each of the characteristics of self listed above (and possible links to spiritual experiences). The first is *continuity*, or the sense of time running through the mind: a person remembers the past, feels the present and anticipates the future. You do not wake up in the morning a different person.[11] A feeling of loss of continuity may be experienced both in health (after a traumatic or life changing emotional situation) and in neuroses and personality disorders. The person knows that both people (before and after) are truly himself, but feels different from what he was. In a healthy person, this temporary state does not alter the state of reality, it is rather thoughts and feelings that do not seem to keep up with the person as he has come to accept himself (Oyebode 2008). However, for someone with schizophrenia, for instance, it takes the form of a passivity of experience, and the patient claims he has completely changed from being one person to another (Jaspers 1959).

An indirect comparison of the state of disrupted continuity is the experience of 'here-and-now' which is identified as one of the fundamental features of spirituality; it means experience of being present in the present, both in time and in space.[12] Most people ('verbal thinkers') are so preoccupied with their thoughts (what to do, where to go, how to manage to keep to the deadline, etc.) that they actually do not physically *experience* where they are and what they are doing; their senses are shut down and do not connect to their conscious awareness. Their 'experience' of the place, for instance, is abstract; they 'know' what is there, without actually *perceiving* the physical environment. In fact, in our hectic life, in the rush to accomplish everything we have planned for the day, we do not feel our *selves* (who or what we are), *knowing* only the 'facades' ('false selves') we have created to play the roles in our social life. The experience of 'here-ness and now-ness' with its intensity and immediateness is different to (and more important than) any theoretical belief for the person who is experiencing it. It is analogous to the state of 'simply be', in contrast to 'appear' (Donna Williams' terminology) that is easily available to some autistic people. 'For me the ability to be open in the now has not been lost. I do not meditate to enter this state, only some time without interruptions from "outside". The state of here-and-now is a state of delight' (Mar, personal communication, 2012).

The second feature is *unity or coherence*, or experiencing oneself as a unity, one person, despite the diversity of one's experiences, memories and beliefs. Ramachandran (2003) notes that the self (by definition and its very nature) can be experienced only as a unity; experiencing two selves may be logically impossible, because it would be unclear who or what is experiencing these two selves. In some psychiatric conditions, however, the assumption of unity can be lost, for instance, in dissociative identity disorder (multiple personality disorder). From the neurological perspective, the idea of the *unification* of the self looks problematic:

> while we subjectively experience ourselves as single and unified beings, the brain is actually composed of millions of individual neurons...but even if we fully understood the mechanism of neuronal synchronization, there still appears to be a fundamental difference... between the unified self and the divisible brain. (Feinberg and Keenan 2005, p.672)

Ramachandran (2003) writes about an interesting phenomenon that can be seen in split-brain patients whose two brain hemispheres have been surgically disconnected: in this case, the person does not experience two selves (each hemisphere's 'self' is aware only of itself). The researcher describes a study that showed that the non-verbal right hemisphere of a split-brain patient can lie: for instance, after receiving instructions from researcher A (to lie to B), the patient (non-verbally) signed the wrong answer to researcher B. They also tested the personality and aesthetic preferences of the two hemispheres' 'selves' by training the right hemisphere to communicate 'yes' or 'no', or 'I don't know' non-verbally by picking one of three abstract shapes with the left hand, and received surprising results that showed that the two hemispheres can simultaneously hold contradictory views. For example, in patient LB the left hemisphere said it believed in God whereas the right hemisphere insisted that it was an atheist! This very example illustrates a possibility of at least two 'selves' in one body, each residing in a different hemisphere, and indicates how little we know about our 'selves'. For example, which of the two (the right or the left) is the 'true self'?

The third characteristic, *sense of embodiment*, or the feeling of self, is rooted in the body; for most of the time we are not conscious of our body, but we *know* that we possess the integrated body which comprises the self. The loss of 'felt sense' can result in *dissociation*, which can range from mild detachment from one's immediate surroundings to a severe detachment from physical and emotional reality. In mild cases, dissociation can be regarded as a defence mechanism to cope with stress. Ramachandran compares these disabling states with normal states of emergency, when emotions are shut down but the person is alert and hypervigilant (the anterior cingulate – part of the frontal lobe – becomes extremely active, suppressing the amygdala and other limbic emotional centres). If this mechanism is triggered (when there is an emergency) by chemicals or brain disease, the person's world becomes devoid of emotional meaning, and derealisation or depersonalisation occurs. Severe prolonged cases of dissociation lead to dissociative disorders, such as partial or complete identity confusion; Cotrad's syndrome, when the person claims that he is dead; depersonalisation ('I am not real' – when the person feels like a zombie living in a dream); derealisation ('The world is not real'); multiple personality disorder (dissociative personality disorder), the embodiment of at least two personalities (identities). The latter phenomenon raised doubts about the intuitive assumption that an individual human being is indivisible (Oyebode 2008). However, (nonpathological) dissociation is, in fact, a universal phenomenon. All people experience it from time to time, during absorption in a book, daydreaming, and so on.

Out-of-body experience (OBE), near-death experience (NDE) and anomalous perception in general are also seen as belonging to this category. However, if we consider them pathological, then there would be hardly any healthy people around – numerous polls and surveys show that many presumably 'normal' people report anomalous or so-called psychic experiences.[13]

The phenomenon of being able to see one's own body and others around it during OBEs can be induced by stimulation of the right parietal cortex with an electrode, by certain drugs, meditative practices, or spontaneously (for instance, during NDEs), or by some traumatic event, makes this characteristic (embodiment) questionable – does it represent a part of self or just one of its possible 'locations'?

Ramachandran gives an example of stimulation of the right parietal cortex with an electrode while a person is conscious, when the person will momentarily feel an out-of-body experience – floating near the ceiling watching his or her own body down below – to illustrate the case when the embodiment of self (one of the axiomatic characteristics of self) is temporarily abandoned. However, who (or what) is watching one's body? Doesn't it indicate that self can temporarily leave the body? Can the body not be necessarily seen as a characteristic of self but rather as a means or tool to experience self?

Sense of agency, or free will, is not a straightforward feature, either. Experiments by the American neurosurgeon Benjamin Libet (2002) show that what we call 'readiness potential' is picked up by the electroencephalograph (EEG) three-quarters of a second *before* a person consciously exercises his 'free will' to make a movement (for example, wiggle a finger). So it seems that there is brain activity before a person is consciously aware of any subjective experience of the finger movement.[14] So is free will an illusion?

The fifth feature is *capability of reflection*, or being aware of oneself. Ramachandran (2011, p.202) insists that self-awareness is the 'aspect of self [that] is almost axiomatic; a self that is not aware of itself is an oxymoron'. However, the researcher himself provides an example of right/left hemispheric selves that are not aware of each other. Besides, there is the unconscious part of self that has to be taken into account as well. Some argue that self-awareness is a uniquely human feature, but is it?

Is self-awareness a uniquely human feature?

To find out which animals are 'self-aware', Gordon Gallup (1968) designed the 'mirror test', which has been used on different species. A mirror is placed in front of an animal, and if a creature shows that it recognises its own reflection (for example, by touching a spot painted on the forehead, while ignoring another invisible mark on the head, which shows that the animal is not reacting to touch or smell), it means that the animal knows who stares at it from the looking-glass. Animals who have passed the test are apes, elephants, dolphins, pigeons and some others.[15] Many animals are fascinated by mirrors but, researchers claim, do not seem to realise that what they see is their own reflection.

However, there are several possible explanations why animals do not recognise themselves in a mirror, and lack of self-awareness is *not* one of them. Some animals do not show 'visual self-awareness' because their visual perception is different. For instance, could we expect bats to react to their reflection in the mirror? 'Failing' the mirror test, these animals may be self-aware through other senses (e.g. smell, hearing or body awareness; Anderson 1984) (for instance, a cat wouldn't try to squeeze its body into a mouse-hole, it would use its paw to attempt to get its prey). The mirror test fails to identify modality-specific senses of self-awareness among animals. Besides, there is a connection between the ability to recognise themselves in the mirror and social experience. For example, chimps reared in isolation seemed incapable of self-recognition in the mirror (Gallup 1979), while those who live with others easily learned to recognise their reflections. While discussing animals' abilities, some researchers insist on distinguishing between thinking and cognition. They define *cognition* as processes by which sensory input is transformed, reduced and elaborated. They define *thinking* as attending to the animals' internal images or representations. They say that many animals can *cognate* (i.e. get sensory information and store it in their memory) but are unable to *think* because they have only a very simple level of consciousness (Ristau 1991).

The role of language (It's the language, stupid!)

The main argument used to deny animals the ability to think (and develop self-awareness) is that they lack verbal language. Some insist that acquiring a human language, oral, written or sign language, is a necessary precondition to develop consciousness and self (Dennett 2006). Dennett proposes that human subjectivity is a remarkable by-product of human language, and no version of it should be assumed present in any other species, including pre-linguistic children. Although they can be sensitive, responsive to pain, alert and cognitively competent in many ways, babies and animals are not really conscious, as there is no organised subject to be the enjoyer or sufferer, no owner of the experience. According to Dennett, the rudimentary communication systems of other species cannot compete with the human as they are incomparable; for example, animals' 'languages' have no verbs, nouns, prepositions or tenses. However, to expect 'human categories' in animals' languages and equate communicative ability to gestural and vocal responses is anthropocentric (Menzel 1970). In fact, the concepts noun, verb, and adjective, and so on are arbitrary. The lack of adverbs, for instance, in animals' languages does not mean they do not understand such concepts as 'fast', 'slowly', 'up', 'down', 'left', 'right', and so on. Their world is not one-dimensional; in fact, as their sensory systems are so different, their world can be more 'dimensional' than that of humans.[16]

There have always been strong voices against Dennett's assumption. For example, the German ethologist Otto Koehler (1953) has demonstrated that animals employ 'wordless thinking' with regard to quality. Koehler found that some animals can 'see numbers': they choose the object with a certain number of points on it from a group of objects with points differing in number, size, colour and arrangement, and 'act upon a number' (by repeating an act a certain number of times).[17]

Anderson (2006) argues that even quite simple animals are conscious, including bees, butterflies and cockroaches. To illustrate the point, Anderson employs the German biologist Jacob von Uexküll's concept of *Umwelt*, the world around animals as they perceive it. *Umwelten* of different species (including humans) are diverse but equally real. For example, the objects in the bees' world have meanings that are quite different from our own, but very significant for the bees; that is why their attention is drawn to things humans barely perceive. Anderson defines consciousness as a feeling of 'seeing' the world and its associations. For the bee, it is the feeling of being a bee. Of course, Anderson does not mean that a bee is self-conscious or spends time thinking about its life, but the bee has its own 'feeling' that can be compared to the activity of a human nervous system giving rise to our own 'feelings'. In a way, even tiny creatures are more 'human' than we give them credit for: they can suffer from stress, know their territories well and act on the changing environment. This approach is not anthropomorphic, as animals live in their *Umwelten*, free from human motives (Anderson 2006).

Donald Griffin believes that the best evidence of conscious thinking and feeling in animals is in their actions, and that conscious thought is the most economical explanation of animal behaviour. Animals have to adapt constantly to a changing environment. They are not passive objects; their thinking is rational and conscious. Animals are able to think of alternative actions and choose those they believe will get them what they want, or avoid what they dislike or fear. Griffin states that it is reasonable to attribute this type of consciousness to mammals and birds, on the same basis as it is attributed to pre-linguistic children (Griffin 1984). Simple perceptual and rational conscious thinking is as important for small animals as for those with large brains (Griffin 1998). The difference seems to lie in the level of consciousness, from simple to complex, depending on the complexity of the brain. For example:

- *simple consciousness*: common in insects
- *higher consciousness*, which, in turn, may be subdivided into several levels of consciousness. Humans, with the most complex brains, possess a higher level of consciousness than, for instance, dogs, which have smaller, less complex brains but have consciousness nevertheless (Grandin 1998). Ethologists and cognitive psychologists (some very reluctantly) agree that animals have some consciousness (primary consciousness) because animals do get sensory information and act on it but, unlike humans, they are not self-aware.

- *self-consciousness* or *self-awareness*: humans are said to have this (highest) level of consciousness. However, a lot of evidence for self-awareness has been reported in some other animals.[18]

There is no doubt that 'human consciousness', especially when it is tied up with language, differs from consciousness of other species. That is why it is hard (impossible?) to know what consciousness might be in another animal: we cannot measure it because it is internal and subjective, and we cannot use our own experience as a basis for comparison (LeDoux 2006).[19]

Temple Grandin (1998) puts forward her classification of several levels of self-consciousness where different degrees of consciousness depend on the ability of different brain subsystems to integrate information and make associations. Grandin's approach accounts for many phenomena in the self-awareness of both animals and humans.

- *Consciousness within one sense.* This type of consciousness explains why some animals fail the 'mirror test'. Those animals who do not recognise themselves in the mirror do not lack self-consciousness but rather lack 'visual self-consciousness'. They are self-aware in other sensory modalities, such as tactile-aware, smell-aware, movement-aware, and so on. So some animals may be 'one/two-sense(s) conscious'. Some autistic individuals with severe sensory processing problems may experience hyposensitivity in one or several sensory channels and lack self-consciousness in certain senses but be self-aware in others. For instance, individuals with proprioceptive processing problems may experience difficulty in figuring out their body boundaries and use their vision or hearing to locate themselves among the objects around them. Another group of people with autism, who are easily overloaded, may use one sense at a time to get information about the environment. Some can switch channels and check the information from different sensory modalities but have problems integrating stimuli from several senses simultaneously (Daria 2008). For example:

  > Many times, sensory stimuli are perceived in fragments. The child focuses on one sense, such as sight. Whilst he is examining something with his vision, he sees every minute detail and colours are vibrant, perhaps radiatingly brilliant like the jewel tones of a modern painting. As he brings in the visual stimulus, he loses track of his other senses. So he doesn't make much sense of sounds in the background. Also

his body seems suspended, floating, as he loses knowledge of feeling touch. (O'Neill 1999, pp.24–25)

- *Consciousness where all sensory systems are integrated.* This type of consciousness is typical for those individuals (both with autism and without the condition) whose sensory systems are integrated. Temple Grandin places herself in this category because her thoughts are not connected with emotions.

- *Consciousness where all sensory systems are integrated with emotions.* Some individuals who experience problems with recognising or expressing emotions may have difficulty with this type of consciousness.

- *Consciousness where sensory systems and emotions are integrated and thinking is verbal.* This type is very common in non-autistic individuals.

As children with autism do not share the perceptual world with other people because their experiences are very different from the 'typical' ones, then it is only logical to assume that their self-awareness, thinking and language development do not follow a 'typical' route. However, lack of abstract language consciousness does not mean that 'language-less self-consciousness' is inferior to 'highest self-consciousness with language thinking'. 'Non-language thinkers' do have mental language(s) that are qualitatively different from the conventional one but equally complex. Language-less self-consciousness (typical for some autistic individuals, especially those who lack verbal language, and those who develop it later than 'normal' children) makes them more open to spiritual experiences, pre-linguistic spiritual experiences, which they remember better than 'normal' children as their memories are not 'translated' into verbal (culturally determined) concepts.

Development of self

How do we develop the (conscious, subjective) self and become aware of 'I-ness' or 'me' versus 'not me'?

Neurobiological approach

Approaching the concept of self from a biological perspective, Damasio (2000) argues that a likely biological forerunner for what eventually emerges as the elusive sense of self is the organism as represented inside its own brain. According to Damasio, the deep roots for the self, including the elaborate self which comprises identity and personhood, are to be found in the brain's mechanisms which continuously and nonconsciously maintain the body functions and states that are necessary for survival. 'These devices continually represent, *nonconsciously*, the state of the living body, along its many dimensions.' Damasio calls 'the state of activity within the ensemble of such devices the *proto-self*, the nonconscious forerunner for the levels of self which appear in our minds as the conscious protagonist of consciousness: core self and autobiographical self'. Unlike the infamous homunculus of the old-fashioned neurology textbooks, Damasio's model of the body-in-the-brain 'perceives' and 'knows' nothing, rather it is a collection of brain devices that regulate the organism's life. Although neither these devices nor their regulatory actions reflected in neural maps generate consciousness, their presence is indispensable for the mechanisms that achieve core consciousness (Damasio 2000, p.22). Proposing biological mechanisms of producing consciousness, Damasio distinguishes between two kinds of consciousness:

- The simplest kind of consciousness, *core consciousness*, provides the organism with a sense of self about one moment, now, and about one place, here; there is neither before nor after.

- The complex kind of consciousness, *extended consciousness*, provides the organism with an elaborate sense of self, an identity and a person, and places that person at a point in individual historical time, being aware of the lived past and of the anticipated future and the world around him now.

According to Damasio, the core consciousness is a simple biological phenomenon (of one single level of organisation), is stable across the lifetime of an organism and does not depend on language, memory or reasoning. The extended consciousness, on the other hand, is a complex biological phenomenon of several levels and grades, evolving throughout the lifetime of the organism (in humans and some non-humans). It is built on the foundation of the core consciousness. Impairments of extended consciousness do not cause any problems to the core consciousness but, by contrast, impairments at the level of core consciousness destroy the extended consciousness as well.[20] Damasio believes that these types of consciousness correspond to two kinds of self: the core self and the autobiographical self. The *core self* is a transient entity, recreated for every object with which the brain interacts. The *autobiographical self* is a nontransient collection of unique facts and ways of being that characterise a person.

Damasio describes the birth of self from the emerging consciousness. The process begins:

> when the brain acquires the power...of telling the story without words, the story that there is life ticking away in an organism, and the states of the living organism, within body bounds, are continuously being altered by encounters with objects or events in its environment or...by thoughts and by internal adjustments of the life process. Consciousness emerges when this primordial story – the story of an object causally changing the state of the body – can be told using the universal nonverbal vocabulary of body signals. The apparent self emerges as the feeling of a feeling. (Damasio 2000, pp.30–31)

The body as a filter

In his book *A History of the Mind: Evolution and the Birth of Consciousness* (1992), Nicholas Humphrey states that consciousness is essentially a matter of having bodily sensations rather than having higher level thoughts, and proposes a theory of how consciousness may have evolved, replacing Descartes' famous claim 'I think, therefore I am' (*cogito, ergo sum*) with 'I feel, therefore I am' (*sentio, ergo sum*) (Humphrey 1992, p.115). Humphrey postulates two axioms: '1. Consciousness stems from the having of sensations. 2. The subject of consciousness, "I", is an embodied self' (Humphrey 1992, p.115) and argues that a mind requires boundaries, physical boundaries (skin for humans), to discriminate 'me' from 'not me'.

This is how Bergson described the process of emerging self – with body as a filter providing the boundaries between 'me' and 'not-me':

> My perception, in its pure state, isolated from memory, does not go from my body to other bodies; it is, to begin with, in the aggregate of bodies, then gradually limits itself and adopts my body as a centre. And it is led to do so precisely by experience of the double faculty, which this body possesses, of performing actions and feeling affections; in a word, by experience of the sensori-motor power of a certain image, privileged among other images. For, on the one hand, this image always occupies the centre of representation, so that other

images range themselves round it in the very order in which they might be subject to its action; on the other hand, I know it from within, by sensations which I term affective, instead of knowing only, as in the case of the other images, its outer skin. There is then, in the aggregate of images, a privileged image, perceived in its depths and no longer only on the surface – the seat of affection and, at the same time, the source of action: it is this particular image which I adopt as the centre of my universe and as the physical basis of my personality. (Bergson 2004, p.64)

Anthropologist Ashley Montagu (1978) defines individual self-awareness (corresponding to Freud's ego) as the perception of the bodily self. Whenever one feels (perceives) something, one is simultaneously experiencing the division between self and other, creating finer and finer distinctions in the process (which started *in utero*, accelerated sharply at birth, and has been an ongoing process ever since), with all the experiences and feelings the person experiences through the body. So the first physical boundary between self and Not-self is our skin and the first physical sense to develop (even before birth) is the sense of touch. In his book *Touching: The Human Significance of the Skin*, Montagu describes the function of the embryo's skin which has 'the capacity to resist the absorption of too much water…to respond appropriately to physical, chemical and neutral changes, and to changes in temperature'. All our lives, 'from its earliest differentiation, [the skin] remains in intimate association with the internal or central nervous system' (Montagu 1978, p.2), and though the skin itself does not think:

> its sensitivity is so great, combined with its ability to pick up and transmit so extraordinarily wide a variety of signals, and make so wide a range of responses, exceeding that of all other sense organs, that for versatility it must be ranked second only to the brain itself. (p.230)

With the development of its nervous system, through sensory input – first through touch, then smell – the foetus begins to distinguish between 'in here' and 'out there', and learns to recognise and to react to the chemical information of the mother's different states. According to Jawer (2009), the sensory feelings the foetus experiences are the precursor to emotions that will be expressed after birth. In his book *The Secret Life of the Unborn Child* (1981, p.64), Thomas Verny describes the roles of these initial sensory feelings in the development of self:

the unborn's ego begins to function sometime in [the second trimester]. His nervous system is now capable of transmitting sensations to the higher brain centers...the unborn baby's attempt to make sense of [the mother's states, such as tiredness] involves his brain. [The mother's tiredness creates a primitive feeling in the foetus – discomfort.] After enough of these episodes, his perceptual centers become advanced enough to process more subtle and complex maternal messages... Anxiety, within limits, is beneficial to the fetus. It disturbs his sense of oneness with his surroundings and makes him aware of his own separateness...he starts erecting a set of primitive defense mechanisms. In the process, his experience of anxiety becomes more sophisticated. What began as a blunt, displeasing feeling...acquires a source (his mother), prompts his thoughts about that source's intentions toward him, forces him to conjure up ways of dealing with those intentions, and creates a string of memories that can be referred to later.

Jawer also highlights the role of the body in making us conscious beings, with feelings (and emotions) felt through the body not as merely manifestations of various brain states but rather as 'the product of interaction between raw sensation on the one hand and mental activity on the other':

> we must first be *sentient* (capable of sensory perception) before we can be *conscious* (self-aware)...the premier component of consciousness is feeling – not...thinking... Feeling preceded thought in our evolution... To be conscious requires that you notice, first and foremost, what you're feeling. And what you're feeling has much to do with the body, of which the brain is a part. (Jawer 2009, p.5)

Pert's (1997) research confirms that neuropeptide receptors are not only in the brain but 'in virtually all locations where information from any of the...senses...enters the nervous system', thus the entire body can be considered as a single sensing and feeling organ (i.e. all bodily organs store emotional memories). This explains 'received memories' by organ transplant recipients.

One of the important organs is the gut which rules the enteric nervous system, which is self-contained. Professor Michael Gershon (1998) calls this system the 'second brain': it is huge, containing millions of nerve cells, and operates without any input from the brain or even the spinal cord. In the gut system are found all the neurotransmitters that are found in the brain and the flow of 'messages' between the two is so continuous that some researchers refer to them as one entity, namely the brain–gut axis but, despite a very close connection, the system of the bowel does operate on its own (Jawer 2009). Schulz (1998) notes that original threatening events are usually felt (and triggered) in the body, rather than by verbal recall, so sometimes subconsciously the person may feel uncomfortable because his body reacts to the triggers (which he is not consciously aware of), while unable to explain the feeling (that is often called intuition, or gut feeling). The body (and bodily organs) retain an unconscious impression of the memories, while the conscious brain is unable to comprehend them. If memories are of some traumatic events, in places or with people who are associated with these memories the person may experience 'strange' feelings but cannot explain them (Jawer 2009). Sleep problems and nightmares are quite common in people who have undergone a traumatic experience, and the person may develop psychosomatic problems, such as neck and back pain, ulcers, irritable bowel syndrome, allergies, migraine, vertigo, chronic pain, chronic fatigue or dissociative personality traits (Levine and Frederick 1997). As many autistic individuals are hypersensitive, their gut feeling is more pronounced. For example:

> I can remember walking down the street [at the age of six] and sensing something which was about to happen but then attempting to [interpret] the situation. I…went with the odds of what I'd interpreted and…it hadn't worked out. What I'd sensed had been right. I recall cursing myself for not trusting in sensing… (Williams 1998, p.33)

Another important organ is the heart: it is not just for pumping the blood around the body. Jawer (2009, p.115) believes that the heart's traditional description as the seat of emotions is justified because, when we feel love, for example, it is 'a whole-body phenomenon, a feeling of joy and wonder radiating from our center. That it is not our brain misinterpreting where the feeling comes from or assigning it, whimsically and metaphorically, to our chest. *It is a bodily reality.*'

A broken heart is no longer a mere metaphor – people can die of a 'broken heart': recent research has shown that a 'broken heart' *hurts* in the same way as pangs of intense physical pain.[21] The pain experienced upon bodily injury and social pain (the pain experienced upon social injury when social relationships are threatened, damaged or lost) share neural and computational mechanisms. The same regions of the brain that become active in response to painful sensory experiences are activated during intense experiences of social rejection, or social loss generally.

Embodied self

In his book *The Heart's Code*, Paul Pearsall (1998, p.23) proposes a simple experiment:

> take one hand…and point to yourself. Where is your hand pointing? Most people find their hand touching the area of their heart… No matter how important it thinks it is, the brain that is coordinating the pointing movements seems to know where the major component of the self it shares with the body resides.

Jawer (2009, p.17) suggests that if we want to understand such notions as the 'self', the 'soul', the 'ego' and the 'conscious I', we have to start with emotions as 'feelings may literally be at the *centre of who we are*'. According to Jawer (p.125), self 'occupies' the whole body (bodymind) – 'close awareness of our bodily states – of pressure and vibration, weight and balance, touch on the skin, breathing, heartbeat, blood-circulation, temperature, smell and taste, appetite and thirst, hearing, pain, pleasure, alertness, and all the other bodily perceptions' that he categorises as feelings. This corresponds to the concept of 'the felt sense', the term coined by Peter Levine to describe:

> the medium through which we experience the totality of sensation [and which] blends together most of the information that forms your experience. Even when you are unaware of it, the felt sense is telling you where you are and how you feel at any given moment… It is so integral to our experience of being human that we take it for granted, sometimes to the point of not realizing that it exists until we deliberately attend to it. (Levine and Frederick 1997, pp.68–71)

In the context of spirituality, special techniques and meditations have been designed to restore this felt sense which has been neglected and ignored by the majority in the rush of their busy life.

Many children (and adults) with autism experience problems with body awareness, 'feeling' the body (hypoproprioception); for example:

> I couldn't really feel where the various parts of [my body] were, or where they were in relation to each other. (Gerland 2007, p.86)

> I had no concept of my body…and I never experienced it… My body was a mere reflection in front of the mirror… I never felt any pain. (Mukhopadhyay 2008, p.18)

Being 'loosely' connected to the body, some autistic individuals are more prone to OBEs, 'sensing' others and the environment (merging or resonating with objects, plants, animals and people); for instance:

> When I was younger I went unconscious I think. I experienced letting go of my body and of life. I felt lifted and the higher I got, the warmer I got. I felt a kind of tingling through my 'body' (but my body was 'down there' – I mean my floating non-body body). The tingling and the warmth made me feel an overwhelming sense of beauty and belonging and purity and honesty at once. I felt part of everything around me and it was part of me. I felt like I was now part of 'knowing' without words or sight. (Williams 1999a, p.193)

> I could eventually monitor my own out-of-body experiences…my own mergence with the feel of things around me… (Williams 1998, p.39)

From my personal communication with people on the autistic spectrum, it turns out that the majority of them feel that their 'self' is not restricted to the body but has no boundaries:

> I experience consciousness inside and outside my head, my body, boundless and all pervasive. (Diny, personal communication, 2012)

> By allowing ourselves to realize our significance and insignificance, no longer can 'self' be relied upon as being just body nor mind, it becomes a different awareness. No center, no edges, instead a vast presence of openness to space and a connection to all yet ever changing. (Nancy, personal communication, 2012).

Interestingly, research shows that electrical energy, measured by electrocardiograms (ECGs) and magnetocardiagrams (MCGs), exists not only within the body but also spreads outside it; and it is the heart that produces the strongest electrical and magnetic activity of any bodily organ (including the brain) (Tandy 2001). According to Donna Williams (1998, p.26), 'the "body" is more than a physical form. It is an energy form, generally, but not necessarily contained and expressed through a physical form.' Some people are sensitive to this energy.

Sensory filters

After birth, through the sensory experiences coming from all the senses, infants gradually learn about their environment and themselves and their boundaries. For babies, even their body does not exist as a whole, rather as 'separate organs such as hands, mouth, arms and belly', and they know 'nothing of various parts being related together' (Tustin 1974, p.60). Gradually babies learn to 'feel self' and control their body parts to produce meaningful movements and use other senses to learn about the world and their 'selves'.

Memories of very early experiences (before the appearance of verbal language) become stored and expressed as *sensations* rather than in highly elaborate form (Innes-Smith 1987). These early experiences are remembered and yet not easily accessible. They are affective memories that appear prior to, and to some extent separate from, cognitive memories; they influence secondary processes whether or not this influence becomes conscious (Bucci 1997; Krystal 1988). These are the first signs of emerging *conscious* self (but the unconscious and subconscious signs are always there and will remain with the person for their whole life − though often ignored). As many autistic individuals' memory works in sensory perceptual mode, their subconscious processes are more pronounced.

It is one thing to have faculties (senses), but to use them to function in the environment is a different matter altogether. For example, vision and hearing means the ability to receive sights and sounds. However, infants have to learn how to see and hear with cultural meaning. They develop their visual and auditory processing skills and achieve comprehension through interaction with the environment. Babies actively learn how to discriminate different stimuli from a chaos of sounds, shapes, patterns and movements, and in the first months of their lives they achieve the ability to make fine discrimination between the slightest variations in colour, form, sound and smell. They actually *learn* how to use their sensory organs and connect sensory images with meaning. With development and maturation, and by interacting with their environment, 'normal' infants learn to sort out incoming information and filter irrelevant (for the culture they are born into) stimuli, thus stopping sensory bombardment. Sensory experiences become linked with one another, creating patterns. These are so-called non-verbal (or pre-verbal) ways of knowing about the self and environment. 'The sensation is, in itself, a primary experience' (Matte-Blanco 1975, p.101) which is impossible to describe verbally. They may be seen as 'sensory abstractions' ('non-verbal thoughts') which are still not sufficiently understood and appreciated, or even ignored as irrelevant. According to Winnicott (1960, 1963) these sensory abstractions form the basis of 'true self' experience, which derives directly from the world as experienced and has its origins in the earliest sensations. 'Sensory knowing' of oneself and the environment starts with recognition of patterns, and they are less accessible to conscious, verbal, rational thought (Charles 1999; Stern 1994).

Donna Williams (1998, p.26) hypothesises that before we learn to use our physical body senses, we are still able to see, hear, feel, and so on with what she calls 'shadow senses': when one does not need to touch an object to feel its nature, feeling the object from within, without interference from the mind, and 'using the body not as a tool of sensory exploration or body as self, but as a tool of resonance'. No judging, analysing or prioritising is involved. The experience simply happens.

Mind as a filter

William James (1884) hypothesised that in a way a stream of (unlimited) consciousness is reduced and distorted by intellect which frames it into concepts. By its nature, intellect is the fabricator of concepts, and concepts are static; they leave out the flux of things, omitting too much of experience and losing vital contact with life itself. With development, man has found intellect more valuable for practical use, yet intuition is still there.

'Normal' babies (in the first weeks and months of life) lose the ability to merge and resonate with their surroundings; they begin to develop mind and thinking that filter the information through the available 'templates' (culturally determined concepts) through which they start perceiving the world around them. For some autistic infants, however, this transition is slow and connection to their 'out-of-mind' experiences remains strong. For instance, Donna was still functioning in the earlier phase (of resonance and merging) when she was in late childhood. Until she was about seven or eight she was still privately sure that she could walk through walls or solid surfaces, perhaps because she had the experience from an earlier time:

> I had a memory from the age of about three where I'd got up into the hall cupboard and stepped out but not landed. I'd found myself

about a foot off the floor and I was afraid I couldn't get back down. I had willed myself back down to about two inches off the floor before finally landing… I'd remember this not as a dream but as a memory, feeling vividly the body-memory of the feeling of the wood of the cupboard in my hand and the sense of space around me. Perhaps, without having a good ongoing connection with my physical body, I was having an out-of-body experience at the time and was using shadow senses which I confused with physical-based senses. (Williams 1998, p.27)

In contrast to Damasio's bottom-up approach (1994, 2000), Varela and Depraz (2003, p.214) put forward an interesting suggestion for studying emerging self, with emerging mind filtering the information and creating constraints:

Many will accept that the self is an emergent property arising from a neural/ bodily base. However…the *reverse* statement is typically missed. If the neural components and circuits act as local agents that can emergently give rise to a self, then it follows that this global level, the self, has direct *efficacious actions* over the local components. It is a two-way street: the local components give rise to this emergent mind, but, vice versa, the emergent mind constraints and affects directly these local components.

Mind and bodymind
Mind: (1) the seat of awareness, thought, volition and feeling; attention, concentration; (2) the intellect, intellectual powers; memory.

Lancaster (2010) distinguishes two powerful instruments for understanding the mind – the one brings about 'observation from within' and the other, 'observation from without'; they can be found in spiritual traditions and cognitive neuroscience, respectively. Lancaster analyses three areas of connection between the two domains: the first studies the effects of spiritual practices on the brain and cognitive processes; the second examines their respective analyses of specific functions of the mind, such as perception, thought, memory; and the third explores ideas articulated within the more esoteric aspects of spiritual (and mystical) traditions.

Larry Culliford distinguishes between our *everyday* minds and our *wisdom* minds, which seem to know more than we think, because *wisdom* minds are permanently in tune with the universe, with the 'big picture'. He compares minds to computers:[22]

> We use our everyday minds like laptop computers, carrying them around with us; but it is as if they are also connected to each other's laptops (to those of the other people around you, your family and so on) both directly and via internet. The link between your mental laptop and the world wide web of wisdom, so to speak, is quiet most of the time. Occasionally, however, messages appear on your screen unexpectedly, intruding on the programme you are already running. You can pay attention to the new messages or ignore them. Often, if you delete them, they seem to go away; but the *wisdom* mind is persistent, and will represent the same messages to your everyday mind repeatedly, often in different guises, as a dream, for example, that stays with you on waking, or through some kind of meaningful coincidence. (Culliford 2007, p.14)

An illustration of the wisdom mind at work is a story told to me by my good friend with Asperger syndrome, a writer, when we were talking about the ability to sense and feel. In 2010 she sent her manuscript to a leading neurologist for comments. Two weeks later she saw a dream in which this neurologist was typing an e-mail to her. As if watching a movie, she observed as letters were appearing on the screen of the computer, one by one: 'Frankly, I didn't like it.' As soon as she got up in the morning (with the 'picture' of the e-mail still in her mind's eye) and opened her e-mailbox she found a letter from this researcher, with the same content but expressed in a more polite way.

Some neuroscientists do not limit 'mind' to the brain and see bodily feelings as underlying and supporting higher thought processes, emphasising an important role feelings and emotions play in mental phenomena. Damasio (1994, p.128) states that 'emotions and feelings provide the bridge between rational and non-rational processes, between cortical and subcortical structures'; Pert (1997, pp.189, 143) asserts that emotions are 'at the nexus between matter and mind, going back and forth between the two and influencing both'. Jawer (2009, pp.56–57) argues that 'a view of mind and body as two divergent categories is not just inaccurate but decidedly unhelpful' and expands on the concept 'bodymind' introduced by Ken Dychtwald, defining it as:

> the combination of brain and body, including every aspect of us and everything we feel, think, know, intuit, remember, or have forgotten. Within this conceptualisation, the body is central to the mind and so are feelings…[which are] nothing less than the biological substrate of the mind… 'Bodymind' [is] shorthand for the amalgam of who each of us is physically, mentally, emotionally, and…spiritually.

Tolle (2005, pp.133, 134) writes about unconscious and subconscious instinctive responses of the body as primordial forms of emotions to some external situation, while emotion is the body's response to a thought (i.e. influenced by mind), 'a response to the event seen through the filter of a mental interpretation, the filter of thought' that often misinterprets the reality. The body, though intelligent:

> cannot tell the difference between an actual situation and a thought. It reacts to every thought as if it were a reality. It doesn't know it is just a thought. To the body, a worrisome, fearful thought means 'I am in danger,' and it responds accordingly, even though you may be lying in a warm and comfortable bed at night. The heart beats faster, muscles contract, breathing becomes rapid. There is a buildup of energy, but since the danger is only a mental fiction, the energy has no outlet. Part of it is fed back to the mind and generates even more anxious thought. The rest of the energy turns toxic and interferes with the harmonious functioning of the body.

Placebo and nocebo

The *placebo* effect can be termed as *the power of the mind and the unconscious* to heal in response to something (whether sugar pills or just a suggestion) that the person believes will improve his or her condition.

Scientific studies on placebo focus on the effectiveness of new drugs or treatments, whereas they have confirmed the reality of a mysterious phenomenon – the possibility of thought influencing not only psychological but also physical states of people.[23] The effects appear to be strongest and most reliable in the treatment of pain, where in both clinical and laboratory settings placebos of all kinds – sugar pills, cold creams, saline injections, fake ultrasound, even mere words, *when convincingly presented as medical painkillers* – have been found to bring significant relief (Humphrey 2002). About 35 per cent of all people who receive a placebo treatment will experience a significant effect. The conditions and illnesses that have proved sensitive to placebo treatment include angina, 'migraine headaches, allergies, fever, the common cold, acne, asthma, warts, various kinds of pain, nausea and seasickness, peptic ulcers, psychiatric syndromes such as depression and anxiety, rheumatoid and degenerative arthritis, diabetes, radiation sickness, Parkinsonism, multiple sclerosis, and cancer' (Talbot 1996, p.91). Humphrey notes that when people are unwell, they often start to recover as soon as they receive medical attention – whether the treatment has taken effect, or even if it is a sham. It is often the mere belief that recovery is coming that brings the recovery about.

Buckman and Sabbagh sum it up:

Placebo…seem to have some effect on almost every symptom known to mankind, and work in at least a third of patients and sometimes in up to 60%. They have no serious side effects and cannot be given in overdose. In short they hold the prize for the most adaptable, protean, effective, safe and cheap drugs in the world's pharmacopoeia. (Buckman and Sabbagh 1993, p.246)

Turner (1969) and Paul (1975) researched how healing rituals and symbols 'work' by operating on the self-image of the patient, creating a particular personality with particular emotional patterning (analogous to psychotherapy). There is some evidence from research (Laderman 1987) that the ritual influences body image and, indirectly, impacts on the physiology of the person. We still cannot explain how (and why) the placebo effect affects both body and mind (see Samuel 2009 for a detailed analysis) but it does show that mere imagery (whether visual, verbal, etc.) can create real changes at the physiological level. However, this works only if the person believes it will work. (Prayer has similar effect on those who believe it.)

The *nocebo* effect is the opposite – if a person believes he has been harmed (either by magic or the 'evil eye', for example), he will soon feel the consequences.

There is no clear-cut boundary between mystical and scientific explanations. For example, two contrasting approaches have been distinguished in the causation of ill health: 'naturalistic' and 'personalistic' ones (Foster 1976, p.775):

A personalistic medical system is one in which disease is explained as due to the *active, purposeful intervention of an agent*, who may be human (a witch or sorcerer), nonhuman (a ghost, an ancestor, an evil spirit), or supernatural (a deity or other powerful being). The sick person literally is a victim, the object of aggression or punishment directed specifically against him… In contrast to personalistic systems, naturalistic systems explain illness in impersonal, systemic terms. Disease is thought to stem, not from the machinations of an angry being, but rather from such *natural forces or conditions* as cold, heat, winds, dampness, and, above all, by an upset in the balance of the basic body elements… Causality concepts explain or account for the upsets in this balance that trigger illness.

The naturalistic approach stems from linear causality when something within the external world leads more or less reliably to certain results. The personalistic explanation looks for moral–ethical judgement: who is responsible for things going badly (Samuel 2010).

Cognitive anthropologists usually treat 'mystical' (personalistic) explanations as isolated 'counterintuitive' representations within a logical (and scientific) framework.[24] Geoffrey Samuel (1990, 2010) argues, however, that such cognitive accounts drastically understate the extent to which all our thinking is pervaded by non-rational, moral–ethical, emotional aspects. Samuel stresses that both modes of explanation are characteristic in different degrees of all human societies; these two approaches – naturalistic and personalistic – may work neatly together, for example 'I am sick because you deliberately gave me something bad to eat.' More typically, however, they work on different planes, as assumptions of human malevolence do not necessarily depend on a naturalistic explanation for the harm caused; then idioms of sorcery, witchcraft, the evil eye or spirit attack can easily fill the gap (Samuel 2010). However, far from being isolated elements within a rational frame, non-rational elements in fact structure rational thought and it is no longer adequate to treat them as anomalies or relics of prehistoric thinking. Samuel (2010) argues that biomedical science has issued a blind endorsement of specific types of naturalistic explanation and automatically rejected personalistic ones as pre-scientific and incorrect instead of treating both naturalistic and personalistic styles as alternative modes of explanation, each with true content, validity and usefulness.

Cultural and linguistic filters

Very early in life, cultural and linguistic filters are in place: guided by their carers infants focus their attention selectively on different aspects of experience, integrate them in memory, and construct simulators to represent objects and events.[25] By the time babies are ready for language, a huge amount of knowledge, shared with their carers, is in place to support its acquisition (Barsalou 1999). Infants soon learn to filter out information and start structuring the environment in accordance with culturally constructed concepts introduced by their carers. They learn to 'draw boundaries' around objects, people and themselves, successfully entering the cultural world they are born into. In autism, because of their inability or difficulty in filtering out information (Gestalt perception) the process is delayed, and they may remain 'foreigners' in any culture.

Consciousness through personal experience

A different route to understanding the nature of consciousness has been paved by spiritual seekers in the East, who focus not on studying brain functions and cognitive experiments, but rather on exploring it through direct personal experiences. Many ancient texts (for instance, *The Tibetan Book of the Great Liberation*) contain fascinating insights into the quest for the unknown. In these sources, consciousness is often described as Light (and those who have 'awakened to the meaning of life' are typically referred to as 'enlightened').[26]

A worldview in which consciousness is a fundamental component of reality

But what if we join the (past and present) philosophers who look at consciousness as the only reality that exists? For example, Professor Donald Hoffman believes that spacetime, matter, fields, energy and the like are contents of consciousness, dependent on it for their very being. Then we have to admit that the world around us, with all the objects of different sizes, smells, colours, sounds, and people themselves, can be seen as:

> a species-specific user interface between ourselves and a realm far more complex, whose essential character is conscious… The rules by which, for instance, human vision constructs colours, shapes, depths, motion, textures, and objects – rules now emerging from psychological and computational studies in the cognitive sciences – can be read as a description, partial but mathematically precise of [it]. What we lose in this process are physical objects that exist independent of any observer. There is no sun or moon unless a conscious mind perceives them; both are constructs of consciousness, icons in a species-specific user interface. To some this seems a *reduction ad absurdum* readily contradicted by experience and our best science. But our *best* science, which is our theory of quantum, gives no such assurance, and experience once led us to believe that the earth was flat and the stars were near. Perhaps mind-independent objects will one day go the way of the flat earth. (Hoffman 2006, p.95)

Hoffman's perspective obviates neither methods nor scientific results but rather reinterprets results of scientific studies in a new framework. For example, instead of considering neural correlates as a causal source of consciousness. Hoffman interprets them as a feature of our interface, corresponding to, but never causally responsible for, alterations of consciousness. According to this view, neither the brain nor the neural correlates cause consciousness, but, instead, consciousness constructs the brain:

Damage the brain, destroy the neural correlates, and consciousness is, no doubt, impaired...This is no mystery. Drag a file's icon to the recycle bin and the file is, no doubt, deleted. Yet neither the icon nor the recycle bin, each a mere pattern of pixels on a screen, causes its deletion. The icon is a simplification, a graphical correlate of the file's contents, intended to hide, not to instantiate, the web of causal relations. (Hoffman 2006, p.94)

Russell (2002) suggests that rather than trying to explain consciousness in terms of the material world we should develop a new worldview in which consciousness is a fundamental component of reality. He uses the concept of consciousness – not as a reference to a particular state of consciousness, but as the faculty of consciousness – to indicate what lies beneath any experience or life. He defines the faculty of consciousness as the capacity for inner experience, whatever the nature or degree of the experience. Russell compares it to the light from a film projector on the screen that can be modified so as to produce images; the images are like perceptions, sensations, dreams, memories, thoughts and feelings. The light itself corresponds to the faculty of consciousness, and the images projected on the screen to the forms of consciousness. It does not matter how different the experiences may be (for example, animals have different experiences from those of humans), they all share the faculty of consciousness. Russell considers the faculty of consciousness as a fundamental quality of nature which does not arise from matter (the processes in the nervous system, for example); it is always present. If we look at consciousness from this perspective, then matter (for example, the nervous system) does not produce consciousness but rather amplifies it, increasing the quality of experience; to use the analogy with a film projector: the light is always on the screen but the quality of images depends on the lens in the projector (the nervous system producing the images).

The idea that consciousness is in everything is not new. In philosophy it is known as *panpsychism* (*pan* meaning 'everywhere' and *psyche* meaning 'soul') – all objects/entities have a unified centre of experience. *Panexperientialism* restricts the concept to all entities having precursors to phenomenal consciousness but not mind (cognition), and *panprotoexperientialism* – all entities have precursors to phenomenal consciousness, but not conscious awareness. According to this view, the faculty of consciousness is universal; consciousness is not something that emerges with humans, it is present always and in everything, changing in complexity and reaching human awareness (de Quincey 1994). Recent research (especially in quantum physics) seems to indicate that this view, namely that everything has the faculty of consciousness, is worth exploring further: 'there is nowhere we can draw a line between conscious and nonconscious entities; there is a trace of experience, however slight, in viruses, molecules, atoms, and even elementary particles' (Russell 2002, pp.35–36). Russell concludes that the *faculty* of consciousness seems to be always present, but the *forms* of consciousness, with the various qualities and dimensions of conscious experience, have emerged over the course of evolution; the evolution of the forms of consciousness can be traced from the earliest living organisms (like bacteria, for example) through multicellular organisms with nervous systems (which integrate the different sensory modalities into a single picture for each particular species and enhanced quality of consciousness), through the development of the limbic system of the mammalian brain which adds basic emotions (such as fear) and more complex forms of consciousness (with better memory, attention, thinking), reaching the diversity of qualities which are reflected in humans (Russell 2002). And, at last, the emergence of language, allowing humans to share their experiences, is considered as a huge leap forward in the development of consciousness, but weakens the connection between conscious and unconscious aspects of self.

Unconscious self

If self is defined by consciousness (and we are not conscious all the time), where is 'I' or 'self' when the person is unconscious? The problem here is that we are not conscious of our state of unconsciousness. For example, when we are in a dreamless sleep,[27] under anaesthesia, in a persistent vegetative state (PVS),[28] or coma.[29] However, even being conscious and awake, we are still unconscious of some of our feelings, emotions and behaviours. There are times when we are not aware of our own actions or the causes of these actions. Neurobiologist Robert Provine (2000) investigated unconsciously controlled laughter produced by people who could not accurately explain their actions; his findings led him to consider other unconsciously controlled behaviours. In this context, Provine (2006) raises several questions that await explanation, for example: Are essential details of the neurological process that governs human behaviour inaccessible to introspection? Is it not wiser to wonder whether human behaviour is under no more conscious control than that of animals, instead of arguing whether animals are conscious or have a different, or lesser, consciousness than ours? (If we consider the complex social order of bees and ants, we can see what can be achieved with little if any conscious control.)

If we look at our senses, providing us with sensory information, it is not straightforward, either.

Blindsight, or a 'sighted person' that has nothing to do with 'me'

An example of 'unconscious vision' is a neurological syndrome identified by Larry Weiskrantz (1986), Alan Cowey (Cowey and Stoerig 1991) and Ernst Pöppel (Pöppel, Held and Frost 1974), known as blindsight. Some patients who have become blind after brain damage can still perform tasks which appear impossible because of their blindness; for instance, they can grasp or point at an object, or describe whether a stick is vertical or horizontal, even if they insist it is a guess and they cannot see it. Ramachandran accounts for this interesting phenomenon by distinguishing between conscious and unconscious visual processing: there are two visual pathways in the brain (the old system [called the superior colliculus] in the brain stem, and the new one going to the visual cortex). If only one is damaged, a person loses the ability to see an object but is aware of its location and orientation. Only the new pathway is conscious; the old one going through the colliculus and guiding the hand movement occurs without the person being conscious of it. It is as if, even though the person is oblivious to what is going on around him, there seems to be an unconscious being inside him who can guide his hand with an amazing accuracy (Ramachandran 2003).[30] Ramachandran poses more questions to which we as yet have no answers: Why should one path lead to conscious awareness while the other does its job without being conscious? Why can't the rest of the brain do without consciousness, that is, be all blindsight? Is it only certain styles of processing that lead to consciousness? Are there certain anatomical locations that are linked to consciousness? What are the limits of blindsight?[31]

Nonconscious/subconscious emotions

It was noticed long ago that the faculty of mental photography belongs to subconsciousness, and a voluntary retrieval of the photographic images is difficult (Granville 1899). In autism, it can be easily triggered by sensory stimuli (no language), while in non-autism, a 'language filter' protects verbal thinkers from emotional overload (i.e. the 'label' is stored, not the image). If this filter is absent, the impact of emotional involvement is much greater (Daria 2008). The raw (language-less) 'emotional images' are very different (because no language is involved) and can be accessed easily, without the person realising what influences his decision.

To illustrate the phenomenon of nonconscious emotions, Damasio (2000) describes the case study of David (a patient with extensive damage to both temporal lobes, hippocampus and amygdala) who had very severe deficits in learning and memory and could not learn any new information about places, people, events, and so on. David was unable to recognise or give the names of the people he lived and interacted with but, surprisingly, he did have preferences, such as specific people he would avoid, or those he would approach to ask for something. To explore what was going on, Tranel and Damasio (1993) designed the 'good guy/bad guy experiment': for a week, under controlled circumstances, David was engaged in three distinct types of interaction with someone who was extremely pleasant (the good guy), with someone who was emotionally neutral (the neutral guy), and someone with a brusque manner, who always said 'no' to any of David's requests, and engaged him in boring and tedious activity. In a week, David was asked to look at sets of four photographs, each set containing the face of one of the individuals involved in the good guy/ bad guy experiment, and then asked to whom he would go if he needed help, and who his friend was. David chose the good guy over 80 per cent of the time and the bad guy was almost never chosen. David did not know why he chose one or rejected the other; there was nothing in his conscious mind to give him a reason, he just did. Damasio (2000) speculates that the nonconscious preference David manifested is relayed to the emotions that were induced in him during the experiment. That is, it was not *he* himself who chose to do so deliberately, but rather that his *organism* produced such behaviour. I would suggest it was his subconscious 'self' that acted on uninterpreted raw emotions.

Damasio's research shows that we are not conscious of *all* our feelings, for example, we can feel anxious or uncomfortable, worried or relaxed in certain situations. It is apparent that the particular state we are conscious of has begun not at the moment of knowing but rather some time before we actually felt it, that is, it first emerged in nonconsciousness.[32]

Feelings are mostly subconscious, and emotions can begin so quickly that they can occur before the person becomes aware that they are happening (Ekman 1994). In a way, 'unrecognised feelings' may be perceptions that are detected by the body but not processed by the brain. In autism, they are felt even more strongly and (uninterpreted and disconnected from mind) are often scary. Donna Williams refers to this phenomenon as Big Black Nothingness:

> When I was younger the Big Black Nothingness came to take me again and again and again…and suffocate me in a void. In the void there was no thought… In the void there are no connections… In the nothingness there is no body to be comforted… You must escape because you hear the roar of 'tidal waves' – big, dark 'tidal waves.' (It is the sound of blood washing through the contracting muscles of your own ears)… The tidal waves were my own delayed, out-of-context reactions. These terrifying wailing bouts of Big Black Nothingness were emotional overload triggered by anything from happy to angry and everything in between. (Williams 1999c, pp.90, 91)

Nonconscious parts of conscious self

Does self contain a subconscious/nonconscious part that 'I' is not aware of? So, is 'I' still 'out (in) there' controlling 'me', even if 'I' am not conscious of it? In a way, we are all unconscious of some parts of our selves: we are conscious of that part of self that is a collection of memories, emotions, experiences, and so on that belongs to 'me': 'I' am the subject, the experiencer who experiences, and collects whatever is happening and develops under the influence of the environment and the genetic make-up.

Nonconscious acquisition of information is going on all the time – we are just, well, not conscious of it. Our conscious self is unaware of what the unconscious/subconscious one is absorbing and reacting to. There is evidence from research studies in people without any disorder that preferences can be acquired nonconsciously and very fast (because the brain does not have to process the information).[33]

'Mindlessness'

However, there is another way to look at it:

> When the mind is silent, and the thoughts, feelings, perceptions, and memories with which we habitually identify have fallen away, then what remains is the essence of self, the pure subject without an

object. What we then find is not a sense of 'I am this' or 'I am that', but just 'I am'...[that is] pure consciousness. You are not a being who is conscious. You are consciousness. (Russell 2002, p.81)

Russell calls it 'amness' or 'pure being', which has none of the uniqueness of the individual self; someone's sense of I-ness is indistinguishable from someone else's. So all are identical in the faculty of consciousness. Seen from this perspective, the essential self (pure consciousness) is beyond space and beyond time, it is eternal, it never changes. Some can achieve this state in meditation – time disappears, there is simply now (Russell 2002). Some mystics, who have explored what they call the true nature of self, identify it with God, that is, according to some, the true self without any personal identifications can be seen as God. For example, Thomas Merton (1958, p.71) writes:

If I penetrate to the depths of my own existence and my own present reality, the indefinable *am* that is myself in its deepest roots, then through this deep center I pass into the infinite *I am* which is the very Name of the Almighty.

Similar explanations can be found in many texts of different religions, and can be interpreted as that one's essential self – the 'I am', the pure consciousness – lies behind all the experience and is the source of all, the supreme Being. Like God, consciousness (the sense of 'amness') is omnipresent, it never changes, it is eternal. God is said to be the creator and the source of all creation, and so is consciousness – the creator of everything we know – our sensations, perceptions, thoughts, feelings, and so on – is a form of consciousness that we develop:

[The] concept of God is not of a separate being, beyond us in some other realm, overlooking human affairs and loving or judging us according to our deeds. God appears in each and every one of us as the most intimate and undeniable aspect of ourselves, the consciousness shining in every mind. (Russell 2002, p.89)

Many mystics describe their experience of pure consciousness as their personal quest for knowing the divine.

In autism the experience of 'true/pure self' is often spontaneous, or easily achieved (if voluntary). For example, Gunilla Gerland (1997, p.122) has found it easy to 'sink into myself and stay there. That inner emptiness was perhaps not all that unlike meditation, but with the great difference that I usually did not control the state myself.'

> Personally, I consider it one of the gifts of autism to have the mind emptiness that I can achieve and need as I force myself to interact with society. As my mind empties of all thought and emotion, it is not recharging so much as refinding my own inner balance. There are no thoughts, no sense of self, no awareness of environment, no sense of body or mind...just mindlessness. (Nancy, personal communication, 2013)

> Mindfulness is based on Buddhist principles where meditation is the target. Why fullness instead of emptiness? I strive for emptiness. (Mar, personal communication, 2013)

> I would say mindlessness is a state of perfect bliss, of 'just being' – like I remember it from being little – but sometimes I can also let my thoughts wander consciously which I guess would be mindful. (Barbara, personal communication, 2013)

The state of 'mindlessness' is analogous to the experience of 'pure/true self'.

From pure self to individuality

Anatomy of self

The pure/true self (we are not conscious of it) can be defined as amness, pure Being, or 'simply be' – self undistorted by mind, unrestricted by the body and undetermined by cultural templates:

> [The] definition of ['self'] will never do so it's all about a kind of intuitive understanding beyond words... I don't think the real self is like self in the word 'myself'. The impersonal, 'highest' self is deep within us and our fundamental inspiration but hard to experience... we are not consciously in contact with this pure awareness, although that is where we need to go, in order to be of the most benefit for all living things. (Teun, personal communication, 2012)

> Self existed before its separability from everything external to it... [it] existed before its various phases of relationship to body or mind and its eventual identification of these. Self existed before the

formation of expressed personality or the impact of environment. (Williams 1998, p.19)

This experience can be achieved when the mind is switched off or quiet:

> In this experience of pure Being we find a steady, unshakable peace that is not dependent on what we have or do in life. We find the fulfilment we have always been seeking – the peace of God that passes, or lies beyond, all understanding. (Russell 2002, p.91)

Mind filter

With development of mind, the subjective self evolves – the inner subject of one's experience. Russell argues that everything we experience is a construct within consciousness and our sense of being a unique self is merely another construct of our mind. 'Quite naturally, we place this image of the self at the centre of our perceived world, giving us the sense of being in the world. But the truth is just the opposite. It is all within us' (2002, p.84).

Body filter

Eventually, the inner subject develops subjective experiences of continuity, unity, agency, embodiment and self-awareness that leads to an emerging sense of individuality – one's ego. The majority lose connection with their 'true self' and identify themselves with the ego, while many autistic individuals remain connected to their unconscious/subconscious self (amness).

Contrary to the common assumption that autistic children have no sense of self, some report their quest for 'I' much earlier than normally developing children. This is the recollection of a person with Asperger syndrome:[34]

> When I was very young (before age three, I'm sure, because I remember my bedroom very vividly, and my family moved houses when I was two years and a half) I used to lie in bed at night *feeling* me – not my physical body, but something that was *me*. Sometimes I was scared when the question emerged – 'who am I?' I knew I could get the answer only if I followed this elusive 'me' deeper inside, but I never finished the journey – I was too frightened, and always stopped in the middle to return back. Those experiences were very scary but also fascinating at the same time. I never told my parents

or anybody else till now. I think this is pure consciousness. Religious people would call it 'soul'. (M.P., personal communication)

I spent a great deal of time inside myself, as if in my own world, screened off from everything else. But there was no world inside me, nothing more than a kind of nothing layer, a neither-nor, a state of being hollow without being empty or filled without being full. It just was, in there, inside myself. This emptiness wasn't tormenting in itself. I was inside the emptiness and the emptiness was inside me – no more than that. It was nothing but a kind of extension of time – I was in that state and it just went on. But the sense of unreality and of always being wrong when I was in the world, outside myself, was always harder to bear. (Gerland 1997, pp.19–20)

Most think of self as a *differential image* that distinguishes us as individuals.

When asked 'Who/what are you?', answers may refer to gender, personality, character, appearance, nationality, intellectual/physical abilities, social roles (parent, carer, etc.), profession, belonging to a political party, religion (or lack of it – atheist), and so on. However, these are all better described as constituent parts of ego, which we construct (and protect at any cost!) believing that it is what we are.

Jung emphasised the importance of distinguishing between 'self-knowledge' and 'self':

Most people confuse 'self-knowledge' with knowledge of their conscious ego personalities. Anyone who has any ego-consciousness at all takes it for granted that he knows himself. But the ego knows only its own contents, not the unconscious and its contents. People measure their self-knowledge by what the average person in their social environment knows of himself, but not by the real psychic facts which are for the most part hidden from them. (Jung 1958, pp.3–4)

Jung concludes that what is commonly understood as 'self-knowledge' is, in fact, a very limited knowledge.

Some features are given to us at birth, for example gender, race, temperament; others are conditioned by the culture we are born into, such as the prestige of certain positions, professions, social roles; others are conditioned by the 'nearest environment', for instance violence in the family, that impact on the development of personality; some are combinations of the above.

Roles / characters

We develop our 'self-image' (and identify with it) and protect it from any attack from outside. When our self-image is threatened, we feel our 'very self' is threatened, so we respond to any criticism as to a personal attack. We identify our selves with roles we play in our life, wearing masks to fit in in different social situations, pushing the true self even further away. In contrast, those autistic individuals who develop characters for 'normal' interactions are aware of them as survival strategies — necessary to be accepted by 'normal' people.

As the perceptual experiences and thought processes of autistic individuals are qualitatively different from those around them, it is no wonder that it takes them much longer to figure out that other people think differently. For instance, it took Donna Williams 13 years to understand that others play social games (saying what they do not mean for the sake of being polite, for example) for real, and assume everybody should feel the same:

> When I was 13, I had already bought into the socially learned game of facades but I'd bought into it late and clumsily, unable to fully integrate it. The data base for these facades were picked up mostly from TV characters and I understood mimicry and acting according to stored learned roles. But what had deeply distressed and depressed me around this age was when I tried to get others to stop playing what I saw as a game and to drop their facades. I'd assume their own facades, like mine, were part of a non-integrated database. I could clearly see straight past the surface and assumed they could too. (Williams 1998, pp.85–86)

Notes

1. Kanner borrowed the term from Bleuler (1950[1911]), who coined it to describe withdrawal symptoms in schizophrenic patients.

2. See, for example, Bradley 1983; Flew 1949; Toulmin 1977.

3. For a conceptual history of self, see Berrios and Markova 2003.

4. In descriptive psychopathology, self and ego are used interchangeably (in such terms as 'ego disorders' or 'self disorders') to describe the abnormal experiences of *I-ness* and *me-ness* in different psychiatric illnesses.

5. The word *spirit* is derived from Latin *spiritus*, 'breath'. Other languages in which spirit and breathing are related by a single word include Sanskrit — *prana*; Arabic — *ruha*; Hebrew — *ruach*; Chinese — *chi* (as in *tai chi*); Russian — дух, душа, дышать.

6. See, for example, Laszlo 2009; Tart 1997, 2009.

7.   *Emic* – studying or describing a particular culture in terms of its internal elements and their functioning rather than in terms of any existing external scheme, that is, people's own explanation. *Etic* – studying or describing a particular culture in a way that is general, non-structural and objective in its perspective, that is, the observer's explanation.

8.   In the field of psychiatry, the situation is very similar: various concepts of 'self' have been suggested, for example, the ecological self, the extended self (Zahavi 2003).

9.   *Privacy* – as each individual's qualia and mental life are subjective, unobservable by others, and *social embedding* – the need to feel part of a social environment with which the individual can interact and understand on its own terms (Ramachandran 2011).

10. Based on Jaspers (1959) and Scharfetter (1981, 1995, 2003): (1) an awareness of unity (ego consistency): at any given moment, each individual knows that he or she is one person; (2) awareness of identity (ego identity): the individual has been the same person all the time; (3) awareness of the boundaries of self (ego demarcation): the individual is aware of the boundary between self and non-self; (4) the feeling of awareness of activity (ego activity): the individual knows that he or she is an agent who initiates and executes his or her thoughts and actions; (5) the feeling of awareness of being or existing (ego vitality), fundamental to awareness of self: when one knows that one is alive (Oyebode 2008, p.222).

11. Cf. Galen Strawson's view of many mental 'selves', each one existing only as long as one's attention is focused on something. He calls it the pearl view, because 'it suggests that many mental selves exist, one at a time and one after another, like pearls on a string, in the case of something like a human being' (Strawson 1997, p.424).

12. The importance of 'here-and-now' experiences is emphasised in both Western religions and Eastern traditions, such as Buddhist awareness meditation (Vipassana).

13. See, for example, Gallup and Newport 1991; Palmer 1979; Ross and Joshi 1992.

14. Ramachandran (2003) suggests that there is a neural delay before the signal arising in one part of the brain reaches the rest of the brain to deliver the command to move the finger.

15. Human children under the age of 18–20 months often fail this test.

16. One does not have to compare animals' and human languages to see differences in interpreting the world 'shaped' by the language spoken. Whorf showed the inadequacy of imposing a traditional classification (parts of speech) while analysing languages very different from Indo-European ones. In English, we have to introduce an agent when we say 'it flashed' or 'a light flashed', thus restructuring the phenomenon from non-agented event to an agent and action. 'Yet the flashing and the light are one and the same! The Hopi language reports the flash with a simple verb, *rehpi*: "flash (occurred)"... Undoubtedly modern science, strongly reflecting western Indo-European tongues, often does as we all do, sees actions and forces where it sometimes might be better to see states... [I]t would be better if we could manipulate...a more verblike concept...without the concealed premises of actor and action' (Whorf 1956, pp.243–244).
     Whorf (1956, p.81) concluded his analysis of so-called preliterate 'primitive languages' with a seeming paradox, that many '('primitive') communities, far from being subrational, may show the human mind functioning on a higher and more complex plane of rationality than among civilised men'. And it is even more ridiculous to apply any linguistic classification to such alien systems as animals'

languages. If it were possible to find out animals' 'cognitive concepts' and apply them to classify a human language, we would be considered 'idiots', unable to function in this new world.

17. Koehler's research has shown that the upper limit of both 'seeing numbers' and acting on them for pigeons was five points, for parakeets and jackdaws, six, for ravens, Amazon parrots, grey parrots, magpies and squirrels, seven. The animals were able to translate a heard number into a seen one: for example, to select a five-dotted dish from others on hearing five whistles, drum beats or flashes of light.

18. For example, Patterson (1980) reported self-awareness in gorillas, including recognising themselves in a mirror, use of self-referential signs and behaviours indicating embarrassment, empathy, etc. Leading primatologist Jane Goodall (2001), who worked with chimpanzees in Africa for several decades, reported many characteristics in chimpanzees that were thought to be uniquely human, for instance, chimps feel a range of emotions, such as joy, sorrow, despair, compassion and love. There are numerous similar examples in elephants, dogs, cats, wolves and many other species.

19. Joseph LeDoux (2006) believes that, even if it is difficult to study the contents of conscious experiences, it is still possible to study the processes that make consciousness possible in other animals, for example, studying working memory or visual awareness.

20. There are other proposed dichotomous classifications of consciousness, too. See, for example, Edelman (1989) and Block, Flanagan and Güzeldere (1997). Edelman also separates primary consciousness from higher-order consciousness, but his primary consciousness is simpler than Damasio's core consciousness and does not result in emergence of a self and, unlike Damasio's extended consciousness, Edelman's higher-order consciousness requires language and is strictly human. Ned Block divides consciousness into access, or A-consciousness, and phenomenal, or P-consciousness (Block *et al.* 1997).

21. See, for example, Eisenberger and Lieberman 2004; Kross *et al.* 2011.

22. Digby Tantam (2009) also compares minds to computers but his version is different in that he focuses on conventional (learned) meanings of the 'messages' that are out on the surface for everyone to see and interpret (or misinterpret, in the case of autism).

23. It is interesting that the researchers ignore the possibility of the placebo effect of those taking real pills/medicine when judge the efficiency of a new treatment. Perhaps some in the group of patients (receiving real drugs) improve not thanks to the effects of the drugs but due to the placebo effect and would show the same improvements when given sugar pills.

24. See, for example, Boyer 1996; Boyer and Ramble 2002; Sperber 1975.

25. See, for example, Cohen 1991; Jones and Smith 1993; Mandler 1992.

26. Some contemporary scientists have followed suit. For example, Peter Russell, a physicist and psychologist, having studied neuropsychology and failed to find any satisfactory answers, turned to Eastern wisdom to get to the root of or understand consciousness. His explorations have brought him to the 'inner light' (the faculty of consciousness) that Russell sees as a close parallel with the light of physics: 'Physical light has no mass, and is not part of the material world. The same is true of consciousness; it is immaterial. Physical light seems to be fundamental to

the universe. The light of consciousness is likewise fundamental; without it there would be no experience' (Russell 2002, p.71).

27. During dream sleep, some consciousness is 'on' (Damasio 2000).

28. PVS is lighter form of coma in which there are signs of wakefulness, but consciousness is gravely impaired. PVS is often caused by dysfunction in the upper brain stem, hypothalamus or thalamus.

29. Coma is caused by head injury, fainting, dreamless sleep or deep anaesthesia and leads to the transient loss of consciousness. In the past, it was believed that those who fell into the 'nothingness of coma' and then returned to 'knowingness' could not recall anything of the period between these two points, which can last for weeks or months; it seemed that little or nothing was going on in the mind (Damasio 2000, p.95). However, there have been 'awakenings' from coma when patients reported their awareness of what was going on around them.

30. Ramachandran points out that when it was first described, the blindsight syndrome seemed so bizarre that it was (and sometimes, still is) looked at with scepticism by some researchers. It seems to contradict our common sense, and it is very rare, so not many scientists are familiar with it.

31. Ramachandran argues that in the 'blindsight syndrome' a person has a representation of the object in his old pathway, but with his visual cortex being injured, he has no representation of the representation, that is no qualia to speak of. Interestingly, in Anton's syndrome, a person is blind (because of cortical damage) but denies that he is blind and insists that he can see. Ramachandran hypothesises that someone with Anton's syndrome has a spurious metarepresentation but no primary representation; the dissociations between sensations and conscious awareness of sensations are possible because representations and metarepresentations are dealt with in different brain loci and can, therefore, be damaged or survive independently of each other. Similar dissociations (known as 'hidden observer' phenomena) can be generated during hypnotic induction (Ramachandran 2003).

32. Damasio separates 'three stages of processing along a continuum: *a state of emotion*, which can be triggered and executed nonconsciously; *a state of feeling*, which can be represented nonconsciously; and *a state of feeling made conscious*, i.e., known to the organism having both emotion and feeling... [Damasio suspects] that some nonhuman creatures that exhibit emotions but are unlikely to have the sort of consciousness we have may well form the representations we call feelings without knowing they do so' (Damasio 2000, p.36).

33. See, for example, Kihlstrom 1987; Lewicki, Hill and Czyzewska 1992; Reber 1993.

34. Cited in Daria 2008, pp.75–76. The character described there under the name M.P. (Miss Ponytail) is a real person and my very good friend.

7

'Autistic Personality'

Personality: (1) the quality or state of being a person; (2) the complex of characteristics that distinguishes an individual especially in relationships with others; the totality of an individual's behavioural and emotional characteristics.

Some researchers emphasise the connection between sensitivities (whether sensory or emotional) and personality traits. They have established personality traits in individuals with certain peculiar developmental features. Psychologist Elaine Aron coined the term 'highly sensitive persons' (HSPs) to describe the individuals she has studied who 'are...born with a tendency to notice more in their environment... They are also easily overwhelmed by "high volume" or large quantities of input arriving at once... [They are] unusually empathic' (Aron 1996, pp.7, 10, 12). Aron reports that HSPs tend to have rich inner lives and vivid dreams; they are highly perceptive, creative and intuitive, while often shy, fearful and withdrawn from their surroundings. Gordon Claridge (1997, 2002) has researched human differences based on physical differences between people – he is especially interested in researching openness to unusual experiences (transcendent or transliminal experiences), which he calls 'schizotypy'. All people are on the schizotypy spectrum, with a high score at one end (high schizotype) and low score at the opposite end. Claridge (2010, p.76) suggests that 'there are inherent personality differences between people that are substantially constitutional, even partly genetic, in origin: such characteristics form traits...that run through the general population and describe the structure of human individual differences.' Nancy

McWilliams has studied the subjectivities of individuals with schizoid psychologies.[1] She identifies one of the common characteristics as extreme sensitivity reflected in a constitutionally sensitive temperament, noticeable from birth. Doidge (2001) describes the sense of being skinless, of lacking a protective stimulus barrier, with withdrawal as the preferred adaptation. Other related features of schizoid personality are loneliness, sensitivity to the unconscious feelings of others, oneness with the universe, symmetrical thinking (in the terminology of Matte-Blanco 1975), and animating the inanimate (the sense of relatedness to all the aspects of the environment) (McWilliams 2011).

In the context of sensory and emotional sensitivities, there is another useful concept, developed by Ernest Hartmann in his book *Boundaries of the Mind* (1991): 'thick and thin boundaries'. Hartmann proposes thick and thin boundaries as a way of looking at individual differences:

> There are people who [are] very solid and well-organized; they keep everything in its place. They are well defended. They seem rigid, even armoured; we sometimes [refer to] them as 'thick-skinned.' Such people...have very thick boundaries. At the other extreme are people who are especially sensitive, open, or vulnerable. In their minds, things are relatively fluid... Such people [have] particularly thin boundaries. (Hartmann 1991, pp.4–6)

According to Hartmann, everyone can be placed on a spectrum of boundaries from thick to thin. Interestingly, people develop certain personality types depending on their sensory sensitivities. Without our body, especially the boundary of our body, we would not be sentient individuals. The boundaries allow us to develop our individual personalities, distinct from the personalities around us. It is quite useful to apply the concept of thin boundaries to autism. Among characteristic features of the thin-boundary personality type are:

- a less solid or definite sense of one's skin as a body boundary

- sensitivity to physical and emotional pain both in oneself and in others

- an enhanced ability to remember dreams, and a tendency to experience nightmares.

(Hartmann 1991)

Hartmann believes that differences in thin/thick boundaries are reflected in neurobiological differences as well, and start very early in life.

Another interesting connection between sensory and emotional sensitivities and types of personality development was described by Polish doctor Kazimierz Dabrowski in relation to 'gifted individuals'. Dabrowski identified several recurring traits in these people, which he called 'overexcitabilities':

- psychomotor, reflected in restlessness, curiosity

- sensual – strong reactions (either positive or negative) to sensory stimuli, aesthetic awareness

- strong visual thinking, vivid fantasy life, good recall of dreams, enjoyment of poetry or metaphorical speech

- intellectual – intense focus on special topics of interests, complex reasoning, problem solving

- emotional – heightened emotional reactions, strong attachments, empathy, difficulty adjusting to change.[2]

All these features are common in autism, and following the reasoning of connection between sensitivities and personality traits, we can assume that hypersensitive autistic individuals are likely to develop a certain type of personality that can be termed 'autistic personality'. However, it is important to emphasise that not *all* autistic individuals develop autistic personality, and there are non-autistic people who have autistic personality traits. On the other hand, some autistic individuals can develop other personality disorders as well. There are many influences that may define a person's character, as with any individual whether they are autistic or not.

Autistic personality

Autistic people recognise each other; they seem to be members of the same community.

Many individuals with autism seem to possess a number of unconventional personality characteristics (Schneider 1999) that, collectively, can be seen as a special type of personality – autistic personality.

To me, Autism is a special type of personality. (O'Neill 2000)

What I had thought to be great strength of character (resisting peer pressure in my teens, etc.)...was actually the result of my autism compensating for my social shortcomings. If one does not fear danger, then one cannot be considered a hero for facing it. (Schneider 1999, p.104)

Many autistic people are honest with themselves; they accept limitations (their own and those of others) and find joy and satisfaction in their lives by having found ways to cope with their problems, while building on their strengths. They are kind and compassionate. Instead of focusing on what might have happened 'if...', they are happy with what they have and are keen to share it with others, enjoying a meaningful life characterised by spiritual values. Apart from (sensory and emotional) sensitivities, some other common characteristics of 'autistic personality' are discussed below.

'Non-liars'

This does not mean that all autistic individuals never lie; but it does mean that it is harder for them to deceive others.

> I had always...said what I meant and meant what I said. As a child, I had told many lies as a survival tactic, but soon I recognized that I was no good at that at all, so I told the truth instinctively, realizing, if only pragmatically, that the consequences of telling the truth were invariably less than those of being caught in a lie. (Schneider 1999, p.106)

> Autistic people tend to have difficulty lying because of the complex emotions involved in deception. I become extremely anxious when I have to tell a little white lie on the spur of the moment. To be able to tell the smallest fib, I have to rehearse it many times in my mind. (Grandin 2006, p.156)

However, some do learn to tell lies but their motivations to deceive are different from 'normal' ones. For example, having being bewildered for many years why people tell 'as it wasn't', Gunilla Gerland came to a point when she realised that:

> you could say things differently from the way they really were. Here was a tool to use in order to be more like other children and to get myself out of awkward situations. Saying it as it wasn't became synonymous with saying what the adults wanted to hear. The older I got, the more I learnt to make use of this technique. But not even

when I thought I knew what a lie was did I consider I was lying when I said it wasn't. I wasn't lying, I was trying to survive...

At times this technique could be a great help, and people seemed to get on better with me when I didn't say exactly how things were. But in the long run, it made me lose touch with my own identity. In the end I had said it as it wasn't so many times that I began to forget how it actually was. I believed in what I'd said, and all that was left was a vague sense of something not being quite right. (Gerland 1997, pp.51–52)

Sometimes people with autism tell lies or do what is expected from them just to please people. For example, Gunilla was taken to the hospital (after an injury) and was examined by the doctor. When the doctor tapped her knee her response was logical: 'I knew you should kick up your leg when you were tapped on the knee. I'd seen that in Donald Duck, so I did so' (Gerland 1997, p.61).

'Survivors'

Even before he was formally diagnosed with autism, Edgar Schneider's autistic personality was shining through:

I had encountered a number of reversals in my fortunes of no small magnitude. In each case, I fought back as much as my resources allowed. If the fight proved successful, all well and good. If not, I retrenched and plotted another course for my life. If this retrenchment caused any hardship, I bore it with equanimity until such time as the new course came to fruition. In any case, like a cat, I invariably landed on my feet... I was always a survivor. I always credited this to the fact that, on my mother's side, my ancestry is Russian, and unquestionably, historically, they are a nation of survivors. (Schneider 1999, pp.11–12)

Gunilla Gerland writes about her 'ability to go on and never give up':

My tenacity, consisting mostly of the word *no*, had two sources: my lack of that inner brake combines with a potential for panic that could make me invincible. Quite simply, I couldn't afford to lose. No one around me seemed to have the slightest idea of what my needs were. So I was totally at the mercy of my own judgement in doing those vital things so obviously important to me. (Gerland 1997, p.13)

Despite having problems that he cannot address yet, Tito remains optimistic: 'Yet with all my haves and have nots I remain a total optimistic person [because so many people] constantly encourage me to achieve my dreams' (Mukhopadhyay 2000, p.76).

It is interesting to note that even those we call 'low-functioning non-verbal individuals with autism' seem to be survivors as well. One of the most famous cases is that of Victor, the 'wild boy of Aveyron'.[3] The boy was first seen in 1797 in the forest near Lacaune, France. The villages caught him twice in 1797 and 1798, but the boy managed to escape. He was captured again in 1800, and this time was held. Victor was thought to be about 12 years old at the time. The question is, how could a low-functioning autistic boy survive alone for at least two years in the wild?

'Loners' / 'Outsiders'

I have always felt like an 'outsider'. Even during the times that I have not been explicitly conscious of that, this was something that was made plain to me by others... I was told by someone, when in my mid twenties: 'Ed, the trouble with you is that you're not a mixer; you're not part of the group.' It is not that I did not try. Not being aware, at that time, that I simply did not think as others did. I could never understand why virtually all my attempts to be 'part of the group' came a cropper. (Schneider 1999, p.106)

My family and I did not live in the same world. We scarcely came from the same planet... My life just happened to run parallel to theirs – otherwise, we had nothing in common. I couldn't help that. It was neither my wish nor my idea – it was simply the way it was. (Gerland 1997, pp.13–14)

They typically refuse to give in to peer pressure:

In fact, this shoulder-shrugging is precisely the reaction I have always given to any insult or put-down I ever got from anybody. (Schneider 1999, p.66)

[I was often bewildered at not being able to 'fit in'.] Because of this, the discovery of who and what I was turned out to be the cure for whatever was ailing me. I was able, at long last, to confront my limitations while remaining cognizant of my abilities. One result is that I have, ironically, become, much more of an extravert than I had been before. I found a greater ease in dealing with people, because I knew how I was *not able* to interact with them. (Schneider 1999, pp.109–110)

Some long for friends but find it difficult to establish relationships:

Deep down I had always been hungry for loving (non-sexual) physical contact, but what had been offered, I couldn't bear; just as I had always ached for friends, yet felt the need to withdraw from people. It seemed paradoxical, as I was trying to make sense of it. One thing I discovered…was that only certain types of adults, those who were able to give freely without seeking fulfilment for their own needs, felt safe enough for me to receive physical kindness from, and people like that are unfortunately very rare. As soon as I sense any kind of selfish motive behind someone's approach, I instinctively withdraw. This is not to say that children and animals never have selfish motives when giving or looking for physical contact. But perhaps their needs are different, of an innocent nature and more openly acknowledged. (Kammer 2007, pp.109–110)

Some prefer solitude to meaningless relationships:

I have never felt lonely or a need for what could be called 'the warmth of another human being'… Yet, with people who fervently share interests with me, I have been able to form very close friendships… I have always been able, when needed, to maintain solitude, even in the midst of a large crowd of people… As such, I have never felt what could be called an emotional void that needed to be filled by another person. (Schneider 1999, p.57)

Loyalty
'If you earn our trust, it is for life' (Nancy, personal communication, 2012).

Sense of fairness
Justice and fairness are very important for many autistic people. 'When we see something that is broken, including rules and injustices, we have a tendency to be bluntly honest' (Nancy, personal communication, 2012).

Vulnerability

'Often people with autism are taken advantage of. Paul McDonnell wrote about the painful experience of being betrayed by somebody he thought was his friend, having his money stolen and his car damaged' (Grandin 2006, p.157).

Autistic personality versus autistic personality disorder

Like autistic personality, autistic personality disorder is not a clinical category, but it is interesting to mention the condition referred to as autistic personality disorder by the researcher who first described it – Hans Asperger. In 1934 (in letters to his colleagues) and in his famous 1944 paper, 'Die "autistischen Psychopathen" im Kindesalter', Asperger described a distinctive pattern of abnormal social behaviour and communication in a group of children and adolescents as a separate syndrome, which he called 'autistic psychopathy' (it was translated as 'autistic personality disorder', but Lorna Wing suggested the term 'Asperger's syndrome', instead, to avoid a negative association with psychopathy).[4] Asperger (1979, p.45) describes children with 'autistishen Psychopathen' as 'highly intelligent... with interesting peculiarities' but with very difficult behaviour: 'They may achieve the highest university professorships or become artists – yet their quirks and peculiarities will remain with them for life.'[5] At present, Asperger syndrome is seen by some as interchangeable with HFA, and by others as a separate condition.

In his 1971 paper van Krevelen insisted that Kanner's and Asperger's cases 'differ considerably'. He analysed clinical pictures of both conditions and came to the conclusion that Kanner's early infantile autism should be differentiated from Asperger's autistic personality disorder because 'Kanner described psychotic *processes*, characterized by a *course*. Asperger's autistic psychopathy represented *traits*, which were *static*' (van Krevelen 1971, p.82).[6] These traits seem to be an exaggerated version of the features of 'autistic personality'.

Asperger syndrome versus personality disorders

Not all individuals with ASD develop an 'autistic personality'; there are some who develop other personality problems, for example:

> Recently I went to a large autism meeting here in the U.S. and was appalled at the rude behaviour exhibited by a few adult individuals with AS who were also attending. One of them walked up to me

and said, 'Who the f--- are you?' He also interrupted two major sessions at the conference because he adamantly opposed the notion of finding a cure… What was most distressing to me was that these individuals felt that because they had Asperger's, the people around them should accept their rude behaviour – that their 'disability' made them somehow exempt from the social standards we all live by. Like it or not, social boundaries exist that we are expected to conform to, whether we're members of a 'minority' population or mainstream American society. To be members of a group, we must all learn the rules and act in socially appropriate ways. People with autism and AS may find this more difficult to do, but being on the spectrum is not an exemption from doing so. (Grandin 2008, p.123)

In contrast to autism, other associated psychiatric disorders are quite common in Asperger syndrome (Szatmari *et al.* 1989).

There are other medical conditions that involve a loss of empathy (which can be misdiagnosed as ASD). In his book *The Science of Evil: On Empathy and the Origins of Cruelty*, Simon Baron-Cohen discusses the categories which he has reconceptualised as examples of three forms of zero-negative degrees of empathy (borderline, psychopath and narcissist) and contrasts them with forms of zero-positive degrees of empathy (Asperger syndrome):

People with Asperger Syndrome are Zero-Positive for three reasons. First, in their case their empathy difficulties are associated with having a brain that processes information in ways that can lead to talent. Second, the way their brain processes information paradoxically leads them to be supermoral rather than immoral. Finally…while their cognitive empathy may be below average, their affective empathy may be intact, enabling them to care about others. (Baron-Cohen 2011, pp.99–100)

Personality disorders

Personality is often defined as the unique quality or state of a person; the collection of behavioural and emotional characteristics that distinguish the person from others. The concept of *personality disorder* is 'untidy' and hard to define, but it does possess clinical usefulness (Oyebode 2008, p.401). Many clinicians use the descriptions of personality problems in recognised diagnostic classifications (such as the *Diagnostic and Statistical Manual of Mental Disorders* [DSM] and the *International Classification of Diseases*

[ICD]) to identify and diagnose personality disorders. These disorders are characterised by extreme deviations from the 'normal' behaviours that are accepted in a given culture (Wolff 1995). Rather than being illnesses, personality disorders are enduring and pervasive features of the personality that deviate markedly from the cultural norm. They include the dependent, histrionic, narcissistic, obsessive-compulsive, antisocial, avoidant, borderline (unstable), paranoid and schizoid types. The causes appear to be both hereditary and environmental. The most effective treatment combines behavioural and psychotherapeutic therapies.

Examples of personality disorders are dissociative identity disorder (multiple personality disorder), antisocial personality disorder, borderline personality disorder and narcissistic personality disorder.

Autistic personality (and autistic personality disorder) differ from personality disorders such as narcissistic personality disorder (NPD) (though on the surface the behaviours may look similar). For example:

> I am not ambitious because I do not seek to hold a particular rank in an organisation; to me those are empty honors. Using [my] internal standards...I want to do the work that is up to my level of capability, and which I feel essential to the mission of the organization... Those who are competitive and ambitious put a high premium on 'coming out on top'. They seek out situations in which they can do this... As such, they become confronters, and actually relish confrontations. (Schneider 1999, p.81)

As the diagnosis of both ASD and personality disorders is based on behaviours, sometimes people with other personality disorders can be misdiagnosed as having ASD. For instance, narcissistic personality disorder is a serious mental disorder that severely impairs the person socially (Webb *et al.* 2005).[7] Its full manifestation – a pervasive pattern of grandiosity (in fantasy or behaviour), need for admiration and lack of empathy – is visible by early adulthood. Some of the main features of NPD are:

- a grandiose sense of self-importance: they expect to be recognised as superior, exaggerating their talents and achievements. They believe that they can be understood only by special and unique people, and are furious to be associated with others whom they deem 'unworthy'; for example, 'I don't want *my* name to be in the list with...'

- a sense of entitlement: they expect automatic compliance with their demands, beliefs, and so on. They jump on the bandwagon of whatever they think will bring them 'deserved' recognition and furiously fight their case, imagining that without them it would have never been achieved

- interpersonal exploitative behaviour: they manipulate and take advantage of others to achieve their own ends

- lack of empathy for people who do not support their grandiose self-image

- arrogant, haughty behaviours and attitudes.

Though people with NPD demand excessive admiration, their self-esteem is, in fact, very fragile and their feelings are easily hurt by the slightest criticism. The individual with NPD is capable of rageful outbursts and violence at the slightest provocation (Webb *et al.* 2005), and sees offence anywhere, projecting their own negative attitudes to anyone they happen to talk to, for example, 'I am always polite and ethical but this shameful so-and-so insulted me, he defamed my character – he said that I am a liar! Apologize!' A pathological narcissistic personality tends to be organised around feelings of shame, envy and a fundamental sense of entitlement that covers an underlying sense of deficiency. Pathological narcissism is generally a compensatory arrogance covering an internal emptiness. Often the sense of failure (narcissistic injury) is expressed as rage, which serves to protect a very low self-esteem and ego strength (McWilliams 1994).[8] Unfortunately, unlike autism, NPD is very hard to treat, and in most cases any treatment is unsuccessful, if the person him or herself is unwilling to recognise their problems and is not prepared to deal with them.[9] NPD develops over time, typically beginning quite early in childhood; the characteristics of this disorder once developed are resistant to change, regardless of what kind of interventions are attempted (Webb *et al.* 2005). Paula Jacobsen (2003), a psychotherapist, provides a very good illustration of the differences between children with autism or Asperger syndrome and those with NPD, whose behaviours (on the surface) look very similar:

> [Eric, a five-year-old child's] early developmental milestones were normal except language development, which was precocious, and [delayed] social development... He did not play well with other children. [He benefited from] structured learning which was easy

for him, but he did not develop friendships… Eric had a greatly
exaggerated sense of superior abilities. He was enraged by a
perceived failure in his own performance, because he experienced
this as a narcissistic injury and could not tolerate it. No amount of
understanding of the situation was useful. Eric wanted to demonstrate
his superiority, and he wanted admiration. He was very aware of his
anger and his tantrums at the time and afterwards. He could easily
describe what he had felt and done, and he saw his behaviour as a
reasonable response to his situation… (Jacobsen 2003, pp.25, 26)

Children with AS are very different, though their issues (e.g. anger) look
similar to those with NPD:

Matt was a bright, verbal seven-year-old who had long temper
tantrums. He was overwhelmed by sensory stimuli, such as sounds,
lights, odors, and textures. Matt was unable to control his behaviour
when he felt overwhelmed. He was unable to examine what had
happened afterwards… He had no idea of what he sounded like…
of how long his tantrums were…

Matt did not want to behave that way, although he continued
for years to struggle with tantrums, particularly in certain situations,
situations that felt overwhelming to him… He was oblivious to his
own behaviour as well as its effect on others. (Jacobsen 2003, p.28)

As the surface behaviours are similar in some other conditions and
disorders, and there is still no biological marker of autism, 'autistic
personality' features can help differentiate between different conditions.
However, there can be other co-morbid problems that also should be
taken into account.

Notes

1. McWilliams does not refer to the clinical definition of schizoid personality but
rather to phenomenologically oriented psychoanalytic understanding of schizoid
issues, which corresponds to the Jungian concept of 'introversion'.

2. Cited in Piechowski 1999.

3. Uta Frith (2003) suggests that, judging from the available detailed medical reports
of Victor's behaviour and his reactions to intervention (by Jean Marc Itard), the boy
might have had low-functioning autism.

4. Now it is known as Asperger syndrome and is included in autism spectrum
disorders but it will be merged with autism in future classification systems, such

as the American Psychiatric Association's *Diagnostic and Statistical Manual*, Fifth Edition (DSM-V).

5.   Ssuchareva (1926) and Wolff and Chess (1964) described a group of children whom they diagnosed to have 'schizoid personality disorder', who are oversensitive, emotionally detached, solitary, rigid/obsessive, lacking in empathy, and prone to bizarre thoughts. Some researchers (see, for example, Wing 1996) believe that the 'schizoid personality disorder' diagnosis may be an alternative way of looking at Asperger syndrome, especially in adults, although there is no complete overlap between 'schizoid disorder' and autism.

6.   Wolff (1995) also found the condition to be innate and stable over time and thought Asperger syndrome could be considered as a form of schizoid personality. Children with schizotypical personality (described by Nagy and Szatmari 1986) closely resembled children with schizoid personality; moreover, the majority of children with schizoid personality disorder in adulthood fulfilled the diagnostic criteria for schizotypical personality disorder (Wolff 1995). Wolff concludes that 'it would be wrong to call groups of children with a similar clinical picture and a similar outcome by different names' (p.124).

7.   This is why it is sometimes misdiagnosed in adults as autism or AS: the 'surface behaviours' look very similar.

8.   Not many people want the label of NPD, and when an opportunity arises to jump under the autism spectrum umbrella many immediately catch it. As there is a (very unfortunate) trend at present to diagnose AS by default, or self-diagnose, quite a few individuals with NPD have grasped the badge of autism with both hands, proudly announcing 'we, autistics' and starting the fight against any negative comment against *their* 'autism'.

9.   Differences between individuals with AS and those with NPD are:

   • Both AS and NPD individuals exhibit self-absorption and narrow focus at their interest(s), but AS people seek to understand their topic for themselves, while NPD individuals do it to prove their 'superiority' above others.

   • Both AS and NPD individuals seek to express the abilities and talents that they perceive within themselves without regard for opinions of others, but AS individuals seek out quirky solutions that match their needs rather than seeking the solutions to impress (typical for NPD). These people fight to express what they have, while those with NPD fight to hide a sense of inferiority and personal shortcomings. Besides, people with AS are likely to be truly competent in their special area (Webb *et al.* 2005), while people with NPD are superficial, they tend to disguise their incompetence with 'verbal storm' using many words but actually saying very little.

   • Both AS and NPD people are rigid in their behaviours and insist on sameness of the situations. However, AS people do it because they usually impelled to follow their own path rather than trying to force those around them to become the supporting staff to their 'one-man show', while people with NPD create 'scripts' for those around them and react very badly when people do not behave according to their plan for them (Webb *et al.* 2005).

   • AS individuals show empathy and sympathy for others while NPD people are 'blind' to the hurt they inflict on others, they are on the mission (whatever it might be): to 'save the world'/'defend autistics' from 'unethical normals' or other '(less important) autistics', etc.

- AS people are humble in regard to their own achievements, whereas NPD individuals seek prestige ('I am the first to claim that...' – ignoring hundreds of other researchers, for example, who made the claim decades ago and provided convincing evidence).
- Unlike AS people, who have realistic self-esteem and a strong sense of genuine confidence in their abilities, those with NPD attempt to hide their sense of deficiency and low self-esteem under the cover of arrogance (Webb *et al.* 2005).
- Unlike individuals with AS, individuals with NPD are very good at manipulating people for their own advantage – they will 'perform' differently in different situations and with different people.

8

Spiritual Experiences

Since the earliest times many a wise person has undergone a spiritual quest, exploring different paths to comprehend the seen and unseen worlds and find the spiritual meaning of their lives. The spiritual dimension is implied in their accounts of altered consciousness (Samuel 2009). Those who were not satisfied with what their immediate sensory experiences provided turned to different means to look at the world beyond our limited experience and found it to be more complex, more intense and more powerful than we can encounter in our everyday activities. Humans manage to get along in this universe by:

> a drastic process of cutting down and limiting of experience to a level which our limited perceptions and capabilities can encompass. But reality itself is something hugely beyond our limited everyday picture of it, and, in some terms, we are called on to confront that enormous and frightening complexity. From a theistic point of view, one could speak here of God. (Samuel 2009, p.3)

Many aspirants to the spiritual life have undertaken various techniques to 'open a door into a transcendental world of Being, Knowledge, and Bliss' (Huxley 2004a, p.100), such as mortification of the body, fasting, cultivating insomnia, praying for long periods in uncomfortable positions, using psychedelic drugs, and so on. One of the best-known examples of this is the experiment undertaken by Aldous Huxley with mescalin. Huxley's report is of great significance because his goal was a spiritual one: he wanted to understand the mystery of human consciousness by freeing the mind from the limitations restricting its access to the universe. Huxley documented his experiences in fine detail in his essay *The Doors of Perception* and its sequel *Heaven and Hell.*[1] Under the influence of mescalin, not only were the vitality and hyper-quality of sensory stimuli heightened, but the whole focus on what is meaningful and what is unimportant was shifted in the opposite direction. While in the same physical environment, for a few 'timeless hours' Huxley was 'shaken out of the ruts of ordinary perception' (2004a, p.46), transferred from 'the world of selves, of time, of moral judgments and utilitarian considerations, the world…of self-assertion, of cocksureness, of overvalued words and idolatrously worshipped notions' to the world of 'a Not-self, simultaneously perceiving and being the Not-self of the things' (p.19) around him, to 'the outer and inner worlds, not as they appear to an animal obsessed with survival, or to a human being obsessed with words and notions, but as they are apprehended, directly and unconditionally, by Mind at Large' (p.46). The experience was so overwhelming, significant and beautiful that Huxley repeated several times to his companions: 'This is how one ought to see… These are the sort of things one ought to look at' (p.19). In his essay, Huxley also showed both benefits and dangers of language, influencing our experience with what we call the real (physical) world. Though of great benefit in passing knowledge from generation to generation, language restricts our outlook with 'opaque medium concepts, which distorts every given fact into the all too familiar likeliness of some generic label or explanatory abstraction', so 'we must learn to handle words effectively; but at the same time we must preserve and, if necessary, intensify our ability to look at the world directly' to avoid distortions created by verbal concepts (p.47).[2]

In his essay *Heaven and Hell*, Huxley provides possible explanations of these phenomena, summarised as that, in order to create the internal conditions favourable to spiritual insight, most contemplatives worked systematically to modify their body chemistry. To answer possible objections to the reality of these experiences (e.g. 'since changes in the body chemistry can create the conditions favourable to visionary and mystical experience, visual and mystical experience cannot be what they claim to be' or 'an experience which is chemically conditioned cannot be an experience of the divine'), Huxley points out that '*all* our experiences are chemically conditioned, and if we imagine that some of them are purely "spiritual", purely "intellectual", purely "aesthetic", it is merely because we have never troubled to investigate the internal chemical environment at the moment of their occurrence' (2004b, p.102). Comparing his visionary experience with the accounts of other worlds, inhabited by the gods, spirits of the dead and other unknown entities preserved in cultural traditions, Huxley was struck by the close similarity between induced or spontaneous visionary experience and the descriptions of heavens and fairylands of folklore and religion. Huxley compares the mescalin experience to 'what Catholic theologians call a gratuitous grace' (2004a, p.22).

In search for the exotic, the strange, the unusual, one does not have to go on pilgrimage, or turn away from the world, or convert to a different religion, or visit another country:

> The great lesson from the true mystics, from the Zen monks, and… from the Humanistic and Transpersonal psychologists – that the sacred is *in* the ordinary, that it is to be found in one's daily life, in one's neighbors, friends, and family, in one's back yard, and that travel may be a *flight* from confronting the sacred – this lesson can be easily lost. (Maslow 1970a, pp.x–xi)

Maslow considered searching for miracles elsewhere 'a sure sign of ignorance that *everything* is miraculous' (Maslow 1970a, pp.x–xi).

As our interpretation of reality is shaped by the cultural medium, when Western researchers use criteria for identifying spirituality based on the language of Christianity, they inevitably limit it, significantly distorting the accuracy of their findings. 'In multi-faith and highly secularized nations such as Britain and many other advanced economies, the spirituality of most people is liable to be overlooked' (Hay and Nye 2006, p.50). As Maslow observes, it is unfortunate that many people see organised religion as the only source of the spiritual life and, consequently, use the vocabulary of traditional religion while discussing 'spiritual life'. The lack of any other satisfactory language makes it nearly impossible to demonstrate that 'the common base of all religions is human, natural, empirical, and the so-called spiritual values are also naturally derivable. But I have available only a theistic language for this "scientific" job' (Maslow 1970a, p.4). Maslow suggests that not only should the experiential be emphasised and brought back into psychology as an opponent of the merely abstract and abstruse, of the a priori (of what he calls 'helium-filled words'), it:

> must then also be *integrated* with the abstract and the verbal. We must make a place for 'experientially based concepts', and for 'experientially filled words', that is, for an experience-based rationality in contrast to the a priori rationality that we have come almost to identify with rationality itself. (pp.xi–xii)

There are two distinct ways of knowing: knowing about (logical, scientific) and knowing through experience, which applies two types of logic (rational and transliminal). Clarke (2008, p.41) argues that instead of regarding one as being right and the other wrong, it is necessary to accept that both have their limitations and their strengths: 'The failure to recognise that there are two ways of knowing, and the downgrading of the experiential one, leads to much of the tension between science and religion.' In her book *Madness, Mystery and the Survival of God* (2008), Clarke explores how these two ways of knowing emerge from the very organisation of our brains. The two ways of knowing are based on a constant switching between the two processing modes, with one or the other being in charge.

Here we must mention the different functions of the two hemispheres of the brain. While the main functions of the left hemisphere include analysis, reason, sequence, space and depth perception and language, the right hemisphere is more involved with feeling, aesthetics, nuance, tone and intuition (Schulz 1998). Because of this specialisation, some types of information processed in one hemisphere cannot be recognised by the other. In fact, each hemisphere can not only perceive the same object differently but also store different memories about it. These differing views lead to new perceptions, insights and creativity. The two hemispheres are connected with each other by the corpus callosum, which matures more slowly, which is why what infants and toddlers assimilate and learn before language is stored in the right hemisphere is not easily accessible verbally and not easily articulated (Joseph 1993). However, unconsciously these memories are always there.

It is possible to see everything differently (achieving a new perception or new level of consciousness), when a person can perceive different connections and feel relatedness with everything. Those who achieve spiritual awareness develop the ability to see beyond the 'delusion' of the reality created by the mind. They are able to 'see' beyond the mind-reconstructed world – not through contemplation and theorising but by actually *experiencing* the spiritual dimension. Their knowledge of spiritual reality is achieved not from reading or studying the experiences of others but by experiencing it directly.

In different cultures (and at different times) the same experiences can be seen either as special gifts or pathological experiences – symptoms of psychiatric illnesses or disorders. They can be either spontaneous or induced (for example, in temporal lobe epilepsy or by drugs). Those who in the West are referred to as psychics or mediums in other cultures can be considered healers or shamans. Different cultures interpret what is 'normal' differently. In some, altered states of consciousness, trance, and so on are seen as signs of mental problems, while in others these same phenomena are considered to be highly spiritual states.[3] The most striking difference in the interpretation of 'experiencers' can be found in the Western diagnostic classifications of mental diseases, such as the *Diagnostic and Statistical Manual of Mental Disorders* (DSM), where certain diagnostic criteria for schizophrenia, for example, correspond (or are very similar) to the altered states of consciousness that shamans are able to voluntarily achieve when they perform their rituals. Research into religious/spiritual experiences suggests that there is a tendency to pathologise experiences that people around those who experience them do not understand (Tobert 2010) – the medical and psychological pathology interprets hallucinations as 'inherently abnormal' and caused by a disease of the mind (Thomas 1997, p.24). Thomas provides evidence that social, economic, political and cultural factors are inextricably linked to the nature of schizophrenia and concludes that it is social factors that have a significant influence on the diagnosis and outcome of schizophrenia, with those living in a non-industrial society having a better outcome. For example, 50 per cent of people with schizophrenia are cured in India and Africa, compared with 25 per cent in Britain and 6 per cent in Denmark. Fernando (1991, p.190) suggests that as 'self control' is considered very important in the West, mystical or trance states (associated with the 'loss of ego control') are inevitably seen as pathological, which leads to overdiagnosing of people of African, Hispanic and Native American origin.

It is notable that some religions were started by 'experiencers' of an ultimate, beyond 'normal', reality, who were inspired by voices or visions revealing mysteries, for instance, the Quakers and Shakers, the Seventh Day Adventists, Mormons, Paul on the road to Damascus, Mohammed, Moses (Tobert 2010). Keighley (1999) writes about Florence Nightingale, who heard the voice of God in 1837, inspiring her to start the health services in the UK. And it is not only the founders of religions or some special persons who have these and similar experiences. In fact, in the course of their lives, many people have some sort of experience of a reality beyond, and encounter the divine. These experiences and encounters can be ecstatic or disturbing, or both (Clarke 2008).

Maslow (1970b, p.19) argues that the core, the essence of every known religion has been the private, lonely, personal illumination, revelation or ecstasy experienced by some very sensitive prophet or seer:

> The high religions call themselves revealed religions and each of them tends to rest its validity, its function, and its right to exist on the codification and the communication of this original mystic experience or revelation from the lonely prophet to the mass of human beings in general.

According to Maslow, these mystical illuminations and revelations are, in fact, 'transcendent' or 'transliminal' experiences (Maslow calls them 'peak-experiences') which are natural human experiences, but which were phrased in terms of whatever conceptual, cultural and linguistic framework was available to the particular seer in his or her time. For example, the older reports were 'framed' in terms of supernatural language. If studied today, we can provide different (natural) explanations which can be reflected in the language we use. On the other hand, Maslow also warns against reducing the mystical to the merely experiential, with the experiencer turning away from the world in search for triggers of these wonderful subjective experiences, eventually losing compassion and becoming 'not only selfish but also evil' (p.ix). In short, one-sidedness is over-extreme and dangerous. Instead of looking at either/or, black/white, exclusiveness and separativeness:

> the profoundly and authentically religious person integrates these trends easily and automatically. The forms, rituals, ceremonials, and verbal formulae in which he was reared remains for him experientially rooted, symbolically meaningful, archetypal, unitive. Such a person may go through the same motions and behaviors as his more numerous co-religionists, but he is never *reduced* to the behavioural, as most of them are. (Maslow 1970a, pp.vii–viii)

Geoffrey Samuel (2009) draws a parallel between such experiences and Buddhist concepts: the Sanskrit *shunyata* (meaning 'voidness' or 'emptiness') and the Tibetan *rigpa*. Similar experiences are achieved through meditation (especially in the Buddhist sense of a calming mind, *shamatha* in Sanskrit). Samuel points out that the logic behind *shamatha* and analogous techniques that can operate as a form of 'stabilisation' (for example, the imaginative identifications with Tantric deities; the so-called *tr'ulk'or* or *yantra yoga* techniques, or similar exercises and processes in Hindu, Taoist or other traditions) used by 'normal' people is 'to calm and centre one's consciousness to the point where it can begin to encounter the enormous and overwhelming complexities of reality' (Samuel 2007, p.4). Teachers in Asian traditions explain that those practising these techniques for spiritual enlightenment or awakening have to be psychologically balanced and mature *before* they start. However, some Tibetan Tantric practices are specifically directed at healing and strengthening the practitioner, and there is no rigid boundary here between physical and psychiatric illness (Samuel 2008). Here we can see possible connections 'between what we might classify as psychiatric illness and what we might classify as a process of spiritual cultivation' (Samuel 2009, p.4). In Tibetan tradition, the process of self-cultivation and of the eventual attainment of Buddhahood is seen not only as self-identification with a Tantric deity (the *yidam*, which represents aspects of the awakened state) but also with internal flows, currents or winds within the *subtle body* (Samuel 2005). To grow towards spiritual awakening, one has to learn to control the flows of *prana* (in Sanskrit) or *lung* (in Tibetan) through physical exercises and internal visualisations. In the Chinese self-cultivating techniques (*yangsheng*) the internal flow is represented by *qi* (a term approximately corresponding to *prana* and *lung*). Samuel (2009) provides a fascinating analysis of different interpretations of experiences in Western medicine and Tibetan medical practice: what might be classified as 'psychiatric illness' in the West, in Tibet is described in terms of 'lung imbalance'. In Chinese practices of self-cultivation, *qi* is central to both spiritual practice and health care theories of psychiatric illness (Lo and Schroer 2005; Low and Hsu 2007; Samuel 2009). In general, in South, Southeast and East Asia, spiritual development is seen through refining and purifying internal winds and forces which can be 'out of balance' and can be helped by various techniques (for example, acupuncture), whereas in the West, the 'unbalanced winds/forces' would be considered as psychiatric illness (Laderman 1993; Low and Hsu 2007; Samuel 2009).[4]

Mystical experiences
The definitions of a mystical experience vary considerably, ranging from Neumann's (1964) 'upheaval of the total personality' through Greeley's (1974) 'spiritual force that seems to lift you out of yourself' to Scharfstein's (1973) 'everyday mysticism'. The most commonly accepted

definition is a transient, extraordinary experience characterised by feelings of unity, harmonious relationship to the divine and everything in existence, as well as euphoria, sense of noesis (access to the hidden spiritual dimension), loss of ego, alterations in time and space perception and the sense of lacking control over the event.[5]

Newberg and colleagues suggest that the states of 'unity and oneness' (transcendent or transliminal experiences when self blends into other and mind and matter become one) can be experienced by anyone (to a varying degree) and proposed the notion of a 'unitary continuum' ranging from the experience of separateness from the world to the experience of the sages and mystics of unity or oneness. In the state of absolute unity, 'self blends into other; mind and matter are one and the same' (Newberg *et al.* 2001, p.156). It shows that anyone can discover what is sometimes called a 'spiritual force' that can bring a powerful transformation. Even if it is only experienced in brief moments during life, this force takes over the whole person, redefining their objectives and giving meaning and purpose to their life. The spiritual force is devoid of opposites and contradictions. During such experiences, thought, emotion, speech and action are unified; the subjective self ('I') disappears, the self becomes a part of the unifying whole (Culliford 2007). Although most people have their spiritual experience(s) when they are alone, it does not mean that spiritual experiences cannot occur to many people simultaneously in large religious gatherings.[6]

There are two opposite views on explanation of religious/spiritual experiences (consciousness and brain functions). The first (a reductionist view) considers consciousness and subjective experiences to be products of neural activity of the brain (e.g. Dennett 1991). The second argues that subjective experiences cannot be 'reconstructed' from neural activity and cannot be validated using scientific methods (e.g. Nagel 1974). Fenwick (2010, p.10) argues that it is impossible to predict subjective experience by studying objective firing patterns of neurons, and 'therefore impossible to explain the subjective aspects of mind or consciousness. Conscious stuff and brain stuff are different. The idea of a mechanical universe which excludes consciousness is unsatisfactory from an experiential point of view.'

To understand what it is like to experience the state of consciousness when there is no distinction between self and other (absolute unitary being, Newberg *et al.* 2001), we have to turn to the insights of mystics and to research studies in the field of transpersonal psychology. Potentially, it is attainable by all people irrespective of whether they are religious or not. Some people claim to 'go between' the worlds on a regular basis. They include those (shamans, mediums and psychics) who claim to work interdimensionally by altering their consciousness and interacting with non-physical entities, others who achieve consciousness-shift either with drugs or through meditation, and also those whose experiences are involuntary, such as out-of-body experiences (OBEs) or near death experiences (NDEs) or what can be termed as spontaneous 'religious/ spiritual experiences'.

Having studied electromagnetism's effects within the brain, Michael Persinger argues that some individuals have high temporal lobe lability that makes them prone to tiny epileptic-like seizures. According to Persinger, such individuals are more artistic and creative, and more likely to experience 'anomalous perception' (such as telepathic and clairvoyant experiences) than others. The researcher suggests that extremely low frequency electromagnetic radiation (less than 3 kHz) in the earth's atmosphere (undetected by the majority) affects the temporal lobes, causing the experiences of flying, floating or being out of the body, as well as hearing voices, having visions and feeling presences, with hallucinations based on the cultural background (Persinger 1977, 1987). Persinger has found that in bereavement people become even more susceptible to these experiences – seeing vivid images of deceased loved ones and, with the decrease of overnight melatonin, they may be woken up by the apparitions of the deceased (Persinger 1988). Other studies by Persinger and colleagues (Persinger *et al.* 2010; Ruttan, Persinger and Koren 1990), designed to investigate different effects of subtle stimulation of the temporal lobes,[7] have revealed that the participants experienced a 'sensed presence' and other mystical experiences and altered states of consciousness. Persinger has put forward several hypotheses, the first known as the vectorial hemisphericity hypothesis (Persinger 1993b), which proposes that the human sense of self has two components, one on each side of the brain, which ordinarily work together but in which the left hemisphere is usually dominant (Persinger and Healey 2002; Persinger *et al.* 1994). Persinger argues that the two hemispheres make different contributions to a single sense of self, but under certain conditions can appear as two separate 'selves'. Persinger and Koren designed a 'God helmet' in an attempt to create conditions in which contributions to the sense of self from both cerebral hemispheres is disrupted.

Persinger's second hypothesis is that when communication between the left and right senses of self is disturbed (while the person is wearing the helmet the usually subordinate 'self' in the right hemisphere intrudes into the awareness of the left-hemispheric dominant self), it causes what Persinger calls 'interhemispheric intrusions'. The third hypothesis is that 'visitor experiences'/hallucinations could be explained by such 'interhemispheric intrusions' caused by a disruption in 'vectorial hemisphericity' (Persinger 1989). Persinger believes that paranormal experiences (1993a), feelings of having lived past lives (1996), sense of presence of non-physical beings (1992), ghosts (Persinger, Tiller and Koren 2000) and other 'spiritual beings' (Persinger and Makarec 1992) are examples of interhemispheric intrusions. According to Persinger, religious and mystic experiences are artefacts of temporal lobe function.

So far there has been only one attempt to replicate Persinger's study, by a group of Swedish researchers (Granqvist *et al.* 2005). As the effects reported by Persinger have not been independently replicated, his theory has been criticised, and dismissed by many academics and non-academics.[8] However, Persinger (Persinger and Koren 2005) argues that the replication was technically flawed, there were differences in the magnetic fields used by the Swedish researchers and they did not expose the subjects to magnetic fields for long enough to produce an effect. Interestingly, though the Swedish researchers say that they do not know what neurological mechanisms could generate the experiences, the personality tests they conducted with the participants revealed that people with spiritual interests and those who were more suggestible were more likely to feel a supernatural presence than those who have never been interested in this or were 'strong non-believers'.

But do the results obtained in the laboratory indicate that low magnetic stimulation of the brain *produces* anomalous perceptions or *facilitates* access to information that is (and has always been) in the environment? Persinger himself did not exclude the second possibility. Jawer (2009, p.182) supposes that both paths are possible, depending on different people's 'inherited neurobiology, their degree of sensitivity to external *and* internal stimuli, their life experiences, and the way in which they typically process energy associated with feeling'.

Another (very important) variable is sensitivity. Certain groups of people (sometimes called highly sensitive persons, or HSPs) can sense much better than those who are dumb to their environment, and if we add lack of suggestibility (not as a negative trait, but as a refusal to 'see' anything that is not included into their 'culturally constructed world'),[9] then the results of experiments with volunteers are very telling. For instance, Susan Blackmore, a psychologist based in Bristol, and the science writer Richard Dawkins, whose works on evolutionary biology and criticism of religion are well known, participated in the experiment.[10] Blackmore is reluctant to dismiss Persinger's theory just yet. She has firsthand experience of Persinger's methods. 'When I went to Persinger's lab and underwent his procedures I had the most extraordinary experiences I've ever had,' she says. 'I'll be surprised if it turns out to be a placebo effect'.[11] In contrast, Dawkins (who also volunteered for the experiment) reported in the BBC science documentary series *Horizon* that he did not have a 'sensed presence' experience, but rather felt at times 'slightly dizzy', 'quite strange' and had sensations in his limbs and changes in his breathing. He summarised his experience as follows: 'It pretty much felt as though I was in total darkness, with a helmet on my head and pleasantly relaxed'.[11] Persinger explained Dawkin's limited results in terms of his low score on a psychological scale measuring temporal lobe sensitivity.

Jawer believes that considering these and similar experiences as occult inevitably prevents us from considering that they could have mundane biological origins.

> The transmutation of an *internal* unseen, but subconsciously registered stress reaction to the *external*, shadowy, but nonetheless sensate world of the anomalous is something exceedingly strange. [But still] the connections to our own physical reality are there. As Sir Isaac Newton was able to infer the existence of an invisible force (gravity) from the known motion of objects, so it remains for us to discern the existence of a realm coincident with the one we take for granted. The gateway into the dimension is *emotional* and *energetic*. (Jawer 2009, pp.137–138)

Many researchers recognise that what we call 'mystical experiences' or 'mystical states' are part of normal human experience and are reflected on the biological level. It has been suggested that these experiences are triggered by neural (electrical and biochemical) activity in the right hemisphere. The evidence for this assumption is the ineffability of the experience – no concepts or words are adequate to characterise them, meaning that the left hemisphere (responsible for categorisation and language) cannot play a major role in them (Fenwick 2010). Research seems to confirm this: for instance, the experience of merging with one's surroundings, losing the boundaries between the 'self' and the world, a deep feeling of unity with the universe, seems to be caused by an alteration in the right hemisphere. Feeling time alterations such as disorientation points to the right temporal function (Davidson 1941); speeding up or slowing down of subjective time can be caused by right temporal lobe seizures (Penfield and Perrot 1963). Fenwick and colleagues (1985) report the results of a test on 17 mediums from a college of psychic studies, which showed that those who claimed to have psychic gifts and two subjects in the control group who had had mystical experiences after a head injury had had more right hemisphere deficits than the rest in the control group. There is also some evidence that mystical states involve the frontal lobes and thalamus as well (Fenwick 2010). However, it is one thing to establish the affected areas of the brain and distinctive patterns of neural activity, but we cannot be sure whether these neurological changes are caused by objective or subjective reality (Lancaster 2010). Some researchers do claim that the evidence supports the view that individuals who have religious, spiritual or mystical experiences 'do in fact contact an objective real "force" that exists outside themselves' (Beauregard and O'Leary 2007, p.290). Sometimes they are compared to bodily pain. William James cited Saint Teresa, who describes the experience of these 'celestial joys' as 'penetrating to the marrow of the bones, whilst earthly pleasures affect only the surface of the senses' (James 1985, p.412).

James (1985, p.379) believed that personal spiritual (religious) experience 'has its root and center in mystical states of consciousness' and though admitting that he himself had not had firsthand experience of them, James was sure that these states were real and had very important functions. Recognising the difficulty and ambiguity of the definition of such concepts as 'mysticism' and 'mystical', James proposed a solution of providing certain restrictions to describe 'mystical experiences' – four characteristics that if present would justify us in calling them mystical.

The first is *ineffability*: the experience defies expression, it cannot be described verbally, 'its quality must be directly experienced; it cannot be imparted or transferred to others. In this peculiarity mystical states are more like states of feeling than like states of intellect.' The second feature is the *noetic quality* of the experience:

Although so similar to states of feeling, mystical states seem to those who experience them to be also states of knowledge. They are states of insight into depths of truth unplumbed by the discursive intellect. They are illuminations, revelations, full of significance and importance, all inarticulate though they remain; and as a rule they carry with them a curious sense of authority for after-time. (James 1985, pp.380–381)

The third characteristic is *transiency*, as the mystical states cannot be sustained for long and soon fade, 'but when they recur it is recognized; and from one recurrence to another it is susceptible of continuous development in what is felt as inner richness and importance'. The last feature is *passivity*: when this sort of consciousness has set in, 'the mystic feels as if his own will were in abeyance, and indeed sometimes as if he were grasped and held by a superior power'. What distinguishes the passivity of the mystic experience from such phenomena as prophetic speech, automatic writing or the mediumistic trance (all examples of 'alternative personality') is that the latter leave no recollection and have no significance for the subject's inner life, making a mere interruption, while mystical states are never merely interruptive; they have a profound sense of importance, modify the inner life of the experiencer and leave long-term memories of the event (James 1985, pp.380–381). James emphasises that, while all four characteristics are necessary to qualify the experience as mystical, there exists a wide range of experiences, with the simplest rudiments of mystical experience without any special significance at one end of the spectrum, to extreme religious experiences at the other. The example of the simple mystical experience can be the sense of deeper significance that cannot be confined to rational explanations; it can be triggered by 'single words, and conjunctions of words, effects of light on land and sea, odors and musical sounds, [that] all bring it when the mind is tuned aright' (James 1985, p.383). James gives examples of experiences caused by certain words which 'haunt' or 'fascinate' some individuals, thus having a power to 'transport' them to a different reality.[12]

Such experiences may be comparable to a subtype of 'peak-experiences' explored by Maslow. Maslow's 'peak-experiences' include what was called 'direct revelations from God', indicating that these experiences are characteristic not only of special people (prophets) but (potentially) of any human. According to Maslow, these revelations or 'peak-experiences' are valid psychological phenomena that are to be scientifically (rather than metaphysically) studied, in order to better understand a peculiarly 'human' aspect of man's existence. In addition to 'peak-experience', Maslow also distinguishes 'plateau-experience', which is a calmer, less intense, serene response to the miraculous and the awesome. From Maslow's analysis, the high plateau-experience always has a noetic and cognitive element that is absent from peak-experience, which can be purely and exclusively emotional. Plateau-experiences are also far more voluntary than peak-experiences are. One can learn to see everything in the unitive way almost at will. 'It then becomes a witnessing, an appreciating, what one may call a serene, cognitive blissfulness which can, however, have a quality of casualness and of lounging about' (Maslow 1970a, pp.xiv–xv).

Anyone, at times, can get a transient glimpse of peak-experience, but to achieve the high plateau of unitive consciousness (experiencing life at the level of Being) is a lifelong effort – it takes time, discipline, study and commitment. Maslow points out that the knowledge revealed was there all the time, and what has been perceived during peak-experiences is neither a change in the nature of reality nor the invention of a new piece of reality. It is all due to a perceiver's readiness, perspicuity and efficiency, comparable to the efficiency of his spectacles. On top of 'the truest and most total kind of visual perceiving or listening or feeling', these experiences also bring changes in the cognitive function:

> which can be best described as non-evaluating, non-comparing, or non-judging cognition. Figures and ground are less sharply differentiated...there is a tendency for things to become equally important rather than to be ranged in a hierarchy from very important to quite important. (Maslow 1970a, p.60)

Similar experiences may also be triggered by sensory stimuli (sounds, sights, smells, etc.), or thoughts emerging spontaneously. However, it seems that, for a true breakthrough experience to occur, a person requires preparation, either by life's events or through special tuition. Spiritual practices, such as Zen meditation or koan,[13] teach people to shatter logical thinking and reach for the truth at a deeper level. They are not about what we know as intellectual ability, but about natural wisdom (Culliford 2007). Culliford draws a parallel between 'a meaningful coincidence' and what Jung called 'synchronicity'. As most of the 'messages' are transmitted in the form of pure, raw emotion, we have to be able to first, correctly interpret them and, second, to distinguish genuine messages from false ones, which can be compared to infective viruses, aiming to lead us astray by persuasive and deceitful communication. Only by learning how to both maintain and improve the quality of communication between our everyday minds and the wisdom minds will we be able to interpret the messages we receive (Culliford 2009).

The experiences achieved in meditation practices are reflected on the biological level. James Austin addresses the biology of spiritual experience in his book *Zen and the Brain* (1999) in relation to meditation and koan. For centuries, Christians have followed the example of Christ, withdrawing from the complexity of everyday life to the simplicity and austerity of a harsh environment.[14] 'Such a life of sensory deprivation and prayer lent itself to visionary experience, both ecstatic and demonic... Austerity, prayer and rhythmic chanting all encouraged the crossing of the threshold into the transliminal state' (Clarke 2008, pp.55–56).

Buddhism and Zen

Buddhism: a widespread Asian religion or philosophy, founded by Gautama Buddha in India in the fifth century BC, which teaches that elimination of the self and earthly desires is the highest goal – reaching *nirvana* (perfect bliss and release from karma, attained by the extinction of individuality).

Zen: a form of Mahayana Buddhism emphasising the value of meditation and intuition.

The next step forward on the spectrum of the mystical experiences is 'dreamy states' (or 'sudden invasions of vaguely reminiscent consciousness') – the term coined by James Crichton-Browns: 'They bring a sense of mystery and of the metaphysical duality of things, and the feeling of an enlargement of perception which seems imminent but which never completes itself.'[15] According to Dr Crichton-Browns, they are connected with the disturbances of self-consciousness which sometimes precede epileptic attacks, and eventually can lead to insanity. James strongly disagrees with this conclusion and stresses the fact that the outcome depends on the state of the person, 'for we make it appear admirable or dreadful according to the context by which we set it off' (James 1985, p.384). Crichton-Browns illustrates the phenomenon of 'dreamy states' with the example of a 'waking trance' that he himself frequently experienced from childhood onwards when he was alone:

> This has come upon me through repeating my own name to myself silently, till all at once, as it were out of the intensity of the consciousness of individuality, individuality itself seemed to dissolve and fade away into boundless being, and this was not a confused state but the clearest, the surest of the surest, utterly beyond words

— where death was an almost laughable impossibility — the loss of personality (if so it were) seeming no extinction, but the only true life. I am ashamed of my feeble description. Have I not said the state is utterly beyond words?[15]

James includes in this category other quite frequent phenomena, for instance, déjà vu: 'that sudden feeling, which sometimes sweeps over us, of having "been here before", as if at some indefinite past time, in just this place, with just these people, we were already saying these things' (James 1985, p.383).

According to James, the next steps into mystical states are caused by intoxicants and anaesthetics. He cites the example of a mystical experience with chloroform, given by J.A. Symonds, which brings the experiencer to question the physical reality:

Is it possible that the inner sense of reality which succeeded, when my flesh was dead to impression from without, to the ordinary sense of physical relations, was not a delusion but an actual experience? Is it possible that I, in that moment, felt what some of the saints have said they always felt, the undemonstrable but irrefragable certainty of God? (p.392)

And at last — the religious mysticism — sudden realisation of the immediate presence of God.

Having researched numerous accounts of mystics, James comes to the conclusion that our normal waking consciousness (rational consciousness) is but one special type of consciousness, while there exist potential forms of consciousness entirely different from it.

We may go through life without suspecting their existence; but apply the requisite stimulus, and at a touch they are there in all their completeness, definite types of mentality... No account of universe in its totality can be final which leaves these other forms of consciousness quite disregarded. How to regard them is the question, — for they are so discontinuous with ordinary consciousness. Yet they may determine attitudes though they cannot furnish formulas, and open a region though they fail to give a map. At any rate, they forbid a premature closing of our accounts with reality. (p.388)

James was convinced of the existence of mystical moments as states of consciousness of an entirely specific quality that make a very deep impression on those who have had them. Sometimes this type of consciousness is called 'cosmic consciousness' – a term coined by Canadian psychiatrist R.M. Bucke, not simply an expansion of self-consciousness but rather the superaddition of a function that is very different from that the average person possesses. According to Bucke:

> The prime characteristic of cosmic consciousness is a consciousness of the cosmos, that is, of the life and order of the universe. Along with the consciousness of the cosmos there occurs an intellectual enlightenment which alone would place the individual on a new plane of existence – would make him almost a member of a new species. To this is added a state of moral exaltation, an indescribable feeling of elevation, elation, and joyousness, and a quickening of the moral sense, which is fully as striking, and more important than is the enhanced intellectual power.[16]

It was Dr Bucke's own experience of cosmic consciousness that led him to investigate it in others. Those who have ever experienced it do not need any proof of its existence, while those who are closed to these experiences would not believe it whatever proof has been provided to them.

Mystical experiences may occur spontaneously, for example:

> All at once, without warning of any kind, I found myself wrapped in a flame-colored cloud... Directly afterward there came upon me a sense of exultation, of immense joyousness accompanied or immediately followed by an intellectual illumination impossible to describe. Among other things, I did not merely come to believe, but I saw that the universe is not composed of dead matter, but is, on the contrary, a living Presence; I became conscious in myself of eternal life. It was not a conviction that I would have eternal life, but a consciousness that I possessed eternal life then; I saw that all men are immortal; that the cosmic order is such that without any peradventure all things work together for the good of each and all; that the foundation principle of the world, of all the worlds, is what we call love... The vision lasted a few seconds and was gone; but the memory of it and the sense of the reality of what it taught has remained during the quarter of a century which has since elapsed. I knew that what the vision showed was true... That view, that conviction, I may say that consciousness, has never, even during periods of the deepest depression, been lost.[17]

Though these experiences vary from individual to individual, their value leaves a very strong impression of being revelations of new depths of truth.[18]

> The kinds of truth communicable in mystical ways, whether these be sensible or supersensible, are various. Some of them relate to this world – visions of the future, the reading of hearts, the sudden understanding of texts, the knowledge of distant events, for example; but the most important revelations are theological or metaphysical. (James 1985, p.410)[19]

In the medical field (in the West) more often than not such experiences are classified as pathological but, as James remarks, 'Undoubtedly these pathological conditions have existed in many and possibly in all the cases, but that fact tells us nothing about the value for knowledge of the consciousness which they induce' (p.413).

Features of mystical experiences

Fenwick (2010) summarises commonly listed features characterising the main elements of mystical experiences that have been quoted in the mystical literature:

- feelings of unity
- feelings of objectivity and reality
- transcendence of space and time
- a sense of sacredness
- deeply felt positive mood (joy, blessedness, peace, bliss)
- containing paradox (mystical consciousness which is felt true despite a violation of logic)
- ineffability (when language is inadequate to express the experiences)
- transiency
- positive change in attitude or behaviour after the experience.

Spiritual emergency

Stanislav and Christina Grof coined the term 'spiritual emergency' to identify a variety of psychological difficulties, and to distinguish them from *spiritual emergence* (a gradual evolvement of spiritual potential).[20]

When a person experiences the extreme forms of the transliminal, his 'journey' can become dangerous. To illustrate a much more extreme state of mystical consciousness James cites the description by J.A. Symonds, who struggled to express it in words: the experience always came suddenly when he was relaxed (reading or at church, for example):

> I felt the approach of the mood. Irresistibly it took possession of my mind and will, lasted what seemed an eternity, and disappeared in a series of rapid sensations which resembled the awakening from anaesthetic influence... It consisted in a gradual but swiftly progressive obliteration of space, time, sensation, and the multitudinous factors of experience which seem to qualify what we...call our Self. In proportion as these conditions of ordinary consciousness were subtracted, the sense of an underlying or essential consciousness acquired intensely. At last nothing remained but a pure, absolute, abstract Self. The universe became without form and void of content. But Self persisted, formidable in its vivid keenness, feeling the most poignant doubt about reality, ready, as it seemed, to find existence break as breaks a bubble round about it. And what then? The apprehension of a coming dissolution, the grim conviction that this state of the conscious Self, the sense that I had followed the last thread of being to the verge of the abyss, and had arrived at demonstration of eternal Maya or illusion, stirred or seemed to stir me up again. The return to ordinary condition of sentient existence began by my first recovering the power of touch, and then by the gradual though rapid influx of familiar impressions and diurnal interests. At last I felt myself once more a human being; and though the riddle of what is meant by life remained unsolved, I was thankful for this return from the abyss... What would happen if the final stage of trance were reached? (James 1985, pp.385–386)

Types of spiritual emergencies

Several types of spiritual problems have been identified (Lukoff, Lu and Turner 1998):[21]

- *Loss of faith.*

- *Near-death experience:* the NDE is a subjective event experienced by persons who 'died' but were resuscitated and recover or by those who find themselves in a potentially fatal situation and escape uninjured. It usually includes dissociation from the physical body, strong positive affect and transcendental experiences. Typically, there is reported a characteristic temporal sequence of stages: peace and contentment, detachment from the physical body, entering a transitional region of darkness, seeing a brilliant light, then passing through the light into another realm of existence (Greyson 1983, 1997). Although a NDE typically brings positive personality transformations, significant intrapsychic and interpersonal difficulties may also arise (Greyson and Harris 1987).

- *Mystical experience:* Grof and Grof (1989) identify three major categories of the contents of these experiences: (1) the *biographical* category: experiences closely related to an individual's life history; (2) the *perinatal* category: experiences around issues of dying and being reborn;[22] (3) the *transpersonal* category: closely related to the Jungian collective unconscious, they involve images and motifs that have a source outside the individual's personal life history.

- *Kundalini:* according to the yogis, Kundalini is a form of creative cosmic energy, residing in a latent form at the base of the spine. It can be activated by meditation, special exercises or, sometimes, spontaneously. The 'awakening Kundalini' is a form of crisis, analogous to the descriptions of the awakening of the serpent power (or Kundalini) in historical Indian literature. The activated Kundalini works through the channels of the 'subtle body' (a field of non-physical energy in and around the body), clearing old traumatic imprints and opening the centres of psychic energy (chakras). The effects are physical (intense sensations of energy and heat arising up the spine accompanied with violent shaking, spasms and twisting movements) and psychological (powerful waves of seemingly unmotivated emotions, such as anxiety, anger, sadness or joy). Visions of bright light or various archetypical beings, internally perceived sounds or memories from past lives are also quite common (Grof and Grof 1989).

- *Shamanistic initiatory crisis:* the career of many shamans starts with an involuntary visionary episode, which anthropologists refer to as 'shamanic illness'. During this episode, the would-be shaman loses any contact with his environment and experiences inner journeys into 'the underworld and attacks by demons who expose [him] to incredible tortures and ordeals. These often result in experiences of death and dismemberment followed by rebirth and ascent to celestial regions' (Grof and Grof 1989, p.14).

- *Psychic opening*: an increase in intuitive abilities and perception of psychic or paranormal phenomena (precognition, telepathy, clairvoyance, etc.).

- *Past lives*: experiences of events taking place in other times and other countries, often associated with powerful emotions and physical sensations.

- *Possession*: feelings of one's psyche and body having been invaded and being controlled by a hostile entity.[23]

- *Meditation-related*, for example, altered perceptions that can be scary, and 'false enlightenment', bringing either delightful or terrifying visions (Epstein 1990).[24]

- *Separating from a spiritual teacher*: during the transition period from the 'culture of embeddedness' with their teachers into more independent functioning some might seek psychotherapeutic help (Bogart 1992).

- *Other spiritual problems*.

Grof and Grof (1989) also add to this list: episodes of unitive consciousness (peak experiences), psychological renewal through return to the centre, communications with spirit guides and 'channelling', experiences of close encounters with UFOs.

Grof and Grof (1989) identify various possible triggers of transformational crisis, including primarily physical factors (such as a disease, accident or operation, prolonged lack of sleep, childbirth or miscarriage); a powerful emotional experience (such as the death of a child or another close relative, loss of an important relationship) a serious of failures (at work or in a personal life); and, in predisposed individuals, the 'last straw' can be an experience with psychedelic drugs, a session of experiential psychotherapy, or deep involvement in various forms of meditation and spiritual practice.

Whether experiences are induced or spontaneous, the outcome of the shift from the 'normal' constructed reality to the unknown (subliminal/ transcendent) is unpredictable: it can go either way, and can lead to the 'dark night of the soul' or 'spiritual emergency' (a turn towards the dark and uncontrollable during a process of spiritual growth [spiritual emergence]) (Grof and Grof 1986, 1989). Huxley elaborates on two sides of visionary experiences in his essay *Heaven and Hell*: the visionary experience is not always blissful (heaven) and sometimes it can be terrible (hell). Both visionary heaven and visionary hell have preternatural light and its preternatural significance but the divine light can become burning, purgatorial fire, and significance can become appalling. Huxley illustrates his point with the example of Renee, a young girl with schizophrenia:

> For [Renee], the illumination is infernal – an intense electric glare without a shadow, ubiquitous and implacable. Everything that, for healthy visionaries, is a source of bliss, brings Renee only fear and a nightmarish sense of unreality... And then there is the horror of infinity. For the healthy visionary, the perception of the infinite in a finite particular is a revelation of the divine immanence; for Renee, it was a revelation of what she calls 'the Systems,' the vast cosmic mechanism which exists only to grind out guilt and punishment, solitude and unreality. (Huxley 2004b, pp.88–89)

Huxley points out another difference in 'heaven versus hell' experiences, which is the bodily sensations: while blissful experiences are associated with a sense of separation from the body and a feeling of deindividualisation and connectedness to the universe, during the 'hell experience' the world becomes transfigured for the worse, individualisation is intensified and the connection with the body grows 'progressively more dense, more tightly packed', until the person finds him- or herself 'reduced to being the agonized consciousness of an inspissated lump of matter, no bigger than a stone that can be held between the hands' (Huxley 2004b, p.90).[25]

The dark side of this sort of experience is well recognised in the communities of meditation and prayer, and wisdom has been accumulated to teach how to use it in a positive and balanced manner. 'The technology has been developed for managing the dark side of the transliminal: uncontrollable, terrifying states in which the individual can become lost in madness. Nevertheless, there are no absolute guarantees.' These various traditions emphasise different aspects of such experiences. Some see a mystical experience as a means to the end, while others seek it for its own sake, and devote their lives to this way of experiencing; 'to relationship with God, or however they conceptualise the ultimate within their tradition' (Clarke 2008, p.53). Clarke cites St John who introduced the concept of 'the dark night of the soul': 'This dark night of the soul is an inflow of God into the soul that purges it of its habitual ignorance and imperfections... God teaches the soul secretly and instructs it in the perfection of love. The experience of divine love is so overwhelming that the contrast with human imperfection is almost unbearably painful' (p.60).

According to Clarke, there are a number of factors that can determine which way it goes, including: (1) the strength of the individual to withstand the onslaught of a full transliminal experience without fragmenting, and (2) the context (for example, under spiritual guidance). Depending on the outcome, some emerge deeper and wiser, while others lose their way, with their sense of self fragmented, still others may stay in the transliminal for the rest of their life (Clarke 2008). For some, the mood they are in can be reflected in how they perceive their environment, for instance:

> [O]n Sundays I attended the service in the chapel. One day, in the middle of the sermon, I suddenly had the impression that the ceiling was caving in. it wasn't an entirely new sensation to me, as I often felt uneasy in tall or crowded buildings, but this time it felt so overwhelming that I had to run out. Usually, under the open sky I felt better, but on that morning the fear of being hit by the chapel ceiling was just replaced by the fear of being hit by a tree. Then it wasn't the hitting any longer, but the feeling of my flesh rotting and my hair falling out. Had there been a nuclear disaster somewhere and a poisonous cloud was descending on us? I looked around, but the other people seemed as unconcerned as ever. (Kammer 2007, pp.78–79)

Spiritual experiences in autism

Some people may never have transcendent/subliminal experiences, while others are more susceptible to them. And, of course, there are those who are more prone to these experiences because of their differences in perceiving and processing information, for example, people with psychosis (Clarke 2010),[26] schizophrenia,[27] individuals with ASD and some other conditions in which 'connectedness' is felt much stronger than in the 'normal' population.

What are the factors that allow the person to achieve spiritual experiences more easily, and what are the features of spirituality experienced in autism?[28]

Several features of spirituality have been identified in children.[29] However, nurturing spirituality in children implies helping them remember the experiences of early childhood, before they were conditioned out of them by cultural traditions; these newly discovered spiritual views are incorporated into the cultural worldview with the cognitive framework firmly in place, whereas in such conditions as autism, the conditioning does not work most of the time.[30]

Expanding the filtering model,[31] we may formulate a hypothesis to account for unconventional experiences in autism. The absence of filters (physical/bodily, sensory, cognitive, linguistic, cultural) may result in delayed embodiment of self.

The reality of out of body experience (OBE) is accepted (at least by some researchers). What is important in this phenomenon is that the person experiencing it can actually see his body and perceive what is going on around him (other people talking, etc.); he does not use his physical senses to perceive it. The best explanation so far is provided by Donna Williams, who has introduced the term 'shadow senses' that let the person perceive (see, hear, feel, etc.) without using the physical senses:

> It was as though some part of 'me', of my 'be-ing' could see without my eyes, hear without my ears, touch without my hands and feel bodily without my body making direct physical contact. It was as though 'I' had two sets of senses, the physical ones, and non-physical ones. (Williams 1998, pp.36–37)

Donna speculates that it is possible to experience 'me' outside of oneself – not by appearance or its physical substance – while not experiencing your own appearance or physical substance: the energy bound up in these physical forms can be experienced beyond them because this energy can escape the boundaries and experience other energies beyond their boundaries (Williams 1998). She describes this phenomenon in the context of self-development: from selfless self (when the experience simply happens) through merging and resonating with the environment (no self, no other – which does not require the use of body – the 'oneness with the world'; the state, 'though mindless, is the place where the soul is in its purest state' before the 'mind filters'), through a fluctuating state of all self, no other; all other, no self (using the body as a tool of resonance), to using the body as a tool of sensory exploration and body as self, to simultaneous self and other. In 'normal' development the moving from the 'boundaryless realm…[and] away from the 'God' in all things…begins…in the first weeks or months of life and most begin to leave it for the next phase – that of simultaneous self and other – between around two and five years old', while some autistic individuals are late moving out of the phase of no self, no other, 'identifying self too strongly with the system of all self, no other; all other, no self, mastering its mechanics, its strategies and adaptations for navigation in a world based on simultaneous self-other' (Williams 1998, p.28).

Donna hypothesises that we are born into our bodies before being born into the world, and develop a perceptual sense of body connectedness even before we are born, with the senses becoming physically based. But there are those (whom Williams terms 'being born unborn' or 'born only partially born')[32] who have not got fully into their bodies and 'may still be "there" in some earlier form… Perhaps babies who become children and adults who don't use their functional physically-based senses, may still be using non-physical senses from an earlier developmental stage.' These born unborn people either outgrow this at least to some extent or 'are called late developers or people with developmental differences or even developmentally disabled' (Williams 1998, p.52).

Bill Stillman also speculates that:

> some with autism have not fully integrated with their bodies and this results in some compensation – creating a special alignment with their subconscious mind or spiritual selves. This aptitude for accessing a non-ending stream of consciousness may cause division with the physical body, a neurological motor-and-spatial disconnect… Because of this shift in orientation, those with autism may hold capacity for spiritual connectedness, heightened awareness, and exquisite sensitivity beyond what is considered typical. These abilities are gifts and blessings. (Stillman 2006, p.18)

Quite a few other autistic individuals have commented on problems they experience in connection with their bodies, for example:

> The boy refused to accept the existence of his body, and imagined himself to be a spirit… The main difficulty was that the boy was losing control over his body. A sense denying its existence was so strong, that he could not respond to a situation the way it should be done. [His mother wondered why he did not make any fuss when

he got hurt.] The boy wondered too. 'But how should I make a fuss? I am the spirit, and above the reach of all pains – a free being,' thought he. (Mukhopadhyay 2000, p.17)

Some autistic people experience severe problems with body boundaries. Jim Sinclair reports that sometimes he cannot find his body. Others, if they cannot see their legs, do not know where they are (Grandin 2006).

Features of spiritual experiences

Most reported features of 'autistic spirituality' are: experiencing 'true self', 'simply being'; OBEs; heightened awareness, including what is beyond 'normal' perception; visions; acute appreciation of nature; connectedness: resonance and merging; special connection with animals; empathy to people (feeling with); so-called 'psychic abilities'.

'SIMPLY BEING'

Donna Williams saw 'Her World' (or 'simply be') as a place of richness and beauty where language was not through words. 'Her World' outside of 'simply be' was a place where the only state of security she could achieve was through non-existence. 'The system of "simply be" was a way to experience the self you normally are deaf, blind, and dead to in the world' (Williams 1999b, p.176). Further, Donna hypothesises that some autistic individuals had their own worlds but they had either never known the addictive beauty and peace of 'simply be' or else they had lost it too long ago to remember.

When she was a young child Gunilla Gerland often retreated into her own world – simply being. She used to sit in the garden, staring at a flower or a leaf, completely absorbed in them; feeling just being at the moment, with nothing else happening. When she was upset with something Gunilla found the place to be left in peace – behind the armchair, where she was able to shut out everything and simply be – absorbed in the material of the brown armchair (Gerland 1997).

OBE

There have been many accounts of autistic individuals who are able to 'leave their body behind' and travel at will. These are just a few examples:

The OBE-experience was awesome, but more important was the realisation that Self is not an individual entity. We are all part of consciousness, we are the experience consciousness is having, we are all one. (Diny, personal communication, 2012)

We are independent and frolic as our free will inclines when we leave our bodies behind. When we are in the body suit, our independence is fettered and we must rely on the duties of others to trudge through living... I am more detached from my body than most folk. I leave it often – always have. (Rentenbach 2009, pp.44, 45)

[Once] I visited [in an OBE] my friend but found myself in a different house. I moved from room to room and found what felt like her room. When I saw her again she told me she'd moved house and I told her I knew... I described the house and the layout of the rooms and my description had been precisely in accordance with where the family had moved. (Williams 1998, p.35)

Heightened awareness, including what is beyond 'normal' perception

People with highly hypersensitive vision can actually...see positively charged air particles which look like minute silvery sparks in the surrounding air. (Williams 1998, p.94)

Autistic individuals experience their environment intensely, with heightened sensations. They can appreciate sensory information much more deeply and acutely than the 'normal' population. Their hypersensitivity is well known, but there have also been reports that some of them are able to perceive what is beyond not only 'normal' but also heightened perception.

Having read some accounts of those who experimented with drugs (including Huxley's 'Doors of Perception') I suddenly realised that I have always experienced my environment like them – as if I had been on drugs all my life. I hadn't got a clue that others couldn't see vibrating colours, blurred boundaries around things, and intoxicating brilliance of 'stars' and shapes floating freely in the air. (Nick P., personal communication)

Very few researchers admit that some individuals are able to perceive what is considered 'beyond the reality we know', and many interpret their accounts as hallucinations. However, if we are prepared to assume that it is possible, then research on Charles Bonnet syndrome[33] and sensory deprivation[34] can shed some light and let us look for other possible explanations of these phenomena.

Research on sensory deprivation[35] reveals that lack of sensory input can result in 'altered states of consciousness', hallucinations and acuteness of the senses after the experiments. In his fascinating book *Hallucinations* (2012), Oliver Sacks explains that the deprivation of normal visual input, for example, can stimulate the inner eye instead, producing dreams, vivid imaginings or hallucinations. The hallucinations seem external, with little relevance or reference to the individual or situation and arouse little, if any, emotion. None of the participants in an experiment had any voluntary control over their hallucinations, which seemed to exist independently. Very similar phenomena have been reported in patients with Charles Bonnet syndrome.

Sireteanu and colleagues (2008) report an fMRI study of a visual artist who was blindfolded for 22 days and underwent several sessions in an fMRI machine, where she reported the exact time when her hallucinations started and ended; she was also asked to imagine her hallucinations using her ability to produce powerful visual imagery. It turned out that during hallucinations the activations were recorded in the occipital cortex and in the inferotemporal cortex, whereas during the sessions of voluntary visual imagery, there was activation in the executive areas of the brain, in the prefrontal cortex, that is, areas that had been relatively inactive when she was hallucinating. This shows that at a physiological level visual imagery and hallucinations are radically different: the former is the result of a top-down process, while the latter is caused by a direct bottom-up activation of regions in the ventral visual pathway which become hyperexcitable due to a lack of sensory input.

Can we draw a parallel between the explanation of the 'inner eye' (Sacks 2012) and 'shadow senses' (Williams 1998)? There are many things we cannot explain yet but, for those who experience them, they are very real. The interpretation of 'strange happenings' depends on the person's 'framework of mind'. This is just one example that can be interpreted differently by different individuals, but for those who were involved it felt very real: when a child, Donna had a friend Robin. One afternoon the girls were sitting beneath a tree; it was getting darker.

Donna saw a man approaching them, who stopped at a distance and waved. Robin could not see anyone, so Donna described his appearance and the clothes he was wearing. The description was unmistakable – it was Robin's grandfather. He died three days later (Williams 1999a).

VISIONS

> On the morning of my baptism I had a vision while I was praying. I was looking into a deep dark hole, when suddenly out of nowhere a huge stone was rolled over it to seal it up. Without being told, I knew that it was a symbol for God sealing the 'black hole' of fears and compulsive thoughts which haunted me so much at day and night. A great relief swept through me so much and yet, at the same time I somehow knew that one day the hole had to open again to let me face and come to terms with what lay at the bottom. (Kammer 2007, p.68)

It is easy to assume that all 'visions' and 'voices' are hallucinations, but they can be interpreted as 'waking (symbolic) dreams' – when the universe 'communicates' with a person who feels (senses) and interprets whatever is there (call it energy, vibrations or anything else) in his or her 'language' – enveloping the information in either symbolic or concrete images. It is possible that this information comes from within rather than without, but then we need to explain what is known as 'premonitions' – when a person 'sees' or 'is told' about future events. This phenomenon is much more common than was previously thought, but there is (understandable) reluctance to share it. From my experience, very few autistic individuals are prepared to talk about such experiences in public. For example, a woman with Asperger syndrome (M.P.) told me about the experience that shook her to the core and is still vivid in her memory after nearly 30 years:

> I was 28 when I started having a recurring dream – but I don't know how to describe it, because it was 'dream of feelings' – no words, no images, just feelings, and they were very disturbing. The first time it happened, I dismissed it as a nightmare (though I could not explain what it was about), but when the same dream returned three or four times a week for two months it really freaked me out. I *knew* something bad was happening, but I had no idea what and where. As I lived far from my family, my first thought was that something

bad was happening at home, so I started calling them three–four times a week. Both of my parents were bewildered by my calls with my first question 'Is everything OK?' Each time they assured me that 'everything *was* OK, why are you asking?' What would they think of me if I'd told them I was 'seeing a bad feeling' in my dream? So the answer was 'I'm missing you.' The night I was nearly suffocated by the 'feeling' in my dream the phone rang – my father was taken to hospital, operated on but the doctor said they could do nothing, it was too late – bowel cancer. I rushed home to help and my mother and I made sure he wasn't alone and spent most days in hospital. It was the beginning of June, when I saw a dream of my father sitting on the settee in the living room, quietly smiling at me. It was like watching the movie – with my father on the screen. And then I heard a voice 'He will die on the 17th of June.' When my mother came from the hospital in the morning, crying – 'He is leaving us, he won't survive another night.' I was adamant – 'No! He will die on the 17th.'... My father lived for 10 more days and died on the 17th. (M.P., personal communication)

M.P. has had more visions and was given more information about her family and friends; it was happening in her dreams. She does not like to talk about it.

Many (and I do mean many) parents of autistic children (especially with severe autism) have confessed to me about their visions related to their children: usually they were positive, giving them reassuring messages about their loved ones. They also told me about their suspicion that their children are 'visited' by (interpretations were different but the general meaning was) their guardian angels.

APPRECIATION OF NATURE

James (1985) notes that certain aspects of nature seem to have a peculiar power of awakening mystical moods and experiences. Because of the acuteness of the senses, many autistic individuals are fascinated by nature. For example, Wendy Lawson (1998) could not understand the apparent apathy of others to the rich intensity and feelings in colours and the beauty of plants. She could watch a nectarine growing on the tree for hours – a miracle that never ceased to amaze her.

I could sit for hours on the beach [studying for hours] each grain of sand as it flowed between my fingers… As I scrutinized their shapes and contours, I went into a trance… (Grandin 2006, p.44)

I was fascinated by [a ladybird], so sat down on the pavement and watched it closely as it climbed over and under the sides of each small leaf and branch, stopping and starting and stopping again at various point along its journey. Its small back was round and shiny and I counted dots over and over…at the time I did not think of anything but the ladybird in front of me. (Tammet 2006, p.70)

CONNECTEDNESS

Individualism, so valued in Western cultures, is, in fact, an illusion. The philosopher Alfred N. Whitehead criticised the notion of independent existence because everything and everybody are interconnected and, for any single entity to be understood, it should be seen as interwoven with the rest of the universe.[36]

RESONANCE

Some autistic individuals seem to be able to surpass the most 'skilled normal' people in resonating with their surroundings. They seem to have an inner sense of things.[37] Those who experience this state can be 'in resonance' with colours, sounds, objects, places, plants, animals, people. For example:

I could resonate with the cat and spent hours lying in front of it, making no physical contact with it. I could resonate with the tree in the park and feel myself merge with its size, its stability, its calm and its flow. (Williams 1998, p.44)

When I see or think about the wind, I am the wind. I see flying leaves around me, as I hear a powerful wuthering noise, which can invite those dark pirate clouds to fly and fight each other for territorial expansion across the sky… How do I perceive it? I do not need to perceive that because I am that when I think of that. Alive and all-powerful. (Mukhopadhyay 2008, p.118)

MERGING WITH THE ENVIRONMENT — DISSOLVING SELF

Connectedness may result in merging with the environment and becoming 'being Not-self', a simultaneous experience of dissolving self (losing any individuality) into the surroundings, that is 'being one with the universe'. Aldous Huxley provided numerous examples of this state or experience, when everything looked 'miraculous' (including trivial objects), and time disappears when the person experiencing it loses his or her self, bringing an extraordinary transformation in one's views and attitudes to life in general:

> This participation in the manifest glory of things left no room, so to speak, for the ordinary, the necessary concerns of human existence... I was now Not-self, simultaneously perceiving and being the Not-self of the things around me. To this new-born Not-self, the behaviour, the appearance, the very thought of the self it had momentarily ceased to be, and of other selves, its one-time fellows, seemed...enormously irrelevant. (Huxley 2004a, p.20)

This is the feeling that is close to what Bergson calls 'intellectual sympathy'. Because of their different route of development and greater 'openness' to the environment (lack of filters), for some autistic individuals (especially those who are skilled in 'resonating with their surroundings') 'losing oneself' and dissolving into the environment can be a common experience. For example:

> I would resonate with the sensory nature of the object with such an absolute purity and loss of self that it was like an overwhelming passion into which you merge and become part of beauty itself. (Williams 1998, p.15)

> When I was about ten years old I used to have a certain colour billiard ball – a pink one. I used to spend around an hour with it before I could reach the point of resonance with it where I would merge with the colour. To anyone else this would have looked like someone 'psychotic' but if they'd known the physical alteration felt in that moment of becoming one with a colour some people would perhaps see it as far less crazy than other ways many people may have spent an hour of their lives at the same age. (Williams 1998, p.22)

> [The] street lights were yellow with a hint of pink but in a buzz state they were an intoxicating iridescent-like pink-yellow. My mind

dived deeper and deeper into the colour, trying to feel its nature and become it as I progressively lost sense of self in its overwhelming presence. Each of the colours resonated different feelings within me and it was like they played me as a chord, where other colours played one note at a time. (Williams 1999a, p.19)

The experiences of 'oneness' with the world are comparable to spiritual or religious feelings:

[Once, working in a slaughterhouse]…my religious feelings were renewed… I felt totally at one with the universe as I kept the animals completely calm while the rabbi performed shehita. Operating the equipment there was like being in a Zen meditation state. Time stood still, and I was totally, completely disconnected from reality… It was a feeling of total calmness and peace… The experience had been… strangely hypnotic… I thought about the similarities between the wonderful trancelike feeling I had had while gently holding the cattle in the chute and the spaced-out feeling I had had as a child when concentrating on dribbling sand through my fingers on the beach. During both experiences all other sensation was blocked… Maybe the monks who chant and mediate are kind of autistic. I have observed that there is a great similarity between certain chanting and praying rituals and the rocking of an autistic child. I feel there has to be more to this than just getting high on my endorphins… When the animal remained completely calm I felt an overwhelming feeling of peacefulness, as if God had touched me… As the life force left the animal, I had been completely overwhelmed with feelings I did not know I had. (Grandin 2006, pp.204–205)

There is no deeper experience than the total encapsulation of self within an experience until one is indistinguishable from the experience. It is like knowing 'God'. (Williams 1998, p.58)

The experiences achieved during meditation are similar to the experiences which are natural to some autistic people, for example:

People think of reality as some sort of guarantee they can rely on. Yet from the earliest age I can remember I found my only dependable security in losing all awareness of the things usually considered real. In doing this, I was able to lose all sense of self. Yet this is the strategy said to be the highest stage of meditation, indulged in to achieve inner peace and tranquillity. Why should it not be interpreted as such for autistic people? (Williams 1999a, p.178)

According to Culliford, the calm mind (for instance, in meditative tranquillity) has capabilities not only of self-healing but also such 'higher powers' as creativity and intuition, and even (in some cases) more extreme and subtle capacities, like the healing of others, telepathy and clairvoyance. Culliford admits that many are sceptical about these abilities and prefer to ignore the limited but still available research evidence, but for those who have experienced them, it is not about understanding the mystery but rather it is about living it. They describe it like a breakthrough, like a 'Wow!' experience of pure amazement. Culliford warns, however, that not all such amazing experiences will be an authentic breakthrough from mundane to cosmic reality; besides, at such moments, the ego is absent – so no one seems to *have* the experience, but, instead, the experience 'has itself through us', and it is difficult (if not impossible) to explain to anyone who has not experienced it; and, last, the experience does not last long, with ego-mind beginning to reassert itself within minutes (sometimes, within seconds). Yet in authentic cases even a few seconds' experience is enough:

> You have caught a blissful glimpse of non-duality, of infinity and wholeness at the same time, in other words of perfection. You have felt the inexhaustible energy of the universe, the pure wind, the gentle breath, the loving spirit of the cosmos, and are bound forever to identify with that, rather than anything less complete... You may acknowledge it as a blessing; for, in this life-changing moment, you will have found and become your true self. (Culliford 2007, p.168)

Individuals with autistic personality feel equally strong connectedness to objects, animals and people.

EMPATHY WITH OBJECTS

Some individuals with autism treat objects as if they were alive: their empathy embraces everything, and some may cry if a toy or an object 'gets hurt'. Intellectually, they do understand that objects are not alive, but it does not change their emotional connectedness to them.

When her little brother threw away one of his soft toys, an elephant with a damaged ear, and their mother rescued it, Elkie Kammer offered to take care of it because she felt such deep empathy for this toy that she could actually hear it cry. All children of a certain age relate to their toys in this way, identifying with their perceived feelings. But there is a difference – Kammer has never grown out of it:

> The problem for which I could never find a satisfactory answer was the perception of feelings and thoughts in the objects around me. The bench in the park would smile at me when I approached it and began to cry if I didn't sit down for a minute. The tree was waving its branches as a welcome and couldn't understand why I jogged past instead of climbing up. They all wanted to be acknowledged and valued and involved in my daily routine. It had more or less always been like that. The objects around me had always been alive to me, enriching my lonely world while at the same time exhausting me with their demands. There wasn't an onset of this 'mental abnormality'. I simply hadn't developed past the stage in which it was seen as normal (the pre-realistic phase or mystical age, according to Piaget). (Kammer 2007, pp.80–81)

SPECIAL CONNECTION WITH ANIMALS

Some autistic children and adults develop very special connectedness with animals:

> Earthworms were one of my great delights and I developed a... passion for them. I fondled them and kissed them. I dug them up in the garden and cautiously patted them. (Gerland 1997, p.36)

> I loved our cat (Knatte)... Love in the cat way, a love with one's integrity maintained, suited me very well. (Gerland 1997, p.37)

> Arthos, the Hungarian sheepdog, became my most important friend. He made up for the human friends I did not have and especially for the lack of physical contact. While it was often even too much for me to shake hands with people without feeling 'burned', I enjoyed hugging Arthos, being licked all over and rolling around in the grass with him. Somehow his clumsy movements and his fluffy fur didn't feel threatening to me like human touch. (Kammer 2007, p.22)

> I have a sensory empathy for the cattle. When they remain calm I feel calm, and when something goes wrong that causes pain, I also feel pain. I tune in to what the actual sensations are like to the cattle rather than having the idea of death rile up my emotions. My goal

is to reduce suffering and improve the way farm animals are treated. (Grandin 2006, p.94)

EMPATHY TO PEOPLE (FEELING WITH)

People often pretend to be something they are not – for the sake of politeness, perhaps. Some autistic people can sense the real nature, and not just 'appearances'. Despite the assumption that autistic individuals do not understand non-verbal communication (like body language, for example), they develop an acute sensitivity to subtle cues people unintentionally (and nonconsciously) emit – this is often referred to as subliminal non-verbal communication, and many autistic people are very good at it. For example, Tito physically felt the attitudes of the people around him:

> Personally I am…sensitive to the attitudes of the people. When I know that someone is watching me with curiosity, I feel uneasy. My body reacts to it immediately. I become hyperactive and flap my hands to release some of the stress… I have a special instinct which allows me to know where I shall be welcomed. Till now, I have never went wrong. (Mukhopadhyay 2000, p.66)

Some autistic individuals find it hard to distinguish between what is their own and what is others' experiences. Stephen Shore (n.d), an adult with Asperger syndrome, calls this phenomenon 'echoemotica', or taking on other people's moods and emotions and not being able to separate them from his own. The experience can be very overwhelming and often quite scary – trying to figure out what the individual is feeling him- or herself and what is someone else's emotional load.

Donna Williams (1998, p.94) hypothesises that:

> mood changes one's own energy field as can changes in the state of consciousness and proximity to another person (and I would say this can be physical or sometimes even spiritual 'proximity' or relatedness). This can have an effect on the energy field of others, whether a room, a creature, a material, object or person.'[38]

PSYCHIC ABILITY, TELEPATHY

Referring to telepathy, the philosopher Bergson hypothesised that people are far less definitely cut off from each other, soul from soul, than they are body from body. He believed that human consciousness is partially independent of the human brain, and that it was probable, or at least possible, that a subtle and subconscious influence of soul to soul was constantly taking place, which was unnoticeable to active consciousness. He argues that:

> our ignorance does not entitle us to say what may be natural or not. If telepathy does not square at all well with our preconceived notions, it may be more true that our preconceived notions are false than telepathy is fictitious… We must overcome this prejudice and seek to make others set it aside. Telepathy and sub-conscious mental life combine to make us realize the wonder of the soul. It is not special, it is spiritual.[39]

At first sight, this statement sounds unscientific and just plain impossible. However, recent research seems to catch up with many 'impossible explanations' of the past. For many centuries, for example, those who talked to plants have been ridiculed, because everyone *knew* that plants could not feel, see, hear, or understand and communicate with each other. In 1973, South African botanist Lyall Watson (1974) claimed that plants had 'emotions' that could be recorded on a lie detector test. For many years, Prince Charles has been mocked for his confession that he talked to the flowers while gardening. And in the last decade results of research studies have been published showing that (if translated into human concepts) plants can 'smell' (chemicals in the air) 'taste' (chemicals in the soil), 'see' (respond to) light, 'hear' sounds (vibrations), 'sense' neighbouring plants and even 'communicate' to them about dangers. For example, Daniel Robert, a biology professor at Bristol University, reported that plants produce frequent little clicks to communicate between their roots; researchers at Western Australia University (Gagliano, Mancuso and Robert 2012) found cabbage plants emitted a volatile gas to warn others of dangers such as caterpillars or garden shears, providing solid evidence that plants have their own 'language' of smells and sounds to communicate. In the article Gagliano said the research opens up a new debate on the perception and action of people towards plants which are not objects but should perhaps be treated as living beings in their own right. It makes sense for plants to produce and respond to sound vibrations, as it gives them information about the environment around them. She hypothesises that sound waves can travel easily through soil and she suggests it could be a way of picking up threats, such as drought, from their neighbours further away. It is possible that certain types of sound wave interfere with the normal behaviour of plant genes. Scientists from South Korea's National Institute of Agricultural Biotechnology (Jeong *et al.* 2008) propose that two genes (which are involved in a plant's response to light) are turned on by music at 70 decibels. The higher the frequency of the sound, the more active is the gene response. With more research, more scientific explanations will be found for 'unscientific and impossible' phenomena.

Even water is said to react to stimuli, including human thoughts and emotions: experiments by Japanese researcher Masaru Emoto show that positive thoughts can change the molecular structure of the world around us. His theory reveals how water is deeply connected to our individual and collective consciousness. In his book *The Hidden Messages in Water* (2005), Emoto describes the ability of water to absorb, hold and even retransmit human feelings and emotions. He found that crystals formed in frozen water reveal changes when specific, concentrated thoughts are directed toward them. Emoto hypothesises that, since water has the ability to receive a wide range of frequencies, it can also reflect the universe in this manner.

In his book *Earthquakes and Animals* (2004) Ikeya meticulously describes the simple laboratory evidence of the behaviour of animals, plants and objects when they are subjected to intense electromagnetic pulses of the kind created by rocks under stress before an earthquake. It turns out that in many cases they behave in ways that have been recorded for centuries – and are still reported today – as earthquake-related. Ikeya's work demonstrates, using many experiments, that the old earthquake legends are, in fact, describing natural phenomena.

So if plants and animals can be 'psychic', why do we deny similar abilities in humans? Even if we cannot explain them yet, they should be taken seriously. In the context of 'feeling plants', those who maintain the ability to 'fantasise' about them as equally important beings, in fact, are responding to their interaction. The reason we find it childish and dismiss it as anthropomorphising is that the only language available to describe this connection is restricted to words we use in relation to humans. If there existed more exact terms to label these experiences, they could be taken more seriously. But before we can create new terminology we should understand the phenomena we want to name. Alas, at present we do not know much about them, so the best we can do is to admit our ignorance and look for ways to learn more. If we had known the processes and mechanisms involved in subliminal interaction and the interconnectedness of everything, we could have replaced anthropomorphic terminology in the example below, then the whole meaning of the experience described by Kammer would have been different:

> And sometimes, when there was nothing to distract myself with, I would hear the plants or the tools talk to me. I didn't hear them with my ears. I rather perceived their message without sounds or gestures. I knew what they were thinking and feeling and what they wanted to communicate to me. They were like the little elephant that my brother had rejected and which I rescued out of compassion. Sometimes they just smiled at me or thanked me for watering and feeding them... Some of the larger trees wanted me to pat them and greet them. If I forgot, they would cry in despair. If I remembered, they were happy... Part of me knew, of course, that plants and tools and other objects couldn't possibly have thoughts and feelings like that, but at the same time their cries were so clear that ignoring them felt impossible. Perhaps I can compare it to a 5-year-old giving a tea party to her dolls and teddies. If one is missed out, she will surely hear it cry. How do you grow out of this? Perhaps it's just one area in which my mind stopped developing. (Kammer 2007, pp.56–57)

Some introduce their own terms and religious references to describe their experience in a way 'normal' people can understand. For example, Donna Williams remembers 'the drug-like addictive effect' of resonating or merging with objects. She recalls such experiences as 'merging with God' because she would:

> resonate with the sensory nature of the object with such an absolute purity and loss of self that it was like an overwhelming passion into which you merge and become part of the beauty itself. It was the ultimate in belonging and 'company'. (Williams 1998, p.15)

We teach autistic children and adults to understand theory of (our) mind and educate them about (our) world. However, we can learn a lot from them about the spiritual dimension, and about the diverse world they live in.

> Autistic and other meditative types travel light. We carry nothing. Only our essence wisps through space/time, enjoying and truly living... We are independent and frolic as our free will inclines when

we leave our bodies behind… Capering in the infinite ethereal zones is so captivating that I have only recently decided to reside there part time. I used to think of the limitless adventures, otherworldly experiences, and indescribable beauty accessed through this portal as my autistic dacha – my rules, my universe. I now think less egocentrically and believe my autism only made it easier for me to get a passport. Like when applying to be a disciple to follow Jesus… (Rentenbach 2009, pp.44, 45)

In his book *Love, Healing and Happiness* (2007) Culliford enumerates several spiritual principles that are universally beneficial for all human beings. The first is that personal growth often depends on experiencing a period of adversity and distress. It is when people face great loss, for instance, that they appreciate much more what they actually have, and re-evaluate their values and priorities. As a result, they experience a revitalised sense of meaning and purpose, often accompanied by a renewed sense of belonging to their family, community and humanity in general. Some call it a kind of a gift that is both precious and long lasting. The second principle is reciprocity, when both a giver and receiver benefit in spiritual terms. Spiritual values that are beneficial for everyone are kindness, tolerance, patience, perseverance and honesty. The reciprocity principle in action is when people repay respect with respect and affection with affection.

Spirituality underlies morality and ethics and one of the important principles of spirituality is *reciprocity*, the basis of the golden rule, *to do as you would be done by* (Culliford 2007), or what goes around, comes around. According to this principle, harming others will bring harm to yourself or is harming yourself, and helping others will benefit you as well. Thus helping others can be seen as both a spiritual practice and a moral principle.

Notes

1. Another valuable feature of his report is that his approach is realistic (he was certain that he would never know what it felt like to be someone else but he wanted some approximation to what it might be like for someone with 'unrestricted' perception to experience it from inside), not blinded by the bias of what he expected but open to any unexpected phenomena (or lack of them).

2. Snyder and colleagues interpret autism as a delayed acquisition of concepts; see Snyder 1997; Snyder, Bossomaier and Mitchell 2004; Snyder and Mitchell 1999; Snyder *et al.* 2003.

3. On the other hand, some psychiatric treatments (for example, hypnotherapy and psychotherapy) produce a trance-like state when patients are encouraged to release supressed emotions, resulting in a cathartic shaking of the body and 'cleaning tears'.

4. The processes of treating 'out of balance' winds or forces are complicated by the fact that mediators working directly with *lung*, for example, can themselves easily fall into states of serious imbalance, so, in Tibetan Buddhist practice, the role of the spiritual teacher (*lama*) is of paramount importance (Samuel 2009).

5. See, for example, Allman *et al.* 1992; Hood 1974; Lukoff and Lu 1988.

6. Durkheim (1976) called the phenomenon 'social effervescence'.

7. The participants wore what is known as the 'Koren helmet' – sometimes called the 'God helmet' – which generated very weak fluctuating magnetic fields.

8. The theoretical basis for the God helmet, especially the connection between temporal function and mystic experiences, has also been questioned (Aaen-Stockdale 2012).

9. The mind's templates restrict the observer, similar to the language that 'shapes' what we can see.

10. Dawkins has written several books expressing his views, one of them with the telling title *The God Delusion* (2006).

11. Cited in Khamsi 2004.

12. These experiences are very common in autism – see, for example, Grandin 2006; Lawson 1998; Williams 1999a, b, c.

13. Koan is a paradoxical riddle without a solution, used in Zen Buddhism to demonstrate the inadequacy of logical reasoning and provoke enlightenment.

14. Cf. some modern 'Christian politicians', consulting 'God' about the decision to start a war, inflicting suffering on thousands of people, with 'consultation' taking place in a luxurious apartment.

15. Cited in James 1985, p.384.

16. Cited in James 1985, p.398.

17. Cited in James 1985, p.399.

18. The experiences resulting in achieving a shift in consciousness have been methodically cultivated as elements of the religious life, for instance, in India, yoga based on exercise, the diet, posture, breathing, intellectual concentration, moral discipline; Buddhism; Hinduism – training in achieving higher stages of contemplation; in the Christian church – 'orison' or meditation, the methodological elevation of the soul towards God.

19. James poses a question: 'Do mystical experiences establish the truth of those theological affections in which the saintly life has its roots?' (1985, p.415). In James' opinion, it is possible to interpret the outcome of the majority of them in terms of two philosophical directions – optimism and monism: 'We pass into mystical states from out of ordinary consciousness as from a less into a more, as from a smallness into a vastness, and at the same time as from an unrest to a rest. We feel them as reconciling, unifying states. They appeal to the yes-function more than to the no-function in us' (p.416).

20. Benedictine monk, Brother David Steindl-Rast, describes the process of spiritual emergence as 'a kind of birth pang in which you yourself go through to a fuller life, a deeper life, in which some areas in your life that were not yet encompassed

by this fullness of life are now integrated or called to be integrated or challenged to be integrated' (cited in Bragdon 1994, p.18).

21. 'Religious or Spiritual Conflict' was introduced as a new diagnostic category (Code V62.89) in the DSM-IV in 1994. The acceptance of this category in DSM shows the importance of recognising the occurrence of forms of distress associated with spiritual experiences and of increasing the competence of mental health professionals with regard to such spiritual issues. The DSM-IV emphasises the need to distinguish between psychopathology and meditation-related experiences: 'Voluntarily induced experiences of depersonalization or derealization form part of meditative and trance practices that are prevalent in many religions and cultures and should not be confused with Depersonalization Disorder' (p.488).

22. According to Grof and Grof, the perinatal level of the mind represents the interface between the individual and the collective unconscious.

23. Using 'the two logics' approach (that of 'either-or' and that of 'both-and') to look at the same phenomenon, Clarke (2008, p.23) gives examples in the context of psychosis, when people 'who have crossed the boundary into what is popularly known as madness…[psychosis] frequently report the experience of being possessed by another person or being'. (This experience is also associated with some religions and is interpreted differently in different cultures.) From her extensive clinical experience, working with people with these sorts of problems, Clarke explored and discussed with these individuals links between their particular possession experience and traumatic events in their lives. At the same time, she does not rule out the idea of possession, as she believes that 'there is enough evidence that the contents of minds can transfer from one person to another to take this possibility seriously'. Following a model of the organisation of thinking Clarke points out that it supports evidence provided by reports of past life regression and the phenomenon of channelling. As these types of experience are very complex, Clarke suggests that our theories and constructs should be flexible enough to allow for several possibilities. According to Clarke (2008, pp.24–25), 'our minds exist in connectedness and relationship [that] is an integral part of what we are. The fact that connection beyond the limits of what is precisely knowable has been a common experience throughout human history, and is an experience that continues to be reported today, suggests that it should not be dismissed lightly. Such reports imply that our capacity to connect and be in relationship operates beyond our connections with our fellow creatures on this earth, human and non human.' Clarke argues that this wider sense of connection is very significant not only for our well-being but also for the well-being of the planet.

24. Epstein (1990, p.27) describes a 'specific mental disorder that the Tibetans call 'sokrlung' (a disorder of the 'life-bearing wind that supports the mind' that can arise as a consequence…of strain[ing] too tightly in an obsessive way to achieve moment-to-moment awareness'). When meditative practices are brought into Western contexts, similar problems can occur. However, anxiety, dissociation, depersonalisation, altered perceptions, agitation and muscular tension observed during these practices (Bogart 1991; Walsh and Roche 1979) 'are not necessarily pathologic and may reflect in part a heightened sensitivity' (Walsh and Roche 1979, p.1086).

25. Huxley draws a parallel between such negative visionary experiences and a doctrine in *The Tibetan Book of the Dead*, where the departed soul is described as shrinking in agony from the Light of the Void, 'in order to rush headlong into the comforting darkness of self-hood as a reborn human being, or even as a beast, an

unhappy ghost, a denizen of hell. Anything rather than the burning brightness of unmitigated Reality – anything!' (Huxley 2004a, p.34).

26. One difference between spiritual experience and psychosis is that usually if the experience is solicited it does not overwhelm the individual (Brett 2010; Tobert 2010). Psychosis is said to be an incomplete withdrawal from the spirit state, a failure to return to this reality, whereas the mystic is in control and comes back completely to everyday reality (Tobert 2010).

27. Schizophrenia: the individual loses control and may remain in the spirit world, becoming unable to function in everyday reality.

28. In order to help people with whom we live or work, we have to learn the ways they experience and express their spirituality, and the language (both verbal and non-verbal) they use to talk about it. In some cultural contexts this will be more visible than in others, and expressed through different means; for example, children brought up in certain religious environment will use the language of their particular religion, and may follow particular rituals.

29. For example, Hay and Nye (Hay and Nye 2006; Nye and Hay 1996) have singled out a set of three interrelated categories of spiritual sensitivity or awareness: (1) awareness-sensing (here-and-now; tuning; flow; focusing); (2) mystery-sensing (wonder and awe; imagination); (3) value-sensing (delight and despair; ultimate goodness; meaning).

    Brendan Hyde (2008) identifies four characteristics of children's spirituality: the felt sense, integrating awareness, weaving the threads of meaning and spiritual questing. (Hyde also considers two 'negative' factors which may inhibit children's expression of their spirituality: material pursuit and trivialising.)

30. The term 'autistic culture', sometimes used to refer to the autistic way of perceiving, understanding and reacting to the world, seems to be justifiable (even if used only metaphorically). Any culture emerges from a *shared* sensory perceptual experience, *shared* knowledge about the world, patterns of behaviours, traditions, beliefs, etc. As 'autistic experiences' are so different, individuals with autism do not share the cultural worldview, and so they are sometimes referred to as 'foreigners in any culture'.

31. Mentioned in Chapter 5, note 4; Bogdashina 2010.

32. In spiritualist literature they are described as 'being not yet fully incarnated'.

33. Charles Bonnet syndrome is a condition that causes people with visual loss to have complex visual hallucinations, ranging from simple patterns of lines and shapes to detailed pictures of people, buildings and scenery. The images appear 'from nowhere' and can last from a few minutes to several hours. It was first described by Charles Bonnet in 1760 when he observed that his grandfather, who was almost blind, suffered 'hallucinations', 'seeing' patterns, birds, buildings and people that were not there.

34. For connection between sensory deprivation and autism, see Bogdashina 2010.

35. See, for example, Bexton, Woodburn and Scott 1954; Forrest 1996; Merabet *et al.* 2004; Robbins 2008; Zubek *et al.* 1961.

36. The notion of a highly interconnected universe has been acknowledged in quantum mechanics with its non-separability as one of the most certain general concepts in physics (d'Espagnat 1973). Each and every particle seems to 'know' what other particles are doing and reacts accordingly. These findings from the Aspect experiment provide us with a very different worldview from what we had before.

We are all as much parts of a single system as two photons flying away from each other and still reacting to the changes happening to one of them (Gribbin 1991).

37. However, it is one thing to have this 'inner sense' of things, this unique perspective to perceive it, but to interpret what is sensed is a different matter altogether (Isanon 2001).

38. Tantam (2009) illustrates the idea of emotional and mental connectedness with examples from group therapy (where it feels as if the individuals in the group have fused into a matrix, in which emotions and ideas circulate and resonate like signals between transistors in a radio) and links it to a number of theoretical perspectives, including Jung's 'archetypes'.

39. Cited in Gunn 1920, p.45.

9

Sense of Right and Wrong

Morality and ethics

These two terms are often used interchangeably, and dictionary definitions are somewhat circular, for example:

Moral adj.: concerned with goodness or badness of human character or behaviour, or with distinction between right and wrong.

Morality: the science of morals; the degree of conformity of an idea, practice, and so on to moral principles; knowing the difference between right and wrong.

Morality is a social phenomenon; it emerges in the interactions between and among individuals. Morality has both emotional (affective) and cognitive components.

Ethics is defined as the science of morals in human conduct, or moral philosophy: the study of rightness and fairness. Why does fairness exist? Why is one action considered fair and another isn't?

Philosophers, however, distinguish between morals and ethics, insisting there are subtle differences between these two concepts. Some researchers do not define them but plunge into the discussion of morals/ethics, on the assumption that readers will know what they mean.[1]

William James argued that the whole concern of both morality and religion is the manner with which we accept the universe: either only in part and grudgingly, or heartily and altogether; whether our protests against certain issues in it are radical and unforgiving, or we accept that even with evil, there are ways of living that might lead to good. He summarised the differences between morality and religion (which can be interpreted as spirituality):

> Morality pure and simple accepts the law of the whole which it finds reigning, so far as to acknowledge and obey it, but it may obey it with the heaviest and coldest heart, and never cease to feel it as a yoke. But for religion [spirituality], in its strong and fully developed manifestations, the service of the highest never is felt as a yoke. Dull submission is left far behind, and a mood of welcome, which may fill any place on the scale between cheerful serenity and enthusiastic gladness, has taken its place. (James 1985, p.41)

The difference at the emotional and practical level between accepting the universe out of necessity and welcoming it with passionate happiness is as great as the difference between passivity and activity. Accepting circumstances uncomplainingly can be seen both as 'accepting the universe out of necessity' and 'welcoming it with passionate happiness'. 'The *anima mundi*, to whose disposal of his own personal destiny the Stoic consents, is there to be respected and submitted to, but the Christian God is there to be loved.' James illustrates this point by comparing the attitude of Marcus Aurelius ('If gods care not for me or my children, here is a reason for it') to that of Job ('Though he slay me, yet will I trust in him!') (James 1985, p.42).

Is morality a uniquely human feature or do other animals possess it as well?

There are still some scientists who insist that morality is exclusively human and resist the idea that it actually can be shared with other beings (animals). However, more and more researchers (biologists, neuroscientists, ethologists and philosophers) are beginning to consider morality as an adaptive strategy that has evolved in many species. Of course, animal moral behaviour is not the same as human moral behaviour, but it is a phenomenon that is a biological necessity for social living, and animals do possess basic features of morality: cooperation, empathy, fairness, justice and trust. 'In the context of animals, morality refers to a wide-ranging suite of social behaviors; it is an internalized set of rules for how to act within a community. Moral behavior includes (but may not be limited to) cooperation, reciprocity, empathy, and helping' (Bekoff 2007, p.88). Sapontzis (1980) argues that animals' intentional, kind and courageous actions are moral actions in the same sense we accept moral norms. We can find plenty of examples when animals seem to display the highest moral principles. Based on his long-term studies of play in social carnivores – including wolves, coyotes, red foxes and domesticated dogs – Bekoff believes that we can make the stronger claim that some animals might be moral beings because 'animal play appears to rely on the universal human value of the Golden Rule – do unto others as you would have them do unto you' (Bekoff 2007, p.87). Bekoff argues that if animals can be shown to display a sense of justice along with a broad range of cognitive and emotional capacities (such as empathy and reciprocity), this indicates that the differences between humans and all other animals are a matter of degree rather than kind. He suggests that some animals have moral codes of behaviour but not that animals have ethics. According to Bekoff, many species, to varying degrees, have social standards for their behaviour; they understand them, and they understand that there are social consequences if they break these standards. It shows that we can find evolutionary roots of human morality by studying the behaviour of non-human animals. A.N. Whitehead recognised that animals are capable of morality (because morality emphasises the 'detailed occasion'), but are not religious (because religion requires a grasp of pure ideality).[2]

Charles Darwin suggested that human moral sentiments were a product of the evolutionary process and could be rooted in animals' behaviour. In other words, Darwin viewed morality as a natural extension and outgrowth of social instincts, with many moral behaviours originating in the emotional centre in the brain which humans share with other animals (Bekoff 2007). Exploring the biological roots of morality and drawing on both Darwin and recent scientific research, primatologist Frans de Waal (2006) puts forward a very convincing argument that human morality is on a continuum with animal sociality and it is futile to seek the origin of human morality in human culture rather than in evolution – we are not moral by choice but by nature.

What is moral and what is not? For centuries people have been struggling to find the answers to these questions and to define the 'gold standard' of moral/ethical behaviour that can be applicable in any society at any period of history. 'Many have turned to God, or Allah, or Yahweh, or Jehovah, or whatever other name they have used to designate Deity, and have relied on their understanding of *What God Wants*' (Walsch 2005, p.53). The research shows a strong connection between spiritual awareness and ethical behaviour, as most people link their spiritual or religious experience with a moral principle, commenting that the initial effect of their experience is to make them look beyond themselves with increasing desire to care for their nearest and dearest, to take issues of social justice more seriously, and to be concerned about the environment in general. Hay and Nye report that 'People say things like, "I behave better; it touches the conscience." One person said, "I now have far more respect for my physical surroundings as well as fellow humans... I don't think they were important to me before"' (Hay and Nye 2006, pp.47–48). The researchers conclude that 'morality has its source at a deeper level than specific religious adherence, since it arises in the first place out of spiritual insight' (pp.29, 47–48). Margaret Knight (1955) agrees that morality does not require a religious belief, despite the fact that morality and religion share similar notions (love, honesty, justice, etc.), as the basis for moral behaviour. However, some people (including autistic individuals) strongly associate morality with religion; for example, for Edgar Schneider (1999), his religious beliefs and social conscience are totally interdependent.

Stages of moral development

One of the best-known theories of moral development was suggested by psychologist Lawrence Kohlberg (1981). He based his model on Piagetian theories of cognitive development, and singled out six stages classified into three levels. (According to Kohlberg, none of these stages can be skipped: each one provides a foundation for the next.)

Level 1: Pre-conventional morality

0. *Egocentricity:* The child makes judgements about what is good vs. bad on the basis of what he wants or likes, vs. what he does not like or what hurts him.[3]

1. *Obedience and punishment orientation:* The child responds to cultural rules of what is considered good or right to avoid punishment. Goodness and badness are determined by outside authority, independently of the child's wants and likes.

2. *Individualism and exchange:* The child's actions are aimed at what instrumentally satisfies his or her needs (and occasionally the needs of others). Reciprocity and elements of fairness are present but on a pragmatic basis.

Level 2: Conventional morality

3. *Interpersonal accord and conformity* (often referred to 'good boy–good girl'): The child seeks to do what will gain approval by others. Individuals identify themselves with their group (family, community, nation) and the main tendencies are conformity and loyalty to social order.

4. *Law and order maintaining orientation:* The individual is oriented towards what is considered right by authority, following the fixed rules, doing one's duty and respecting authority.

Level 3: Post-conventional morality

According to Kohlberg, this third level of moral thinking is not reached by the majority, especially stage 6.

5. *Social contract orientation:* The individual critically examines rights and wrongs and is aware of the relativism of personal values and opinions; rules of laws are important but there should be agreed standards.

6. *Universal ethical principles:* The main emphasis is on the universal principles which are abstract and ethical; the right is defined by the decision of conscience. The individual follows his or her internalised ethical principles of justice, even if they conflict with established rules and laws.

Like Piaget, Kohlberg believes that moral development occurs through social interaction, with the individual moving from stage to stage as a result of cognitive conflicts at each stage.[4]

Morality: Sense of right and wrong in autism

It seems that problems autistic individuals experience with social interaction might obstruct, or at least delay their moral development. Besides, some researchers suggest that lack of Theory of Mind in autism and difficulty to imitate hinder moral development. However, a contrary view has been proven right – that Theory of Mind and morality are developmentally separate.[5] There is growing evidence that indicates that high-functioning individuals with autism are capable of a significant degree of moral agency.[6]

From my experience working with parents of autistic children, many of them are amazed at the very strong sense of justice in their offspring; even so-called low-functioning non-verbal children seem to know what is right and fair and what is wrong and unjust. My son with classic autism (who was non-verbal till he was seven years old) did not seem to understand what was going on around him, but from a very early age he had a profound sense of fairness, the sense of right and wrong.

Another 'bonus' for many autistic individuals is that they are not inclined to give in to peer pressure, and form their own judgements about situations, though they do experience difficulties with understanding cultural rules, and because of their literal interpretation can find themselves in trouble.

There are certain characteristics of self and personality development in autistic individuals that have an impact on their moral development:[7]

- less developed ego (but stronger connection to 'true self')
- logical approach
- difficulty in seeing deception
- difficulty in interpreting social situations.

Less developed ego

This makes it easier to empathise, leading to a strong sense of social justice. Those who feel connectedness or oneness with the world are unlikely to harm others (people, animals, plants, even objects).[8] Damage any part of reality and you damage yourself. The sense of social justice, fairness and compassion for others is very strongly developed in many autistic individuals. (As it is not centred on their selves but rather on fairness for others, it is ironic that 'normal' people look at them as self-centred while being blind to fairness when they are involved personally, and believe that they are in the right.)

> For me, the only thing I do genuinely *feel* (it hurts inside) is a kind of 'injustice/feel sorry for' thing that often compels me to buy my things from the smallest stall (that does not seem to make good business), or to take part in something because I feel sorry for the organiser because the idea seems 'naff' to most people and nobody is showing interest. (Barbara, personal communication, 2004)

I did not understand that people have egos, and that protecting their egos was often more important than loyalty to the company. I naively believed that all...employees would always act in the best interest of their employer. I assumed that if I was loyal and always worked for the good of Swift's [the company Temple worked for], I would be rewarded. The other engineers resented me. They sometimes installed equipment wrong, and they never consulted me. They did not like that 'nerd' telling them how to do it. Technically I was right but socially wrong... I wrote a letter to the President of Swift about a bad equipment installation which caused cattle to suffer. The President was embarrassed that I had found a fault in his operation. I thought he would be pleased if I informed him of the mistake, instead he felt threatened and told [the manager] to get rid of me. (Grandin 1997)

For the individual with autism, personal feelings towards someone do not interfere with their logical analysis of the situation, for example:

I can provide an objective evaluation of another scientist's work even if I hate him as a person. I have observed that most people have a hard time doing this. I can lay my dislike for the person aside and look at his scientific work without letting my dislike for him affect my judgment. (Grandin 1992, p.6)

Logical approach

[M]y morals are determined by logic. (Grandin 2008, p.xxvii)

Autism enables a logical approach to social and economic problems:

For all of my adolescent and adult life, I have been socially conscious, advocating equality and help for the poor and disadvantaged... This was something born out of an intellectual conviction that this was morally right, rather than an identification with the people I was trying to help.

People tend to dismiss a logical approach to social and economic problems, claiming that, being 'unfeeling', it has to lead to self-interest. An example is, if one is hungry, it would be logical to steal food from someone else who has it. However, a powerful factor mitigating against that sort of thing is an intellectual appreciation of the difference between right and wrong. (Schneider 1999, p.49)

Schneider (writing about Gautama Buddha):

> came to a conclusion that was, if nothing else, quite logical. One
> only needs so much in order to live; everything else is optional.
> Beyond what is needed for survival, if what one has exceeds what
> one wants, the result is unhappiness. If what one wants exceeds
> what one has, the result is unhappiness. (That is not to say that one
> should choose living at the barest substance level. Perhaps it could
> be summed up by asking oneself a series of questions about personal
> acquisitions. 'Do I need this?' 'If not, do I really want it, or do I only
> want others' envy?' 'If I get it, will I be depriving someone else of
> something important?' 'If not, can I get it ethically and responsibly?'
> There is an important aspect of 'ethically and responsibly'. One
> should not, to satisfy a want, deprive another of a need.) (Schneider
> 1999, p.112)

Difficulty in seeing deception

As they themselves are painfully honest and experience significant
difficulty with lying, they find it hard (if not impossible) to detect
deception; so they can be taken advantage of by unscrupulous people:

> It's hard for me to tell when someone is lying. It took me a very
> long time, and a lot of painful experience, just to learn what lying is.
> (Sinclair 1992, p.302)

> Autistic people don't really understand how somebody could have
> bad intentions, yet still act friendly on the outside. That paradox
> is confusing for a person who needs to see things literally as they
> are, and not befogged with deceit. A person like this simply can't
> grasp how another person can be acting nice only to play tricks or
> really harm the disabled individual. An autistic person can learn that
> things like that do happen, yet can never actually understand why
> they happen...autistics do need to be guarded from people with bad
> intentions. They are naïve socially. Their innocence and literalness
> prevent them from being able to distinguish between foe or friend
> in many cases... Autistic people generally don't know the things
> others know naturally. They can't be taken for granted, and they
> can't be expected to know something just because others know it.
> (O'Neill 1999, pp.86–87)

Difficulty in interpreting social situations

> And in the social area, as with everything else, I have trouble keeping track of everything that's happening at one time. I have to learn things other people never think about. I have to use cognitive strategies to make up for some basic instincts that I don't have. In the social area, as with everything else, there are a lot of things that I don't understand unless someone explains them to me. (Sinclair 1992, p.302)

Many autistic individuals agree that learning the rules is vitally important for them. The rules of what to do or what not to do in different situations help them survive 'social chaos'. Temple Grandin (2006) had a strict moral upbringing, and learned as a child that stealing, lying and hurting other people were wrong. Growing up, she discovered that some rules could be broken but not others, so she classifies all 'wrongdoings' into three categories that help her negotiate every new situation she enters:

- 'Really bad' rules must never be broken; they include stealing, destroying property, injuring people. These were easy to understand.

- 'Sins of the system' rules have very stiff penalties for seemingly illogical reasons.

- The 'illegal but not bad' rules can often be broken with little consequence, for example, slight speeding and illegal parking.

Not all autistic people have 'autistic personality', so we cannot say they all are perfect and cannot do anything wrong. However, despite their difficulties with imitation and Theory of Mind, the majority develop moral and ethical principles (even if their 'route' of moral development differs from a 'normal' one). Those who experience 'cleansed perception' seem to see spiritual values in their lives more clearly.

> It appears to me that kindness and generosity are extremely logical and rational. It is gratuitous cruelty that has no logic about it, and would seem to spring from the emotions untempered by any rationality whatsoever…as far back as I remember, I always had my own set of values (which were invariably arrived at by intellectual criteria), and, as such, did not hesitate to question the values of others if they seemed to be illogical. (One example is the questioning of my family's values that eventually led to my adoption of Catholicism.) (Schneider 1999, pp.27, 102)

Notes

1. See, for example, Barnbaum 2008.

2. Cited in Armstrong-Buck 1989.

3. However, there is research evidence that humans have a natural tendency to be altruistic. A research study by Felix Warneken and Michael Tomasello (2006) shows that babies as young as 18 months of age will help people in need, for example when they are looking for a lost object. Interestingly, the infants will only help when they believe that a person needs the object to complete a task. For instance, they would only retrieve a clothespin if it seemed to have been dropped unintentionally by the researcher, not if it was thrown on the floor deliberately.

4. Kohlberg's theory has been criticised for overemphasis of one aspect of morality (justice) while ignoring such factors as, for example, compassion and caring. Besides, moral reasoning does not necessarily lead to moral behaviour: knowing what ought to be done does not necessarily mean it will be done.

5. See, for example, Blair 1995, 1996.

6. See, for example, Downs and Smith 2004; Krahn and Fenton 2009; Leslie *et al.* 2006.

7. Huxley remarks that at least half of morality (moral rules) is negative and consists in keeping us out of mischief; thus the Lord's prayer is less than 50 words long, and six of them are devoted to asking God not to lead us into temptation. He cites Pascal, who said that the sum of evil would be diminished if people could only learn to sit quietly in their rooms. Unlike the one-sided contemplative who leaves undone many things he ought to do, but to make up for it refrains from doing things he ought not to do, the contemplative 'whose perception has been cleansed' (heightened, unfiltered and conceptless) does not have to stay in his room and can go about his business, being completely satisfied to be part of 'the divine Order of Things', so that he will never be tempted to mischief: 'When we feel ourselves to be sole heirs of the universe, when "the sea flows in our veins...and the stars are our jewels", when all things are perceived as infinite and holy, what motive can we have for covetousness or self-assertion, for the pursuit of power or the drearier forms of pleasure? Contemplatives are not likely to become gamblers, or procurers, or drunkards; they do not as a rule preach intolerance, or make war; do not find it necessary to rob, swindle or grind the faces of the poor. And to these enormous negative virtues we may add another which, though hard to define, is both positive and important. The *arhat* and the quietest may not practise contemplation in its fullness; but if they practise it at all, they may bring back enlightening reports of another, a transcendent country of the mind; and if they practise it in the height, they will become conduits through which some beneficent influence can flow out of that other country into a world of darkened selves, chronically dying for lack of it' (Huxley 2004a, p.25).

8. Some autistic children and adults do exhibit self-injurious and what can be seen as aggressive behaviour towards others, but the causes of these behaviours are very different; they are not planned and not rooted in the desire to hurt others. When the person exhibits a meltdown, it is triggered by his or her inability to cope (whether it is sensory overload, or severe anxiety/panic attack, etc.) – the person does not lash out at someone because he or she wants to inflict pain, but because he or she is overwhelmed (and possibly in pain) or bewildered by an incomprehensible situation.

10

Spiritual Development

The 'spiritual dimension' is sometimes referred to as one of five interconnected dimensions of human experience: physical, biological, psychological, sociocultural and spiritual. Unlike the first four, the spiritual dimension is not directly accessible to either science or reason, but it can be contacted through direct perception. The spiritual dimension seems both to underpin and surpass the other main dimensions and it connects every part with the whole (Culliford 2007). In the spiritual dimension everyone and everything are interconnected and that is why any action, word, thought, movement, and so on alters and influences the whole; it is a sort of butterfly effect: whatever you do will change (for better or worse) the fabric of the whole and that, in turn, will affect you.[1] In the light of this, individual responsibility is of paramount importance.

We all start our lives as immature beings – whether physically, mentally, psychologically, socially or spiritually. However, as spirituality is innate, immaturity in this aspect of development can be seen in the unawareness of it – the 'spiritual (pre-linguistic) self' connected to the universe is there from the very beginning, but it takes time to develop self-awareness, which allows reflection on it. To follow this line, regress is also possible. Based on her analysis, Bindl (1965) detected a pattern of spiritual development which she presented as four stages: (1) children up to about seven years old exhibit what she called 'naïve relatedness to the Wholly Other'; (2) with the introduction of a conceptual framework and education, children start to show 'decline in spontaneous experience of the numinous'; (3) with puberty, self-obsession leads to 'narcissistic reversion toward one's own self' which effectively shuts down awareness of the Wholly Other; (4) in late adolescence, some individuals have 'consciously striven for relation to transcendence'.

We all go through the stages of development that are part of growing up. Here we will look at the stages of spiritual development the person goes through. There are several models of spiritual development, the most influential being James Fowler's theory of stages of faith described in *Stages of Faith: The Psychology of Human Development and the Quest for Meaning* (1981). Fowler, a psychologist and theologian, suggests that it is faith (rather than religion, or belief) that 'is the most fundamental category in the human quest for relation to transcendence' (p.14).

Faith versus belief

It is useful to distinguish between faith and belief. The dictionary definitions do not help much because they define each of these concepts through the other, for example:

Faith: firm belief, especially without logical proof; belief in religious doctrines; spiritual apprehension of divine truth apart from proof.

Belief: a person's religion; religious conviction; a firm opinion; an acceptance (of a thing, fact, statement, etc.).

In the specialist literature these two concepts are clearly distinguished. For instance, Wilfred Cantwell Smith, a historian of religion (1979), defines *faith* as 'a quality of the person not the system', including 'an orientation of the total person, giving purpose and goal to one's hopes and striving, thoughts and actions' (p.12); unlike *belief*, which involves assenting intellectually to concepts as set forth in different religious doctrines, thus dividing people belonging to different religions, faith unites them. For Fowler (1981), as well, faith is theologically neutral and is applicable to both religious and non-religious perspectives.

> Faith...may be characterized as an integral, centering process underlying the formation of beliefs, values and meanings that (1) gives coherence and direction to persons' lives, (2) links them in shared trusts and loyalties with others, (3) grounds their personal stances and communal loyalties in the sense of relatedness to a larger frame of reference, and (4) enables them to face and deal with the limited conditions of human life, relying upon that which has the quality of ultimacy in their lives. (Fowler 2000, p.56)

According to Culliford, experiencing faith is different from holding a belief in that faith includes all possibilities, where opposites cancel out and negate each other and where all contradictions are resolved by 'both/and' thinking, and that is why faith cannot be challenged successfully, whereas belief implies the simultaneous possibility of doubt; beliefs are strong forms of attachment to an idea or a set of ideas about something, like a strongly held opinion, which we choose in accordance with our personal agendas. The choice may be conditioned by upbringing and certain circumstances, or it may be unconscious (Culliford 2007).

Stages of faith development (and their applicability to autism)

Fowler states that stages in faith development are hierarchical, sequential and invariant and are always experienced in the same order and correlated with life stages; each stage can be characterised by both its positive possibilities and its negative potential. Fowler (1981, p.276) remarks that 'faith stage transitions are not automatic or inevitable', and not all people necessarily attain all the stages of spirituality. Fowler's model is based on the psychological theories of Erik Erikson (1963, 1968) and the cognitive theory of moral development of Lawrence Kohlberg (1971, 1981). Erikson was one of the first to suggest that personality development is life long; he proposed to distinguish between eight stages of development, and believed that later stages build on the successes and failures of the earlier stages, with later stages being able to compensate for the failures occurred during the earlier development, in accordance with what he called the 'epigenetic principle': 'Anything that grows has a ground plan, and out of this ground plan the parts arise, each part having its time of special ascendancy, until all parts have arisen to form a functioning whole' (Erikson 1968, p.92). According to Erikson, movement from one stage to the next is the result of 'crisis'. Similarly, Fowler states: 'The stages are cumulative in that one brings to each new crisis the mixed residue of past solution and contains in it an anticipation of the issues of crisis in future stages' (1981, p.48). 'The stages aim to describe patterned operations of knowing and valuing that underlie our consciousness' (Fowler 2000, p.56). The key concept of Kohlberg's theory of moral development (influenced by Piaget's work) is about the process (in contrast to the content) of children's moral decision-making. It is reflected in investigating how children arrive at judgements in response to different moral dilemmas. Like Kohlberg, Fowler focuses on the process rather than content of various faith traditions 'to find and describe structural features of faith that make comparisons possible across a wide range of "content" differences' (1981, p.99). According to Fowler, not everyone moves on from each stage to the next one at the appropriate time; some get stuck in the earlier stages for longer periods of time, or even stay in one of these early and immature stages all their lives. As Fowler includes both religious and non-religious perspectives in his definition of faith, and focuses on the process and not the content of faith development, his theory becomes inclusive and avoids division among different religious and non-religious traditions.[2] Many researchers have accepted Fowler's classification of stages of faith development, some introducing simplifications to accommodate their own research. We will consider the versions suggested by Peck and Culliford.

M. Scott Peck starts his bestselling book *The Road Less Traveled: A New Psychology of Love, Traditional Values and Spiritual Growth* (1978) with one of the greatest truths[3] – 'Life is difficult': 'Once we truly know that life is difficult – once we truly understand and accept it – then life is no longer difficult. Because once accepted the fact that life is difficult no longer matters' (p.3). Peck warns that if one's goal is to avoid pain and suffering, he would not advise such a person to seek higher levels of consciousness or spiritual evolution. One cannot achieve them without suffering and, when one does achieve them, he or she is likely to be called on to serve in ways that can be even more painful, or at least demanding. Culliford uses the stages of spiritual development to inform his work as a psychiatrist. He simplifies Fowler's classification and uses less technical terms.

Fowler's stages 0, 1 and 2 roughly correspond to the first three stages in Piaget's theory of child development (sensorimotor, preoperational and concrete operational) when children develop their cognitive abilities; their religious or faith conceptions are very much influenced by their immediate environment (carers/parents are their main influence).

Stage 0: Primal faith

Earliest faith is what enables us to undergo...separations [from parents] without undue anxiety or fear of loss of self. Primal faith forms before there is language. It forms the basic rituals of care and interchange and mutuality. And, although it does not determine the course of our later faith, it lays the foundation on which later faith will build or that will have to be rebuilt in later faith. (Fowler 2001, p.103)

In this sense, all babies (in the pre-linguistic stage) are 'universalisers', being unaware of their 'selves', when the 'mind is not in charge yet'. This is the original (pre-verbal) 'here-and-now' awareness (which is considered one of the most important features of spirituality). Margaret Donaldson (1992) terms it as the 'point mode', which she believes is the most basic mode of the mind's operation and which is typical for babies under eight months who do not seem to have any memory of the past and have not developed the ability to plan the future yet. Donaldson believes that the 'point mode' continues to be present in children even when they have developed the 'line mode', that is, the ability to think about the past and future – the 'there-and-then'. According to Lev Vygotsky (1962), before there is a synthesis of language and thought, the consciousness of a child is characterised by pre-verbal thought of 'pure' meaning and the absence of 'marked' time. It is when this type of consciousness (which is typically inaccessible) is reconstructed into the language of the culture the child is born into that the time becomes 'marked' (past, present and future) and the original meaning of the experience (with its intensity, vividness and immediacy of awareness) is lost.

Fowler's Stage 0, *Primal faith*, which forms before there is language, corresponds to infancy, when we first become aware of ourselves as beings separate from others and from the environment. The majority of people have no recollection of themselves till early childhood; that is not surprising as 'language-less memories' are hard to retrieve. Newborns, unlike adults, are probably aware of the raw sensory data available at lower levels of neural processing and they quite possibly have excellent recall of this information but, with maturation, there is a strategy to supress such awareness. Instead, the maturing mind becomes increasingly aware only of concepts (including the body), to the exclusion of the details that comprise the concepts and all the information available, but not reflected, in the cultural concepts and, therefore, ignored. However, in autism the situation can be very different, because many autistic individuals rely on their non-verbal memory well into their adulthood, so there have been reports of persons with autism describing their very early memories, some of them even related to their being born. For example:

> I must have been about 10 months old, for I was crawling on the floor in our living-room. All aunts and uncles were there [it was his mother's birthday]. I remember the sound of their voices and

saw the fresh brushed shoes and the legs...a double sliding-door between the rooms was open... I had a toy wooden truck loaded with wooden milk cans. I remember the colors exactly: creamy white with sprayed light green stripes. It is like a 'video' in my head. (Mar, personal communication, 2012)

My memories, those I actually remember myself (as opposed to knowing of them because my parents told me about events later) are usually just glimpses. The very first is of lying in my cot, probably about 1½ years old, I remember where the walls were and where open space was in relation to my body...and I remember being angry/frustrated because my father wasn't behaving as he should (by visiting my cot before going to work)... Most of my memories are of what some of my toys felt, sounded and tasted like. Like my rocking horse, my clown, my plastic circles on a stick, etc. I remember a few glimpses of terror when Mum made me walk, especially stairs...

Oddly enough I remember some dreams I had quite vividly, the night terrors I had for years as a toddler were about armies of chimney pipes chasing me, and I eventually signed a peace treaty in an Asterix-style Roman field tent many years later in another dream. (Barbara, personal communication, 2012)

Interestingly, while remembering their early childhood, some 'see' themselves as if watching a movie (from outside) with themselves as actors in it.

Stage 1: Intuitive–projective faith
This stage:

emerges in early childhood with acquisition of language. Here imagination, stimulated by stories, gestures, and symbols and not yet controlled by logical thinking, combines with perception and feelings to create long-lasting faith images. Representations of God take conscious form in this period and draw, for good or ill, on children's experiences of their parents and other adults to whom they are emotionally attached in the first years of life... (Fowler 2001, p.103)

It usually occurs between the ages of three and seven, with the positive aspect of it being that children's imagination is uninhibited by logic; they are more open to the unconscious. It is the time when a child acquires self-awareness and learns about his or her culture's beliefs and taboos. The negative potentials are that unrestrained imagination can bring images of terror (from the unconscious) and that the child's worldview can easily be manipulated by the cultural doctrines. This is the stage when the child becomes egocentrically 'self-aware'.

Robert Coles's book *The Spiritual Life of Children* (1992) contains numerous accounts of his interviews with children from different cultural, geographic and faith backgrounds. Instead of applying Piagetian tests to assess the children's spiritual development, Coles focuses on children's experiences, their stories, avoiding any judgement or interpretation. As the children were from different (and none) faith communities, Coles's research confirms that spirituality is a universal feature.

Another approach to the research into children's spiritual experiences is retrospective. The most representative work illustrating it is *The Original Vision* (1983) by Edward Robinson. In his book Robinson provides his findings of childhood recollections of religious or spiritual experiences, collected from about 5000 adult respondents who participated in the study. Despite old age, quite a few of his samples reported childhood experiences which were associated with their personal identity and meaning of their existence; these experiences remained vivid memories for their whole lives. Growing up, children lose this awareness and learn to 'translate' what they see into conventional (cultural) images and notions. The *original vision* of the world is usually lost and forgotten.[4] However, Robinson's research shows that this is not always the case, and some people's childhood experiences remain vivid and bring significance to their lives. A similar but small-scale study was conducted by Lorelei Farmer (1992).[5] All adults in the study said that their childhood spiritually significant transcendent experiences had remained with them all their lives and were interpreted later in life as the truth they had to (and did) follow. However, there are some disadvantages to the retrospective studies: (1) some experiences are lost and forgotten; (2) the spiritual experiences are holistic, and cannot be described in linear format with verbal labels; (3) while describing their childhood experiences, adults inevitably use the language and concepts they have acquired, thus losing certain aspects of the experiences that cannot be described in words or that at the time the experiences happened were not conceptualised because of lack of verbal and conceptual means;

thus, when recollected later, they were inevitably 'distorted' when described through acquired language and cultural concepts.

Stage 1: Egocentric (Culliford 2007)

At an early stage of an individual's psychological and spiritual development (during 'childhood phase'), the external world is seen as a continuation or extension of ourselves: we are egocentric and feel in control, manipulating people and situations to our wilful purposes; dictators are often stuck at this stage. 'Such people develop a kind of grandiose sense of omnipotence, devoting themselves utterly to achieving the outward manifestation of inner sense of power and of being right, whatever the consequences to others' (Culliford 2007, p.234). Culliford suggests that, although such dictators and similar people may be thought of as embodying evil, we may be generous and interpret this evil only in the sense of immaturity – developmentally, they are stuck in Stage 1 and, at least potentially, are capable of further psychological growth. Culliford hopes that it is possible to detect and manage such people within communities. However, in practice, it is very hard to help them if they do not want to recognise their problems.

In contrast, babies and toddlers who are diagnosed with autistim experience the first years of their lives very differently. As we have seen, they remain *connected* to the surroundings without 'me/not-me boundaries' for much longer (though they may appear to be self-absorbed on the surface). Their sensory perception develops very differently from the 'norm', leading to the delayed acquisition of culturally defined concepts, thus developing fluid-mind intelligence.[6]

At the age of two and a half, Tito would change the environment around him with the help of imagination:

> He could go to places that did not exist, and they were like beautiful dreams. One such was that of a staircase, which went high, higher and still higher reaching somewhere – anywhere. But a great disappointment occurred if it took him to nowhere and he had to start elevating again.
>
> There was a funny hope that the staircase would lead him to God. The concept developed probably due to the fact that his Dia was a very pious lady and prayed a lot. (Mukhopadhyay 2000, p.8)

Stage 2: Mythic–literal faith

This stage corresponds to Piaget's 'concrete operational thinking' and occurs when:

> concrete operational thinking – the developing ability to think logically – emerges to help us order the world with categories of causality, space, time and number. We can now sort out the real from the make-believe, the actual from fantasy (i.e. children are conditioned out of seeing what has not been firmly established in each particular culture). We can enter into the perspectives of others, and we become capable of capturing life and meanings in narrative and stories. (Fowler 2001, p.105)

This stage is typical of school-age children (but some may remain in this stage for the rest of their lives), and is characterised by literal interpretations of myths and symbols; the spatial (and unrestricted) imagination gives way to linear thinking and accepting literally interpreted beliefs, moral rules and attitudes. Accuracy in taking the perspective of others increases; children in this stage compose a world based on reciprocal fairness and an immanent justice based on reciprocity. However, literalness and excessive reliance on reciprocity as a principle of constructing reality can result either in an overcontrolling perfectionism or 'righteousness', or the opposite – a sense of badness resulting, for example, from mistreatment or neglect from significant others (Wolski Conn 1986).

Using Fowler's model, in his book *A Different Drum* (1987), Scott Peck offers a simplified version of it. Peck combines Fowler's first two stages into one: 1 – *Chaotic–Antisocial*. Those who are stuck at this stage are usually self-centred and find themselves in trouble due to their unprincipled living. Often it is a very dramatic event in their life that pushes them to the next stage.

STAGE 2: CONDITIONING (CULLIFORD 2007)

Children listen to stories and use narratives as the way to understand their experiences. At this stage they accept stories, myths and symbols literally. They become attached to the beliefs, values and attitudes of their families and communities, opposing contradictory culture-based beliefs. To make progress on the spiritual path one has to give up these learned and conditioned attachments and aversions. Most people, however, carry these allegiances into the next − third − stage (Culliford 2007).

This is when conditioning out of 'unusual experiences' starts. In contrast, in autism, the acquisition of Theory of Mind is delayed because they do not share these experiences and develop Theory of Autistic Mind, which does not coincides with the 'normal' one; however, they compensate in developing a strong sense of 'fairness' that is originated from sensing/seeing unusual connections and certain characteristics of self and personality development.

Göte Klingberg (1959), a child psychologist, studied what he called the 'religious experience' of 630 Swedish children from 9 to 13 years old. The children were asked to complete the statement: 'Once when I thought of God…'. The researcher classified responses into four groups: the majority described situations of stress, followed by experiences in nature, moral experiences and, last, formal worship experiences. According to Klingberg, the tone of the children's essays indicates an immediately felt spiritual dimension in their descriptions. Klingberg's research framework was applied to 144 American adolescents by Elkind and Elkind (1962). The teenagers were asked two questions: (1) When do you feel closest to God? and (2) Have you ever had a particular experience when you felt close to God? The Elkinds distinguished 'acute' experiences (memorably intense and/or unusual) (such as thanking God, meditation, grief, revelation) from others (church, solitude, anxiety, fear, worry, prayer, moral action). Despite different cultural contexts (Sweden and the USA), these research studies confirm that spiritual awareness is quite common in young children and adolescents. In 1967, Long, Elkind and Spilka investigated the concept of prayer in children and adolescents and found that before the age of ten children mostly make requests to God, while, in adolescence, prayer is more like a private conversation with God, when teenagers share their thoughts and confide their secrets. The findings seem to indicate that it is at the age of developing puberty and sexual maturation that children grow spiritually and develop religious awareness.[7] Hay and Nye (2006) point out, however, that this particular pattern of spiritual and religious development is typical for those who grow up in religious (or, at least, not anti-religious) communities, while in a secularised environment this process is very unlikely.[8]

Two studies of Catholic and Protestant children (Thun 1963, 1964), which explored the children's understanding of such existential phenomena as God, Jesus, prayer, death, and so on showed that, starting from the second grade (7 to 8 years of age), the youngsters were able to experience the presence of God and to demonstrate an awareness of what Rudolf Otto (1950) calls the 'mysterium tremendum' and the 'mysterium fascinans',[9] whereas adolescence brings first signs of scepticism and, for many, loss of religious awareness altogether.

Other studies of religious or spiritual development produce similar results. For instance, Tamminen (1991), researching the religious and spiritual development of children and adolescents in Finland, found that up to the age of 12 to 13 years children report spiritual experiences more frequently, while, after that age, there is a noticeable decline; Leslie Francis' research (1987) on British children and adolescents also identifies a decline in religious or spiritual interest at from 8 to 15 years of age.

These and similar studies indicate that, unlike the cognitive development (Piagetian) model, when children acquire linguistic and cognitive skills which improve and mature with age, certain aspects of spirituality are well developed in early childhood and become suppressed (or children are conditioned out of it) with maturity in other areas (linguistic, cognitive, etc.). Young children do not realise that their earliest experiences can be seen as 'extraordinary' by adults; for them, these are their ordinary everyday experiences, bringing delight in their lives and encouraging curiosity. But, then, through education and upbringing, adults introduce them to the 'real' world, and the original vision is often forgotten. Hay and Nye (2006, p.57) offer an alternative way of interpreting the development of spirituality: 'to see it as the process of induction into post-Enlightenment European culture as suppressing or even repressing the natural spiritual awareness of children'. Thus, it is not (as sceptics believe) that spiritual experience is a social construct but rather that it is cultural and social constructs that suppress some aspects of spirituality and cultural and social filters that determine which ones are allowed to develop.

Too much reliance on cognitive development can blind us from 'detecting' spiritual awareness in children, especially children with special needs. For example, Ronald Goldman (an influential psychologist specialising in religious education) approached the subject from the perspective of the mental development of children and when they develop their ability to grasp the meaning of religious concepts and metaphors (Goldman 1965). Based on Piaget's theory of cognitive development, Goldman's (1964) assumptions limited his investigation of spiritual awareness to something extraordinary that can happen only to mystics, thus ignoring young children's experiences as unqualified for the spiritual.[10] If we apply cognitive theories to spiritual development, we will have to interpret childhood spirituality as immaturity and an inadequate, naive or incorrect view of the world that should be replaced with rational and intellectual understanding and explanation.

Stage 3: Synthetic–conventional faith (corresponding to Piagetian formal operations stage)
This stage:

> begins to take form in early adolescence. The emergence of formal operational thinking opens the way for reliance upon abstract ideas and concepts for making sense of one's world. The person can now reflect upon past experience and search them for meaning and pattern. At the same time, concerns about one's personal future – one's identity, one's work, career, or vocation – and one's personal relationships become important. (Fowler 2001, p.107)

Adolescents begin to use logic and hypothetical thinking to evaluate ideas. At the same time, many adolescents do not apply critical thinking to their personal faith but rather conform to the conventional religious beliefs of those they trust (for instance, their peers or influential adults in their lives). The person finds one's identity by aligning with a certain perspective, and lives directly through this perception without reflecting on it critically. 'At Stage 3 a person has an "ideology", a more or less consistent clustering of values and beliefs, but he or she has not objectified it for examination and in a sense is unaware of having it' (Fowler 1981, p.173).[11]

In Peck's version (1987) this stage corresponds to Stage 2 – *Formal–institutional*, when people rely on some sort of institution (whether religious or non-religious) to give them stability; they become attached to the forms of their institutional beliefs and get extremely upset when these are questioned.

STAGE 3: CONFORMITY (CULLIFORD 2007)
This stage is associated with adolescence and begins during the teenage years: it is when teenagers discover boundaries, attempt to push them and see what they can get away with. And this is the time when influences

come from outside the family circle and affect their thoughts, feelings and behaviour. In this stage we conform to a dualistic 'us-and-them' culture, when we are quick to judge and criticise others just because their perspectives are different. During this still relatively immature stage of personal development, as a way of defending themselves from anxiety and the feeling of immaturity, many use the defence mechanism of 'projection', denying aspects of themselves that they feel ashamed or guilty about (unconsciously protecting the idea 'I am without fault') by projecting these negative parts of their selves into other people. They 'are throwing out the unwanted bits to preserve the apparent purity of the ego. This is where the split occurs' and where they lose touch with their 'true, spiritual selves, choosing an identity and adopting as real an incomplete "persona" or mask. It is a fake-identity', created largely by received conditioning:

> This separation of everyday consciousness from the wholeness of the wisdom mind and from our true selves is the origin of the false ego-self. We accept it because we do not know any better at this stage, and have no way of knowing that who we think we are, how we think about ourselves and each other, is a kind of illusion. We accept as real the masks that everyone wears. (Culliford 2007, p.237)

During this stage individuals are dominated by ideas constantly related to 'I, Me and Mine' (in some cases the royal 'We' is used – to make oneself a part of a group that is not necessarily represented by 'We, so-and-so's views). Those who are 'not like Me/Us' are seen as enemies and rivals, created, in fact, by the person's unconscious mechanism of projection, without realising that his or her 'opposition' is his or her own reflection and does not exist in reality. The person is fighting his or her own aspects of self, wrongly attributed to the perceived 'enemy' (Culliford 2007).

In this conformist stage, people tend to feel more comfortable joining together and letting others lead them by making decisions for the group, not realising that they put themselves at the mercy of even less mature people, including persuasive bullies. 'These organizers tend to offer strong leadership, not only through charm and by invoking fear, but also through concealment and dishonesty. They depend upon invoking intolerance within us towards others.' To sustain their 'authority' (in whichever field they opt to 'lead'), their psychological power and influence, such individuals need an identified enemy, a shared foe, both to fear and to fight, using projection, the psychological function of which is to prevent the person from feeling stupid, anxious, afraid, ashamed or guilty (Culliford 2007, p.242). And when you start projecting your own problems onto others, it is hard to stop. Add to this 'herd mentality' and the situation becomes even more complicated – the person's loyal followers endorse him or her even more, complimenting every move and looking for guidance in any situation.[12] The threat from perceived enemies is often non-existent, because the 'enemy' is the projection of their own dark ideas, but it creates a very comfortable emotion of anger that conceals fear and (though falsely) supports the sense of being in the right (while all the rest are in the wrong). Culliford describes what happens during Stage 3 when we prefer anger to fear and uncertainty:

> Paradoxically, even perversely, there are those who enjoy the sensation of anger. The angrier you feel, the easier it may be to convince yourself that you…are strong and in the right; that your defiance is justified. Unfortunately for all concerned, this logic is simply false. (Culliford 2007, p.243)

Despite this stage being 'adolescence' in terms of personal (and spiritual) development, some people even in their middle age are still struggling to move through this conformist stage to the next one.[13] 'Adolescents' in their fifties and sixties are ruled by attachments, possessiveness, desire to control; they mistrust others and are intolerant to any points of view which oppose theirs. According to Culliford, in order to move on, mature and grow beyond the conformist stage:

> a degree of soul-searching, of honest, contemplative self-appraisal is necessary. This eventually results in individuals taking responsibility for how they feel, rather than perpetually seeking someone else to blame and castigate, and from whom to seek recompense. But not everyone is ready to reflect in this way and discover wisdom. Those still in stage three are not yet sufficiently emotionally ripe. (Culliford 2007, p.239)

The 'herd instinct', a characteristic feature of adolescence, though bringing the feeling of safety, has its drawbacks: suppression of individuality, adherence to whatever values are fashionable at the moment, of a superficial, transitory, secular and materialistic nature.

In contrast, many autistic individuals do much better because they do not follow the latest trends and do not feel obliged to follow the majority. For example:

All of my life, I have been an outsider, never feeling part of any group. Even when I do things that are clearly group activities, such as singing in a chorus, I am an individual doing what the others are doing, to be sure, but, nevertheless, as an individual…

I, therefore, by default, exclude myself from most people's conversations. Even when I do talk about interactions between people, it is invariably from an ethical point of view. This, I am sure, carries with it an air of aloofness that, though inadvertent, is perceived as intentional by others… For the NT [neurotypical], from what I have observed, being an outsider is a traumatic situation, causing pain. I, on the other hand, have never been bothered in the slightest by this, being quite content with any resulting solitude. (Schneider 1999, p.102)

I also dressed differently. I had a very particular style of my own and had certain favourite clothes that had nothing to do with the standard fashions the other children followed…and I was quite unaware of anyone thinking differently, or whether that was of any importance anyway. This apparent disregard for the conventions contributed to my appearing brave. In fact, I had absolutely no idea that there *were* such things as conventions. (Gerland 2007, p.90)

Another (negative) feature of this stage is that the 'permanent adolescents' divide the world into two groups, 'us' and 'them'. Culliford observes that there are possible scenarios to deal with those who are not 'like us': either:

to avoid them, to convert them to your way of life, or to destroy them. None of these solutions is satisfactory. All three are difficult to achieve. More to the point, the real location of the problem is not in them but in us… Even if we were to exterminate all our enemies, those into whom we have projected our shadowy parts, the true source of our distress remains unchanged. Unless we are able to recognize, accept this and mature, we will soon be looking around for new foes, including among our former friends and comrades. Transfer conflict from inside to out and it will never end. Understand ourselves, especially in terms of projection, in terms of emotions and the healing process, and we will have a better chance of finding both peace within and harmony with other people. (Culliford 2007, pp.241–242)

The way forward from this stage is when individuals detach themselves from the original group identity, demonstrating the ability to think for themselves, become free to make choices and accept responsibility for the consequences, leaving 'us-and-them' logic behind. 'We must find and follow a new destiny and enter life's stream alone; only then will we have genuinely embarked on stage four' (Culliford 2007, p.262). It seems that autistic individuals find it easier to do just that as they are not really attached to groups (though many would try to fit in superficially to feel more comfortable in social situations).

Stage 4: Individuative–reflective faith

[T]wo important movements have to occur. On the one hand, to move into [this stage], we have to question, examine, and reclaim the values and beliefs that we have formed to that point in our lives. They must become explicit [consciously chosen and critically supported commitments] rather than tacit [i.e. unconsidered, unexamined, uncritically approved] commitments... In the other move...one has to claim...'executive ego'...[unlike a person's identity in the previous stage which is shaped by his or her roles and relationships] one has to face and answer such questions as, Who am I when I'm not defined by being my parents' son or daughter? Who am I when I'm not defined by being so-and-so's spouse? Who am I when I'm not defined by the work I do? Who is the 'I' that has those roles and relations but is not fully expressed by any one of them? (Fowler 2001, p.109)

This is the time when the person takes responsibility for his or her beliefs and feelings. In this stage people develop an independent religious orientation on the basis of critical reflection and differentiate it from the views of those they relied on earlier: 'Stage 4 typically translates symbols into conceptual meanings. This is a "demythologizing" stage' (Fowler 1981, p.182). Religious symbols are reduced to abstract concepts, thus flattening their meaning; for example, religious services are seen as totemic rituals. Because many people rely excessively on rational thinking, reducing the symbolic meaning of religion(s) to (nearly meaningless) rituals, they remain at Stage 4, developing a sort of 'spiritual narcissism' that brings disrespect of faiths of others.[14] The dangers of this stage are in an excessive confidence in the conscious mind, and rational thinking that can lead to 'a kind of second narcissism in which the now clearly bounded, reflective self overassimilates "reality" and the perspectives of others into its own world view.' According to Fowler, only those who go through disillusionment and tragedy proceed to Stage 5: those who recognise 'that life is more complex than Stage 4 logic of clear distinctions and abstract concepts can comprehend' (Fowler 1981, p.183).[15]

Fowler's Stage 4 corresponds to Peck's Stage 3 – *Sceptic–individual*, when people start seriously questioning things and many end up being very non-religious (some stay in it permanently).

In contrast, some autistic individuals recognise the equal validity of all religions. For example, when Temple Grandin was still a child (10 or 11 years old):

> it seemed totally illogical to me that a Protestant religion was better than the Jewish or Catholic religion. I had a proper religious upbringing, with prayers every night, church on Sunday, and Sunday school every week. I was raised in the Episcopal church, but our Catholic cook believed that Catholicism was the only way to get to heaven. [Her] psychiatrist…was Jewish. It made no sense to me that my religion was better than theirs. To my mind, all methods and denominations of religious ceremony were equally valid, and I still hold this belief today. Different religious faiths all achieve communications with God and contain guiding moral principles. (Grandin 2006, pp.222–223)

She has met many autistic people who share her belief that all religions are valid and valuable; however, there are a few people with autism who adopt very rigid fundamentalist beliefs and become obsessed with religion, going to church every day and praying for hours. Grandin interprets this as not a belief but rather an obsession (Grandin 2006, p.223).

Stage 4: Individuality (Culliford 2007)

During the fourth stage of development, we differentiate ourselves from the original family and communal group, living behind the comfort zones, making the critical move towards spiritual maturity. And of course, 'some growing pains are inescapable'. That is why we must expect difficult situations and painful feelings. Problems and crisis during this stage, though threatening, 'can also act as cement, strengthening bonds between people' (Culliford 2007, pp.271, 266). Some can get stuck in this stage, and may remain lonely and unhappy. According to Culliford, some may end up with:

> a kind of spiritual malaise, resulting from failure to connect properly with the positive life force imbuing the sacred whole of the universe. [Some] may even be in denial that any such mysterious source of vital energy exists or can exist, especially when this has not yet been a direct part of [their] experience. (pp.271–272)

The way forward is opening up to new experiences, new teachers and new possibilities. In many families with an autistic child, this is the time when (after a long and painful psychological journey culminating in accepting the child not despite his or her autism but because of it), the parents experience a kind of awakening to new perspectives and priorities in their lives. And it is the time when many either re-evaluate their attitude to religion or acquire spiritual skills.

Stage 5: Conjunctive faith

This stage involves the embrace and integration of opposites and polarities in one's life. It is very rare to reach Stage 5 before 'mid-life':

> Stage 5 knows the sacrament of defeat and the reality of irrevocable commitments and acts. What the previous stage struggled to clarify in terms of the boundaries of self and outlook, this stage now makes porous and permeable. Alive to paradox and the truth in apparent contradictions, this stage strives to unify opposites and experience. It generates and maintains vulnerability to the strange truths of those who are 'other'. (Fowler 1981, p.198)

There are different factors that can trigger the potentially conjunctive encounter with 'other', such as internal contradictions between one's conscious ego and the unconscious, or external encounter with a culture that is very different from one's own, or even revisiting and re-evaluating elements of one's own religious background experienced and abandoned in Stage 4. Stage 5 'implies a rejoining or union of that which previously has been separated' (p.71). Though a very high stage, there are still positive and negative possibilities, summarised by Fowler as follows:

The new strength of this stage comes in the rise of the ironic imagination – a capacity to see and be in one's group's most powerful meanings, while simultaneously recognizing that they are relative, partial and inevitably distorting apprehensions of transcendent reality. Its danger lies in the direction of a paralyzing passivity or inaction, giving rise to complacency or cynical withdrawal, due to its paradoxical understanding of truth. (Fowler 1981, p.198)

He concludes that this stage remains divided because 'it lives and acts between an untransformed world and a transforming vision and loyalties'.

Stage 5: Integration (Culliford 2007)

Those who reach this stage begin to recognise the power of reciprocity, that whatever we do to others equates with doing it to ourselves. But they may still struggle to attain maturity and contentment. For example, they may no longer conceive of people as enemies, but this does not prevent some people from seeing them as a threat. So, during this stage, they have to learn to deal with that harmoniously. Destructive past actions should be psychologically accommodated, and some residual self-seeking tendencies contended and converted. 'Recognizing our shortcomings and making amends will be essential to our integration with the community of our origin and the new global community' (Culliford 2007, p.276). Culliford quotes Christ's commandments, which are important for this stage of development: 'to love God, and your neighbour as yourself'; 'First take the log out of your own eye, and then you will see clearly to take the speck out of your neighbour's eye' (Matthew 7:5) (with reference to projection); 'Do not store up for yourselves treasures on earth...but store up treasure in heaven' (Matthew 6:19–20) (spiritual over secular values); 'If anyone strikes you on the right cheek, turn the other also' (Matthew 5:39) (principles of 'interbeing' and reciprocity).

During this stage, people receive spiritual wisdom and experience profound feelings of joy, inner peace and a sincere gratitude that makes them want to give something back. With fresh insights they begin to take responsibility for their attitudes, values, beliefs and personal lifestyle. They learn to see things from the perspectives of others and become more tolerant and diplomatic. 'No longer interested in winning or losing arguments, [the] aim is not exactly to heal the past. It is more about healing the present, and preparing ourselves and others for a more harmonious future' (Culliford 2007, p.277).

Stage 6: Universalizing faith

> Beyond paradox and polarities, persons...[in this stage] are grounded in a oneness with the power of being God. Their visions and commitments seem to free them for a passionate yet detached spending of the self in love. Such persons are devoted to overcoming divisions, oppression, and violence, and live in effective anticipatory response to an unbreaking commonwealth of love and justice, the reality of an inbreaking kingdom of God. (Fowler 2001, p.113)

Very few achieve this.[16] This is how Fowler (1981, p.202) describes those who have succeeded in reaching the highest stage of faith development:

> [They] have become incarnators and actualizers of the spirit of an inclusive and fulfilled human community... Universalizers are often experienced as subversive of the structures (including religious structures) by which we sustain our individual and corporate survival, security and significance. (p.200)

Fowler gives examples of universalizers, including Mother Teresa, Lincoln, Gandhi and Martin Luther King, emphasising that, even though these individuals showed sacrificial devotion to resolving moral issues of their time, their 'greatness of commitment and vision often coexist with great blind spots and limitations'.

Peck (1987) combines Fowler's stages 5 and 6 into one: Stage 4 – *Mystical–communal*, when those who reach it start to realise that there is truth to be found in both the previous stages and that life can be paradoxical and full of mystery, with more emphasis on community than on individual concerns.

STAGE 6: BECOMING WHOLE (CULLIFORD 2007)
The process of becoming whole can take a long time but as a result:

> mature, selfless and spiritual values assert themselves...[the individuals in this stage become content with] cultivating loving and trusting friendships; taking each day as it comes; being grateful for

what [they] have; sharing it freely, however little; thinking, speaking and acting with kindness and compassion; being honest, especially with ourselves; being tolerant and accepting our limitations. (Culliford 2007, p.280)

Notes

1. My friend with Asperger syndrome interprets this as 'what goes around, comes around' – this is his life philosophy and helps him 'to find the right path at the crossing' (personal communication). He is a person who will go a mile to return a purse he had found at the bus stop; if someone is in trouble (it does not matter whether he knows the person or not), he would do his best to help.

2. Despite being the dominant theory of faith development, Fowler's model has been subjected to criticism for lack of empirical evidence (Batson, Schoenrade and Ventis 1993), being a male-centred theory, thus not necessarily applicable for females (Gilligan 1982); and conceptual flaws (e.g. hierarchical, sequential and invariant characteristics have been questioned) (Piper 2002).

3. This corresponds to the first of the Four Noble Truths taught by Buddha – 'Life is suffering.'

4. Robinson borrowed the title of his book from Edwin Muir's autobiography (1964): '[a child] probably never remembers [a picture of human existence peculiar to himself] after he has lost it: the original vision of the world' (p.33).

5. Both Farmer (1992) and Robinson (1983) believe that the Piagetian model of children's development could not be applied to their religious and spiritual understanding.

6. Professor Allan Snyder and colleagues have introduced an elegant theoretical construct of cognitive differences in autism as key factors of the condition: while 'normal' people are blinded by their 'mental paradigms' or 'mindsets', some autistic individuals are not concept-driven but have privileged access to nonconscious information (Snyder and Mitchell 1999; Snyder et al. 2004).

7. Other studies of children's understanding of God and religious metaphors have been conducted; see, for example, Erricker and Erricker 1996; Heller 1986; McCreery 1996; Tamminen 1994; Taylor 1989.

8. In secularised communities, conversion does happen to some, but much later, sometimes even in their retirement.

9. According to Otto, the numinous mystery of the Holy Other (divine mystery) can be experienced in two ways – *mysterium tremendum* (provoking terror, fear by being overwhelming power) and *mysterium fascinans* (evoking attraction, being merciful and gracious).

10. Goldman's position has been criticised by some researchers of children's spirituality; see, for example, Hay and Nye 2006; Hyde 1968; Langdon 1969; McGrady 1994.

11. Fowler calculated that about one-quarter of adults of 21 or older in his sample were at Stage 3 or lower.

12. At present, autism is a field that attracts quite a number of 'messiahs', who have found themselves artificially inflated to a place of importance, and happily accepted the position, imposing their opinion about things outside their competence, assuming

the role of the 'highest authority' in the field, and from time to time 'modestly' reminding their followers that it is not they who orginated their 'unique abilities to lead and educate' but what can they do if others think them so important?

13. For example, those who have developed personality disorders seem to be stuck in it for life.

14. About 60 per cent of Fowler's sample were in Stage 4 or in the transition from Stage 3 to Stage 4.

15. Only about 20 per cent of Fowler's sample were higher than Stage 4.

16. Only one of Fowler's sample had reached Stage 6.

Endword (and Beyond)

There is research evidence that spirituality is a source of strength, support and joy in the lives of people with learning disability in general (see, for example, Morgan 2004; Swinton 2001), and ASD in particular. However, their spiritual needs are often neglected, and it is not neccessarily because their carers and professionals opt to ignore these needs but rather because they do not know that these needs exist. The widely held assumption that everyone is supposed to *see* the same reality results in dogmatic rules to treat those who experience everything differently as 'abnormal' and in need of psychiatric help. That is why some autistic individuals might feel uncomfortable reporting their inner experiences (and others might feel equally uncomfortable hearing their stories). However, there is much we can learn from their ability to go beyond egocentricity to feel connected to the environment. To do that we have to recognise spiritual (or potentially spiritual) experiences in others and ourselves.

One of the difficulties is that many people are afraid to talk about their inner worlds. It is important to open this subject for discussion and to recognise (and not discredit) the very different ways some people with autism feel and think – a different worldview, because it is valid for them even if it does not make sense to those around them. (In some cases, they have no control over their 'unusual' experiences and will need help from those who can explain what is going on, and why, and teach them strategies to be in control.) Helping others to nurture their spirituality will help us all to rediscover our own sense of the spiritual and reconnect with our own spiritual dimension.

The reality is the same but our perceptions, interpretations and experiences of it are different. It is up to each of us to choose where we live – either in a restricted universe where 'God is dead', or to make acquaintance with the universe that is there for all to see when we are ready to look. Then we can discover numerous ways to *feel* our reality and find our place (and our selves) in it by being at one with the world.

Afterword

The wind whispered and created music as it propelled itself all around me, lightly touching the grass and weaving its way through the branches of the tree. I sail within the wind.

Curled under a majestic tree, I was safe and felt a belonging as I listened in wonderment to the stories the tree told of what it had seen and experienced. On the ground in front of me, the ants methodically worked as a unit for their very survival. I became one of them. I was part of. I was at peace.

Recently, a parent asked me where her autistic child is when he appears as if he has gone away into a different world. I asked her if she goes to yoga or another meditation-type class. She does. Our discussion continued until I finally said to her, where your child goes is the same place you are paying someone to teach you to go…away. Society strives to pull those on the spectrum into a world of confusion and is afraid for them when they appear so distant. Yet society invests a lot of money in their quest to go to this same distant place. Personally, I consider it one of the gifts of autism to have a mind emptiness that can be naturally achieved; ASD individuals need this as they are forced and force themselves to interact exhaustingly within society. Autistic individuals are protected and embraced under the umbrella of the autism spectrum. It is the 'typical' society that is standing in the storm.

Spirituality is referenced throughout history and has been translated diversely to serve humanity's thirst for answers to their yet undiscovered questions: to see beyond what has been scientifically proven, or accepted as true and taught as ideal, to achieve an innate awareness of reality, as to connect with all things in a harmonious reality.

Autism is considered a mystery of the mind, a neurological disorder that seemingly distances an individual into a realm of communication deficits and social blindness so that the person appears lost within a world of different perceptions and awareness.

As a child I could sense all of what was within nature and never did I feel I was observing from a different world but instead was a part of and belonged amongst the trees, the wind and the natural elements of all non-human living things. I could 'go away', not be here nor there, I just was. The natural wonderment and curiosity of childhood innocence allowed me to naturally and willingly succumb to all that was, without an awareness of it being an apparent experience.

As I aged and became infected with the expectations and demands of societal conformity, my connection to the natural essence and harmony of my environment began to fade. I learned about the pressure to excel within the standards and earn entitlement (privilege). I felt as though strings were being attached to a body, my body, the one that surrounded me and held me captive from truly being part of all things that were natural to me. The strings would pull me, and lead me to places where my senses would be bombarded with noise, intrusive sights, continually forcing meaningless information into my memory. Anxiety began to consume me as I was pulled further away from everything that just naturally existed for me. To fight back against the anxiety, I found and began to understand the peace I have inside that is a natural awareness that just is. It is neither timed nor prepared for, it is as if my mind and emotions just know, allowing me to release to all that is and I calm. There are no thoughts, no sense of self, no awareness of environment, no sense of body or mind...just gone...mindlessness. If I am placing effort on finding a balance within, focusing on my breathing, there remains a sense of being, of mindfulness. Mindlessness is no longer possible.

In order to survive, I learned to refine my childhood innocence and wonderment of all things real into an art of emotional achievement. Afraid that I would lose my cherished youthful connection and no longer be able to naturally achieve the experience and essence of awareness, I began to preserve my sense of self as I travelled within the confusing and sensorily overwhelming environment of society. I learned to adapt my connection to all, and discovered I could also express and remain connected with the fundamental nature of my reality, through the art of writing. I could express my thoughts and emotions and thus communicate to others who I was and still am. Where I did not fit in socially and lacked in society's standards of learning, I could effortlessly write. My perceptions, perspectives and internal self that sensed all in my environment, although I did not belong among others, through writing from my spirit, I could share. My capability to write allowed me a sense of comfort and a safe place to return to when 'the world' became overwhelming. At the same time in my life, I also discovered that I could remain connected to the natural world (the non-human world) through the spirit of the horse. Horses became my teachers, my guides. I could sense each of their emotions as though they were speaking to me telepathically. I learned the language of twitches, body movements, vocal sounds, and found balance and acceptance. The spirit of the horses allowed me to remain open and connected to all things as I grazed with the herd.

Temple Grandin tells of her journey as an autistic individual and how her connection and purpose in her life became apparent through her natural connection with cattle. She talks openly of how she could not just sense the cattle but physically and emotionally feel the spirit of the cow, as if she and the cow were as one and the same existence. Temple did not see herself as the cow; she describes how she could, and still does, experience a connection to the sensory and emotional experiences of the cattle and then would place herself into the situation that the cattle were experiencing. I, too, am able to sense and experience through the animal, through the horse.

Religion frightened me as a child. The stories that were told in church taught me how cruel the world could be. The verses that were read and repeated, I understood literally and feared the messages many expressed: 'Now I lay me down to sleep…if I die before I wake.' I became afraid to sleep! I also could not understand why it mattered what I wore to go to church. The itchy frills on the dresses I was required to wear irritated my skin and frustrated me. At church and during Sunday school, I questioned why they spoke about the beauty of all things natural but we should be in a building that was so unnatural and noisy with pictures and windows depicting violence and death. Why should I be praying to achieve a connection to all things when this can be better achieved by the experience of the true connection to nature itself? I felt a deeper connection once services were over and I could exchange my Sunday clothes for my blue jeans and stroll through the forest near our house. In my later years I rediscovered the value of different religious beliefs and the service they provide within different societies as people reach out for guidance and answers. I do not judge nor speak of religion as I have no right to decide or have power over another human being's choices and ideals. I instead choose to communicate through my thoughts and actions for all things, an openness, to not just practise but to 'be' patient, gentle, compassionate and altruistic. My ability to belong within all things will remain as I will not compromise who I am in my existence as an autistic individual. I am content to remain transfixed on the splashes of rain as it synchronises a rhythm in the puddles, to 'go away' and be neither here nor there but instead be mindless with no sense of space, only openness.

Children are taught to suppress their natural openness and are regimentally educated to believe that their perceptions of youth are mundane. In order for them to survive they must let go of such beliefs and conform to what is accepted. In adulthood spirituality is again sought as a connection in order to balance the feelings of a lost existence to all things. Autism is a natural link to a spiritual balance through the connection of the autistic person's sensory realities of awareness. Autism is within the spiritual experience. Science is focused on discovering what appears dysfunctional in ASD when instead research should be aimed at the natural functionality and benefits of what is reality in ASD. Answers to the yet undiscovered questions pertaining to spiritualism may well be found in the unanswered questions and sincere understanding of autism.

As my mind empties of all thought and emotion, it is not recharging so much as rediscovering my own inner balance and it does not cost anything. I jokingly call it a cheap way to go on vacation from chaos.

As you read through the pages, you will have gathered and become absorbed into the theories and facts of both the scientific studies and the mysterious realm of the autism spectrum. Enter with an open mind to all concepts of perception, probabilities and possibilities; which may lead you to an enlightenment and a level of mindfulness to discover an understanding of autism and spirituality.

Nancy Getty
Diagnosed as an adult and the parent of twins,
both diagnosed on the autism spectrum
Founder of A.S.P.I.E.S.
www.aspergerrus.com

References

Aaen-Stockdale, C. (2012) 'Neuroscience for the soul.' *The Psychologist, 25*, 7, 520–523.

Abram, D. (1997) *The Spell of the Sensuous.* New York: Vintage Books.

Adams, K., Hyde, B. and Woolley, R. (2008) *The Spiritual Dimension of Childhood.* London: Jessica Kingsley Publishers.

Adler, L.E., Waldo, M.C. and Freedman, R. (1985) 'Neurophysiologic studies of sensory gating in schizophrenia: Comparison of auditory and visual responses.' *Biological Psychiatry, 20*, 1284–1296.

Adolphs, R. (2006) 'How do we know the minds of others? Domain-specificity, simulation, and enactive social cognition.' *Brain Research, 1079*, 25–35.

Allman, L.S., De La Roche, O., Elkins, D.N. and Weathers, R.S. (1992) 'Psychotherapists' attitudes towards clients reporting mystical experiences.' *Psychotherapy, 29*, 564–569.

Amaral, D.G., Bauman, M.D. and Schumann, C.M. (2003) 'The amygdala and autism: Implications from human primate studies.' *Genes Brain and Behavior, 2*, 295–302.

Anderson, A. (2006) In J. Brockman (ed.) *What We Believe But Cannot Prove: Today's Leading Thinkers on Science in the Age of Creativity.* London: Pocket Books.

Anderson, J.R. (1984) 'The development of self-recognition: A review.' *Developmental Psychology, 17*, 35–49.

Anderson, R.G. and Young, J.L. (1988) 'The religious component of acute hospital treatment.' *Hospital and Community Psychiatry, 39*, 528–555.

Armstrong-Buck, S. (1989) 'Nonhuman experience: A Whiteheadian analysis.' *Process Studies, 18*, 1, 1–18.

Aron, E.N. (1996) *The Highly Sensitive Person: How to Strive When the World Overwhelms You.* New York: Carol Publishing Group.

Asperger, H. (1944) 'Die "Autistishen Psychopathen" im Kindesalter.' *Archiv für Psychiatrie und Nervenkrankbeiten, 117*, 76–136.

Asperger, H. (1979) 'Problems with infantile autism.' *Communication, 13*, 45–52.

Austin, J. (1999) *Zen and the Brain.* London: MIT Press.

Ayer, A.J. (1946) *Language, Truth and Logic,* 2nd edn. New York: Dover.

Bach, S. (1990) *Life Paints its Own Span: On the Significance of Spontaneous Pictures by Severely Ill Children.* Zurich: Daimon.

Bachevalier, J. and Loveland, K.A. (2006) 'The orbitofrontal-amygdala circuit and self-regulation of social-emotional behavior in autism.' *Neuroscience and Behavioral Reviews, 30*, 97–117.

Back, K. and Bourque, L.B. (1970) 'Can feelings be enumerated?' *Behavioural Science, 15*, 487–496.

Banissy, M.J. and Ward, J. (2007) 'Mirror touch synaesthesia is linked with empathy.' *Nature Neuroscience, 10*, 815–816.

Barnbaum, D.R. (2008) *The Ethics of Autism: Among them, but not of them.* Bloomington and Indianapolis: Indiana University Press.

Bar-On, R. (1997) *The Emotional Quotient (EQ-i): Technical Manual.* Mahwah, NY: Lawrence Erlbaum.

Baron-Cohen, S. (2011) *The Science of Evil: On Empathy and the Origins of Cruelty.* New York: Basic Books.

Baron-Cohen, S., Leslie, A.M. and Frith, U. (1985) 'Does the autistic child have a "theory of mind"?' *Cognition, 21,* 37–46.

Baron-Cohen, S., Ring, H.A., Bullmore, E.T., Wheelwright, S., Ashwin, C. and Williams, S.C. (2000) 'The amygdala theory of autism.' *Neuroscience and Behavioral Reviews, 24,* 355–364.

Baron-Cohen, S., Ring, H.A., Wheelwright, S., Bullmore, E.T., Brammer, M.J., Simmons, A. and Williams, S.C. (1999) 'Social intelligence in the normal and autistic brain: An fMRI study.' *European Journal of Neuroscience, 11,* 1891–1898.

Barsalou, L.W. (1999) 'Perceptual symbol systems.' *Behavioral and Brain Science, 22,* 577–609.

Batson, C.D., Schoenrade, P. and Ventis, W.L. (1993) *Religion and the Individual.* New York: Oxford University Press.

Battaglia, D. (1990) *On the Bones of the Serpent: Person, Memory and Morality in Sabarl Island Society.* Chicago, IL: University of Chicago Press.

Beauregard, M. and O'Leary, D. (2007) *The Spiritual Brain: A Neuroscientist's Case for the Existence of the Soul.* New York: HarperCollins.

Bekoff, M. (2007) *The Emotional Lives of Animals.* Novato, CA: New World Library.

Bekoff, M. (2010) *The Animal Manifesto.* Novato, CA: New World Library.

Bergin, A. and Jensen, J. (1990) 'Religiosity of psychotherapists: A national survey.' *Psychotherapy, 27,* 3–7.

Bergman, P. and Escalona, S.K. (1949) 'Unusual sensitivities in very young children.' *The Psychoanalytic Study of the Child, 3,* 4, 333–352.

Bergson, H. (1944[1911]) *Creative Evolution.* New York: The Modern Library.

Bergson, H. (2004[1912]) *Matter and Memory.* Mineola, NY: Dover Publications.

Berrios, G.E. and Markova, I.S. (2003) 'The self and psychiatry: A conceptual history.' In. T. Kircher and A. David (eds) *The Self in Neuroscience and Psychiatry.* Cambridge: Cambridge University Press.

Bexton, W.H., Woodburn, H. and Scott, T.H. (1954) 'Effects of decreased variation in the sensory environment.' *Canadian Journal of Psychology, 8,* 2, 70–76.

Bindl, M. (1965) *Das religiöse Erleben im Spiegel der Bildgestaltung: Eine Entwwicklungs-psychologie Untersuchung.* Freiburg: Herder.

Bissonnier, H. (1965) 'Religious expression and mental deficiency.' In A. Godin (ed.) *From Religious Expression to Religious Attitude.* Brussels: Lumen Vitae Press.

Blackburn, S. (ed.) (1994) *Dictionary of Philosophy.* Oxford: Oxford University Press.

Blackman, L. (2001) *Lucy's Story: Autism and Other Adventures.* London: Jessica Kingsley Publishers.

Blair, R.J. (1995) 'A cognitive developmental approach to morality: Investigating the psychopath.' *Cognition, 57,* 1, 1–29.

Blair, R.J.R. (1996) 'Brief report: Morality in the autistic child.' *Journal of Autism and Developmental Disorders, 26,* 5, 571–579.

Blakemore, S.J., Bristow, D., Bird, G., Frith, C. and Ward, J. (2005) 'Somatosensory activations during the observation of touch and a case of vision–touch synaesthesia.' *Brain, 128,* 1571–1583.

Bleuler, E. (1950[1911]) *Dementia Praecox, or, The Group of Schizophrenias.* Oxford: International Universities Press.

Block, J.R. and Yuker, H.E. (1989) *Can You Believe Your Eyes? Over 250 Illusions and Other Visual Oddities.* New York: Psychology Press.

Block, N., Flanagan, O. and Güzeldere, G. (eds) (1997) *The Nature of Consciousness: Philosophical Debates.* Cambridge, MA: MIT Press.

Bogart, G. (1991) 'The use of meditation in psychotherapy.' *American Journal of Psychotherapy, 45,* 3, 383–412.

Bogart, G.C. (1992) 'Separating from a spiritual teacher.' *Journal of Transpersonal Psychology, 24,* 1, 1–22.

Bogdashina, O. (2004) *Communication Issues in Autism and Asperger Syndrome: Do We Speak the Same Language?* London: Jessica Kingsley Publishers.

Bogdashina, O. (2005) *Theory of Mind and the Triad of Perspectives on Autism and Asperger Syndrome: A View from the Bridge.* London: Jessica Kingsley Publishers.

Bogdashina, O. (2010) *Autism and the Edges of the Known World: Sensitivities, Language and Constructed Reality*. London: Jessica Kingsley Publishers.

Bosacki, S. (2001) 'Theory of mind or theory of the soul? The role of spirituality in children's understanding of minds and emotions.' In J. Erricker, C. Ota and C. Erricker (eds) *Spiritual Education: Cultural, Religious and Social Differences. New Perspectives for the 21st Century*. Brighton: Sussex Academic.

Bosch, G. (1970) *Infantile Autism* (trans. D. Jordan and I. Jordan). New York: Springer.

Boutros, N., Kozuukov, O., Jansen, B., Feingold, A. and Bell, M. (2004) 'Sensory gating deficits during the mid-latency phase of information processing in medicated schizophrenia patients.' *Psychiatry Research, 126*, 203–215.

Boyer, P. 'What makes anthropomorphism natural: Intuitive ontology and cultural representations.' *Journal of Royal Anthropological Institute, 2*, 83–97.

Boyer, P. and Ramble, C. (2002) 'Cognitive templates for religious concepts: Cross-cultural evidence for recall of counter-intuitive representations.' *Cognitive Science, 25*, 535–564.

Bowie, F. (2006) *The Anthropology of Religion: An Introduction*. Oxford: Blackwell.

Bradley, B. (1983) 'Negative self-schemata in clinical depression.' *British Journal of Clinical Psychology, 22*, 3, 173–181.

Bragdon, E. (1994) *A Sourcebook for Helping People with Spiritual Problems*. Aptos, CA: Lightening Up Press.

Brett, C. (2010) 'Transformative crises.' In I. Clarke (ed.) *Psychosis and Spirituality: Consolidating the New Paradigm*, 2nd edn. Oxford: Wiley-Blackwell.

Brewer, W.F. (1986) 'What is autobiographical memory?' In D.C. Rubin (ed.) *Autobiographical Memory*. Cambridge: Cambridge University Press.

Brooks, D.H.M. (1994) *The Unity of the Mind*. London: Allen and Unwin.

Bucci, W. (1997) 'Symptoms and symbols: A multiple code theory of somatization.' *Psychiatric Inquiry, 2*, 151–172.

Buckman, R. and Sabbagh, K. (1993) *Magic or Medicine: An Investigation of Healing and Healers*. New York: Prometheus Books.

Bufalari, I., Aprile, T., Avenanti, A., Di Russo, F. and Aglioty, S.M. (2007) 'Empathy for pain and touch in the human cerebral cortex.' *Cerebral Cortex, 17*, 2553–2561.

Cambridge Dictionaries Online (2013) 'Spirituality.' Available at http://dictionary.cambridge. org/dictionary/british/spirituality?q=spirituality, accessed on 24 April 2013.

Campbell, C.A. (1957) *On Selfhood and Godhood*. London: Allen and Unwin.

Casanova, M.F., Buxhoeveden, D.P. and Brown, C. (2002) 'Clinical and macroscopic correlatesof minicolumnar pathology in autism.' *Journal of Child Neurology, 17*, 692–695.

Charles, M. (1999) 'Patterns: Unconscious shaping of self and experience.' *Journal of Melanie Klein and Object Relations, 17*, 2, 367–388.

Chomsky, N. (1957) *Syntactic Structures*. The Hague: Mouton Publishers.

Claridge, G. (1997) *Schizotypy: Implications for Illness and Health*. Oxford: Oxford University Press.

Claridge, G. (2002) *Personality and Psychological Disorders*. London: Hodder Education.

Claridge, G. (2010) 'Spiritual experience: Healthy psychoticism?' In I. Clarke (ed.) *Psychosis and Spirituality: Consolidating the New Paradigm*, 2nd edn. Oxford: Wiley-Blackwell.

Clarke, A. (2000) *Profiles of the Future: An Inquiry into the Limits of the Possible*. London: Indigo.

Clarke, I. (2008) *Madness, Mystery and the Survival of God*. Winchester: O Books.

Clarke, I. (ed.) (2010) *Psychosis and Spirituality: Consolidating the New Paradigm*, 2nd edn. Oxford: Wiley-Blackwell.

Cloninger, C.R. (2004) *Feeling Good: The Science of Well-Being*. New York: Oxford University Press.

Cloninger, C.R., Svrakic, D.M. and Przybeck, T.R. (1993) 'A psychobiological model of temperament and character.' *Archives of General Psychiatry, 50*, 12, 975–990.

Cohen, L.B. (1991) 'Infant attention: An information processing approach.' In M.J. Zelazo (ed.) *Newborn Attention: Biological Constraints and the Influence of Experience*. Norwood, NJ: Ablex.

Cole, E. and Ochshorn, J. (1995) *Women's Spirituality, Women's Lives*. London: Routledge.

Coles, R. (1992) *The Spiritual Life of Children*. London: HarperCollins.

Cowey, A. and Stoerig, P. (1991) 'The neurology of blindsight.' *Trends in Neuroscience, 14*, 140–145.

Crepeau, L. and Panksepp, J. (1988) 'Dual olfactory system and cat smell-attenuated juvenile rat play.' *Neurosciens Abstracts, 14,* 1104.

Critchley, H.D., Daly, E.M., Mullmore, E.T., Williams, S.C. *et al.* (2000) 'The functional neuroanatomy of social behaviour changes in cerebral blood flow when people with autistic disorder process facial expressions.' *Brain, 123,* 11, 2203–2212.

Culliford, L. (2007) *Love, Healing and Happiness: Spiritual Wisdom for Secular Times.* Winchester: O Books.

Damasio, A. (1994) *Descartes' Error: Emotion, Reason and the Human Brain.* New York: G.P. Putnam's Sons.

Damasio, A. (2000) *The Feeling of What Happens: Body, Emotion and the Making of Human Consciousness.* London: Vintage.

Daria, T.O. (2008) *Dasha's Journal.* London: Jessica Kingsley Publishers.

Davidson, G.M. (1941) 'A syndrome of time-agnosia.' *Journal of Nervous and Mental Disease, 94,* 336–343.

Davies, M., Stankov, I. and Roberts, R. (1998) 'Emotional intelligence: In search of a new elusive construct.' *Journal of Personality and Social Psychology, 75,* 989–1015.

Davies, M. and Whalen, P.J. (2001) 'The amygdala: Vigilance and emotion.' *Molecular Psychiatry, 6,* 13–34.

Davis, T., Hoffman, D. and Rodriguez, A. (2002) 'Visual worlds: Construction and reconstruction.' In A. Noe (ed.) *Is the Visual World a Grand Illusion?* Exeter: Imprint Academic.

Dawkins, R. (1989) *The Selfish Gene.* Oxford: Oxford University Press.

Dawkins, R. (2006) *The God Delusion.* New York: Bantam Books.

Dennett, D.C. (1991) *Consciousness Explained.* London: Penguin.

Dennett, D.C. (2006) In J. Brockman (ed.) *What We Believe But Cannot Prove: Today's Leading Thinkers on Science in the Age of Creativity.* London: Pocket Books.

de Quincey, C. (1994) 'Consciousness all the way down?' *Journal of Consciousness Studies, 1,* 2, 217–229.

d'Espagnat, B. (1973) 'Conceptual foundations of quantum mechanics.' In J. Mehra (ed.) *The Physicist's Conception of Nature.* Boston, MA: Kluwer.

De Waal, F. (2006) *Primates and Philosophers: How Morality Evolved.* Princeton, NJ: Princeton University Press.

Doidge, N. (2001) 'Diagnosing *The English Patient*: Schizoid fantasies of being skinless and being buried alive.' *Journal of American Psychoanalytic Association, 49,* 279–309.

Donaldson, M. (1992) *Human Minds.* London: Allen Lane.

Dostoevsky, F.M. (1930) Письма. т.2, М.–Л.

Downs, A. and Smith, T. (2004) 'Emotional understanding, cooperation, and social behavior in high-functioning children with autism.' *Journal of Autism and Developmental Disorders, 34,* 6, 625–635.

Dritschel, B.H., Williams, J.M., Baddeley, A.D. and Nimmo-Smith, I. (1992) 'Autobiographical fluency: A method for the study of personal memory.' *Memory and Cognition, 20,* 133–140.

Durham, W. (1991) *Co-Evolution, Genes, Culture and Human Diversity.* Stanford, CA: Stanford University Press.

Durkheim, E. (1976[1915]) *The Elementary Forms of the Religious Life* (trans. J.W. Swain). London: George Allen and Unwin.

Edelman, G. (1989) *The Remembered Present.* New York: Basic Books.

Eisenberger, N.I. and Lieberman, M.D. (2004) 'Why rejection hurts: A common neural alarm system for physical and social pain.' *TRENDS in Cognitive Sciences, 8,* 7, 294–300.

Ekman, P. (1994) 'All emotions are basic.' In P. Ekman and R.J. Davidson (eds) *The Nature of Emotion: Fundamental Questions.* New York: Oxford University Press.

Elkind, D. and Elkind, S. (1962) 'Varieties of religious experience in young adolescents.' *Journal for the Scientific Study of Religion, 2,* 102–112.

Elton-Chalcraft, S. (2002) 'Empty wells: How well are we doing at spiritual well-being?' *International Journal of Children's Spirituality, 8,* 2, 151–162.

Emmons, R. (1999) *The Psychology of Ultimate Concern: Motivation and Spirituality in Personality.* New York: Guilford.

Emmons, R. (2000) 'Is spirituality an intelligence? Motivation, cognition and the psychology of ultimate concern.' *International Journal for the Psychology of Religion, 10*, 1, 3–26.

Emoto, M. (2005) *The Hidden Messages in Water.* New York: Pocket Books.

Epstein, M. (1990) 'Psychodynamics of meditation: Pitfalls on the spiritual path.' *Journal of Transpersonal Psychology, 22*, 1, 17–34.

Erickson, E.H. (1963) *Childhood and Society*, 2nd edn. New York: W.W. Norton.

Erikson, E.H. (1968) *Identity: Youth and Crisis.* New York: W.W. Norton.

Erricker, J. (2001) 'Spirituality and the notion of citizenship in education.' In J. Erricker, C. Ota and C. Erricker (eds) *Spiritual Education: Cultural, Religious and Social Differences. New Perspective for the 21st Century.* Brighton: Sussex Academic.

Erricker, C. and Erricker, J. (1996) 'Where angels fear to tread: Discovering children's spirituality.' In R. Best (ed.) *Education, Spirituality and the Whole Child.* London: Cassell.

Erricker, C., Erricker, J., Sullivan, D., Ota, C. and Fletcher, M. (1997) *The Education of the Whole Child.* London: Cassell.

Etzioni, A. (1995) *The Spirit of Community: Rights, Responsibilities and the Communication Agenda.* London: Fontana.

Evans-Pritchard, E.E. (1972) *Theories of Primitive Religion.* Oxford: Oxford University Press.

Farah, M.J. and Feinberg, T.E. (1997) 'Perception and awareness.' In T.E. Feinberg and M.J. Farah (eds) *Behavioral Neurology and Neuropsychology.* New York: McGraw-Hill.

Farmer, L. (1992) 'Religious experience in childhood: A study of adult perspectives in early spiritual awareness.' *Religious Education, 87*, 259–268.

Feinberg, T.E. and Keenan, J.P. (2005) 'Where in the brain is the self?' *Consciousness and Cognition, 14*, 4, 671–678.

Fenwick, P. (2010) 'The neurophysiology of religious experience.' In I. Clarke (ed) *Psychosis and Spirituality*, 2nd edn. Oxford: Wiley-Blackwell.

Fenwick, P., Galliano, S., Coate, M.A., Rippere, V. *et al.* (1985) 'Sensitives, "psychic gifts", psychic sensitivity and brain pathology.' *British Journal of Medical Psychology, 58*, 35–44.

Fernando, S. (1991) *Mental Health, Race and Culture.* Basingstoke: Macmillan.

Feuerbach, L. (1957) *The Essence of Christianity.* New York: Prometheus Books.

Fisher, J. (1999) 'Helps to fostering students' spiritual health.' *International Journal of Children's Spirituality, 4*, 29–49.

Flanagan, O. (1996) *Self Expressions: Mind, Morals, and the Meaning of Life.* New York: Oxford University Press.

Flew, A. (1949) 'Selves.' *Mind, 63*, 355–358.

Fontana, D. (2003) *Psychology, Religion and Spirituality.* Oxford: BPS Blackwell.

Forrest, D. (ed.) (1996) *A Glimpse of Hell.* London: Amnesty International.

Foster, G.M. (1976) 'Disease etiologies in non-Western medical systems.' *American Anthropologist, 78*, 4, 773–782.

Fowler, J.W. (1981) *Stages of Faith: The Psychology of Human Development and the Quest for Meaning.* New York: HarperCollins.

Fowler, J.W. (2000) *Faithful Change.* Nashville, TN: Abington Press.

Fowler, J.W. (2001) *Weaving the New Creation.* Eugene, OR: Wipf and Stock.

Francis, L. (1987) 'The decline in attitudes toward religion among 8–15 year olds.' *Educational Studies, 13*, 2, 125–134.

Frazer, J. (1890) *The Golden Bough: A Study in Comparative Religion.* London: Cassell.

Freedman, R., Olincy, A., Ross, R.G., Waldo, M.C. *et al.* (2003) 'The genetics of sensory gating in schizophrenia.' *Current Psychiatry, 5*, 155–161.

Freud, S. (1928) *The Future of an Illusion.* London: Hogarth Press.

Frey, A.H. and Messenger, Jr., R. (1973) 'Human perception of illumination with pulsed ultrahigh-frequency electromagnetic energy.' *Science, 181*, 356–358.

Frith, U. (2003[1989]) *Autism: Explaining the Enigma.* Oxford: Basil Blackwell.

Frith, U. and Happe, F. (1999) 'Theory of mind and self-consciousness: What is it like to be autistic?' *Mind and Language, 14*, 23–31.

Furth, G. (1988) *The Secret World of Children's Drawings: Healing through Art.* Boston, MA: Sigo Press.

Gagliano, M., Mancuso, S. and Robert, D. (2012) 'Towards understanding plant bioacoustics.' *Trends in Plant Science, 17,* 323–325.

Gallup, G.H. and Newport, F. (1991) 'Belief in paranormal phenomena among adult Americans.' *Skeptical Inquirer, 15,* 137–146.

Gallup, G.G. (1968) 'Mirror-image stimulation.' *Psychological Bulletin, 70,* 782–793.

Gallup, G.G. (1979) 'Self-recognition in chimpanzees and man: A developmental and comparative perspective.' In M. Lewis and A. Rosenblum (eds) *The Child and Its Family.* New York: Plenum Press.

Gardner, H. (1983) *Frames of Mind: The Theory of Multiple Intelligences.* New York: Basic Books.

Gardner, H. (2000) 'A case against spiritual intelligence.' *International Journal for the Psychology of Religion, 10,* 1, 27–34.

Gardner, P.M. (2007) 'On puzzling wavelengths.' In J.-G.A. Goulet and B.G. Miller (eds) *Extraordinary Anthropology.* Lincoln, NE: University of Nebraska Press.

Gazzaniga, M.S. (1988) 'Brain modularity: Towards a philosophy of conscious experience.' In A.J. Marcel and E. Bisiach (eds) *Consciousness in Contemporary Science.* Oxford: Clarendon Press.

Geertz, C. (1973) 'Religion as a cultural system.' In M. Banton (ed.) *Anthropological Approaches to the Study of Religion.* ASA Monographs 3. London: Tavistock.

Geirnaert-Martin, D. (1992) *The Woven Land of Laboya: Socio-Cosmic Ideas and Values in West Sumba, Eastern Indonesia.* Leiden: Centre of Non-Western Studies.

Gelernter, D. (2006) In J. Brockman (ed.) *What We Believe But Cannot Prove: Today's Leading Thinkers on Science in the Age of Creativity.* London: Pocket Books.

Gerald, L.W. (1972) 'Cosmic rays: Detection with the eye.' *Science, 175,* 615.

Gerland, G. (1997) *A Real Person: Life on the Outside.* London: Souvenir Press.

Gershon, M. (1998) *The Second Brain.* New York: HarperCollins.

Gilligan, C. (1982) *In a Different Voice.* Cambridge, MA: Harvard University Press.

Glock, C.Y. and Stark, R. (1965) *Religion and Society in Tension.* Chicago, IL: Rand McNally.

Goldman, R. (1964) *Religious Thinking from Childhood to Adolescence.* London: Routledge.

Goldman, R. (1965) *Readiness for Religion.* London: Routledge.

Goleman, D. (1995) *Emotional Intelligence.* New York: Bantam.

Goodall, J. (2001) 'Foreword.' In S.M. Wise, *Rattling the Cage.* New York: Perseus Books.

Goodall, J. (2008) 'Primate spirituality.' In B. Tylor (ed.) *The Encyclopedia of Religion and Nature.* New York: Continuum International Publishing, pp.1303–1306.

Graham, A. (1968) *Conversations: Christian and Buddhist.* New York: Harcourt Brace Jovanovich.

Grandin, T. (1992) 'Autistic emotions.' *The Advocate,* Spring, 6–8.

Grandin, T. (1997) 'Making the transition from the world of school into the world of work.' Available at www.iidc.indiana.edu/index.php?pageId=599, accessed 30 April 2013.

Grandin, T. (1998) 'Consciousness in animals and people with autism.' Available at www.grandin. com/references/animal.consciousness.html, accessed 28 February 2013.

Grandin, T. (2006) *Thinking in Pictures and Other Reports from My Life with Autism,* 2nd edn. London: Bloomsbury.

Grandin, T. (2008) *The Way I See It: A Personal Look at Autism and Asperger's.* Arlington, TX: Future Horizons.

Grandin, T. and Johnson, C. (2005) *Animals in Translation: Using Mysteries of Autism to Decode Animal Behaviour.* London: Bloomsbury.

Granqvist, P., Fredrikson, M., Unge, P., Hagenfeldt, A. *et al.* (2005) 'Sensed presence and mystical experiences are predicted by suggestibility, not by the application of transcranial weak complex magnetic fields.' *Neuroscience Letters, 379,* 1, 1–6.

Granville, M. (1899) 'Ways of remembering.' *Lancet,* 27 September, 458.

Greeley, A. (1974) *Ecstasy: A Way of Knowing.* Englewood Cliffs, NJ: Prentice Hall.

Greeley, A. (1975) *The Sociology of Paranormal: A Reconnaissance.* Beverly Hills, CA: Sage.

Greyson, B. (1983) 'The Near-death Experience Scale: Construction, reliability and validity.' *Journal of Nervous and Mental Disease, 171,* 369–375.

Greyson, B. (1997) 'The near-death experience as a focus of clinical attention.' *Journal of Nervous and Mental Disease, 185,* 5, 327–334.

Greyson, B. and Harris, B. (1987) 'Clinical approaches to the near-death experience.' *Journal of Near-Death Studies, 6*, 1, 41–52.

Gribbin, J. (1991) *In Search of Schrodinger's Cat: Quantum Physics and Reality.* London: Black Swan.

Griffin, D. (1984) *Animal Thinking.* Cambridge, MA: Harvard University Press.

Griffin, D. (1998) 'From cognition to consciousness.' *Animal Cognition, 1*, 1, 3–16.

Grof, S. and Grof, C. (1986) 'Spiritual emergency: The understanding and treatment of transpersonal crisis.' *Re-Vision, 8*, 7–20.

Grof, S. and Grof, C. (1989) 'Spiritual emergency: Understanding evolutionary crisis.' In. S. Grof and C. Grof (eds) *Spiritual Emergency: When Personal Transformation Becomes a Crisis.* New York: Jeremy P. Tarcher/Putnam.

Gunn, J.A. (1920) *Bergson and His Philosophy.* London: Methuen & Company.

Hall, G.S. (1897) 'Some aspects of the early sense of Self.' *American Journal of Psychology, 9*, 3, 351–395.

Happe, F. (1995) 'The role of age and verbal ability in the theory of mind task performance of subjects with autism.' *Child Development, 66*, 843–855.

Hardy, A. (1965) *The Living Stream: The Restatement of Evolution Theory and Its Relation to the Spirit of Man.* London: Collins.

Hardy, A. (1966) *The Divine Flame: An Essay Towards a Natural History of Religion.* London: Collins.

Hardy, A. (1979) *The Spiritual Nature of Man.* Oxford: Clarendon Press.

Harre, R. (1987) 'Persons and selves.' In A. Peacocke and G. Gillet (eds) *Persons and Personality: A Contemporary Enquiry.* Oxford: Blackwell.

Hart, T. (2003) *The Secret Spiritual World of Children.* Maui: Inner Ocean.

Hartmann, E. (1991) *Boundaries of the Mind: A New Psychology of Personality.* New York: HarperCollins.

Hatfield, E., Cacioppo, J. and Rapson, R. (1994) *Emotional Contagion.* Cambridge: Cambridge University Press.

Hay, D. (1990) *Religious Experience Today: Studying the Facts.* London: Cassell.

Hay, D. (1994) 'Prosocial development.' *Journal of Child Psychology and Psychiatry and Allied Disciplines, 35*, 29–71.

Hay, D. (2001) 'The biological basis of spiritual awareness.' In U. King (ed.) *Spirituality and Society in the New Millennium.* Brighton & Portland: Sussex Academic Press, pp.124–135.

Hay, D. and Heald, G. (1987) 'Religion is good for you.' *New Society*, 17 April.

Hay, D. and Hunt, K. (2000) *Understanding the Spirituality of People Who Don't Go to Church. Research Report.* Nottingham: University of Nottingham.

Hay, D. and Hunt, K. (2002) *Understanding the Spirituality of People Who Don't Go to Church – the Final Report of the Adult Spirituality Project.* Nottingham: University of Nottingham.

Hay, D. and Morisy, A. (1978) 'Reports of ecstatic, paranormal or religious experience in Britain and the United States: A comparison of trends.' *Journal for the Scientific Study of Religion, 17*, 3, 255–268.

Hay, D. and Morisy, A. (1985) 'Secular society/religious meanings: A contemporary paradox.' *Review of Religious Research, 26*, 3, 213–227.

Hay, D. and Nye, R. (2006) *The Spirit of the Child*, rev. edn. London: Jessica Kingsley Publishers.

Heller, D. (1986) *The Children's God.* Chicago, IL: University of Chicago Press.

Heller, S. (2002) *Too Loud, Too Bright, Too Fast, Too Tight: What to Do If You Are Sensory Defensive in an Overstimulating World.* New York: HarperCollins.

Hill, A.A. (1958) *Introduction to Linguistic Structures.* New York: Harcourt.

Hill, P.C., Pargament, K.I., Wood, R.W., McCullough, M.E. *et al.* (2000) 'Conceptualizing religion and spirituality: Points of commonality, points of departure.' *Journal of Theory of Social Behavior, 30*, 51–77.

Hobson, R.P. (1989a) 'Beyond cognition: A theory of autism.' In G. Dawson (ed.) *Autism: Nature, Diagnosis, and Treatment.* New York: Guilford.

Hobson, R.P. (1989b) 'On sharing experiences.' *Development and Psychopathology, 1*, 197–203.

Hobson, R.P. (1995) 'Blindness and psychological development 0–10 years.' Paper presented to Mary Kitzinger Trust Symposium, University of Warwick, September.

Hoffman, D.D. (2006) In J. Brockman (ed.) *What We Believe But Cannot Prove: Today's Leading Thinkers on Science in the Age of Creativity.* London: Pocket Books.

Hood, B. (2009) *Supersense: From Superstition to Religion – the Brain Science of Belief.* London: Constable and Robinson.

Hood, R.W. (1974) 'Psychological strength and the report of intense religious experience.' *Journal for the Scientific Study of Religion, 13,* 65–71.

Hume, D. (1978) *A Treatise on Human Nature.* Oxford: Clarendon Press. (Originally published 1739.)

Humphrey, N. (1992) *A History of the Mind: Evolution and the Birth of Consciousness.* London: Chatto and Windus.

Humphrey, N. (2002) 'The placebo effect.' In R.L. Gregory (ed.) *The Oxford Companion to the Mind.* Oxford: Oxford University Press, pp.735–736.

Huxley, A. (2004a) *The Doors of Perception.* London: Vintage. (Originally published 1954.)

Huxley, A. (2004b) *Heaven and Hell.* London: Vintage. (Originally published 1956.)

Hyde, B. (2008) *Children and Spirituality: Searching for Meaning and Connectedness.* London: Jessica Kingsley Publishers.

Hyde, K. (1968) 'The critique of Goldman's research.' *Religious Education, 63,* 429–435.

Ikeya, M. (2004) *Earthquakes and Animals: From Folk Legends to Science.* Singapore: World Scientific Publishing.

Innes-Smith, M. (1987) 'Pre-oedipal identification and the cathexis of autistic object in the aetiology of adult psychopathology.' *International Journal of Psycho-Analysis, 68,* 405–413.

Isanon, A. (2001) *Spirituality and the Autism Spectrum: Of Falling Sparrows.* London: Jessica Kingsley Publishers.

Jackson, P.L., Brunet, E., Meltzoff, A.N. and Decety, J. (2006) 'Empathy examined through the neural mechanisms involved in imaging how I feel versus how you feel pain.' *Neuropsychologia, 44,* 752–761.

Jacobsen, P. (2003) *Asperger Syndrome and Psychotherapy: Understanding Asperger Perspectives.* London: Jessica Kingsley Publishers.

James, W. (1884) *The Essential Writings.* B. Wilshire (ed.) Albany, NY: SUNY.

James, W. (1950) *The Principles of Psychology.* New York: Dover.

James, W. (1985[1902]) *The Varieties of Religious Experience.* New York: Penguin Classics.

Jaspers, K. (1959) *General Psychopathology.* Manchester: Manchester University Press.

Jawer, M.A. with Micozzi, M.S. (2009) *The Spiritual Anatomy of Emotion: How Feelings Link the Brain, the Body, and the Sixth Sense.* Rochester, VT: Park Street Press.

Jeong, M.J., Shim, C.K., Lee, J.O., Kwon, H.B., Kim, Y.H., Lee, S.K., Byun, M.O. and Park, S.C. (2008) 'Plant gene responses to frequency-specific sound signals.' *Molecular Breeding, 28,* 2, 217–226.

Jewell, A. (1998) *Spirituality and Ageing.* London: Jessica Kingsley Publishers.

Jewell, A. (2003) *Ageing, Spirituality and Well-Being.* London: Jessica Kingsley Publishers.

Jewell, A. (2011) *Spirituality and Personhood in Dementia.* London: Jessica Kingsley Publishers.

Johnson-Laird, P.N. (1989) 'Analogy and the exercise of creativity.' In S. Vosniadou and A. Ortony (eds) *Similarity and Analogical Reasoning.* Cambridge: Cambridge University Press.

Jones, S.S. and Smith, L.B. (1993) 'The place of perception in children's concepts.' *Cognitive Development, 8,* 113–139.

Jordan, R. and Powell, S.D. (1992) *Investigating Memory Processing in Children with Autism.* British Psychological Society Conference, London, 15–16 December.

Joseph, R. (1993) *The Naked Neuron.* New York: Plenum Press.

Jung, C.G. (1958) *The Undiscovered Self.* London: Routledge.

Kammer, E. (2007) *Discovering Who I Am: Growing Up in the Sensory World of Asperger Syndrome.* Inverness: Brandon Press.

Kanner, L. (1943) 'Autistic disturbances of affective contact.' *Nervous Child, 2,* 217–250.

Keighley, T. (1999) 'Woman of mystery.' *Nursing Standard, 12,* 34.

Khamsi, R. (2004) 'Electrical brainstorms busted as source of ghosts.' *BioEd Online,* December 9. Available at www.bioedonline.org/news/nature-news/electrical-brainstorms-busted-source-ghosts, accessed 30 April 2013.

Kihlstrom, J. (1987) 'The cognitive unconscious.' *Science, 237,* 285–294.

Kimball, M. (2005) 'Interpretations of the mind: An exploration of consciousness and autism.' Accessed at www.autism-society.org/site/DocServer/Interpretations_of_the_Mind. pdf?doc%5C on 22 March 2010 (no longer available).

Kircher, T. and David, A. (2003) 'Introduction: The self and neuroscience.' In T. Kircher and A. David (eds) *The Self in Neuroscience and Psychiatry.* Cambridge: Cambridge University Press.

Kish, D. (2011) 'FlashSonar: Understanding and applying sonar imaging to mobility.' *Future Reflections,* Winter. Available at www.nfb.org/images/nfb/Publications/fr/fr30/1/fr300107. htm, accessed 28 February 2013.

Klingberg, G. (1959) 'A study of religious experience in children from 9 to 13 years of age.' *Religious Education, 54,* 211–216.

Knight, M. (1955) *Morals Without Religion, and Other Essays.* London: Dobson.

Koehler, O. (1953) 'Thinking without words.' *Proceedings of the 14th International Zoological Congress.* Copenhagen: Elsevier Publishing Company.

Kohlberg, L. (1971) 'From "is" to "ought": How to commit the naturalistic fallacy and get away with it in the study of moral development.' In Theodore Mischel (ed.) *Cognitive Development and Epistemology.* New York: Academic Press.

Kohlberg, L. (1981) *Essays on Moral Development, Vol.1: The Philosophy of Moral Development.* San Francisco, CA: Harper and Row.

Krahn, I. and Fenton, A. (2009) 'Autism, empathy and questions of moral agency.' *Journal for Theory of Social Behaviour, 39,* 2, 145–166.

Krippner, S. and Welch, P. (1992) *Spiritual Dimensions of Healing.* New York: Irvington Publishers.

Kross, E., Berman, M.G., Mischel, W., Smith, E.E. and Wager, T.D. (2011) 'Social rejection shares somatosensory representations with physical pain.' *Proceedings of the National Academy of Sciences of the USA, 108,* 15, 6270–6275.

Krystal, H. (1988) *Integration and Self-Healing: Affect, Trauma, Alexithymia.* Hillsdale, NJ: Analytic.

Kuhn, T. (1962) *The Structure of Scientific Revolutions.* Chicago, IL: University of Chicago Press.

Labosh, K. (2011) *The Child with Autism Learns about Faith: 15 Ready-to-Use Scripture Lessons from the Garden of Eden to the Parting of the Red Sea.* Arlington, TX: Future Horizons.

Laderman, C. (1987) 'The Ambiguity of Symbols in the Structure of Healing.' *Social Science and Medicine, 24,* 293–301.

Laderman, C. (1993) *Taming the Wind of Desire: Psychology, Medicine, and Aesthetics in Malay Shamanistic Performance.* Berkeley, CA: University of California Press.

Lancaster, B.L. (2010) 'Cognitive neuroscience, spirituality and mysticism: Recent development.' In I. Clarke (ed.) *Psychosis and Spirituality,* 2nd edn. Oxford: Wiley-Blackwell.

Langdon, A.A. (1969) 'A critical examination of Dr Goldman's research study on religious thinking from childhood to adolescence.' *Journal of Christian Education, 12,* 37–63.

Langston, K. (2009) *Autism's Hidden Blessings: Discovering God's Promises for Autistic Children and Their Families.* Grand Rapids, MI: Kregel.

Lannert, J. (1991) 'Resistance and countertransference issues with spiritual and religious clients.' *Journal of Humanistic Psychology, 31,* 4, 68–76.

Laszlo, E. (2009) *The Akashic Experience, Science and the Cosmic Memory Field.* Vermont: Inner Traditions.

Lawson, W. (1998) *Life Behind Glass: A Personal Account of Autism Spectrum Disorder.* London: Jessica Kingsley Publishers.

LeDoux, J. (2003) 'The emotional brain, fear, and amygdala.' *Cellular and Molecular Neurobiology, 23,* 727–738.

LeDoux, J. (2006) In J. Brockman (ed.) *What We Believe But Cannot Prove: Today's Leading Thinkers on Science in the Age of Creativity.* London: Pocket Books.

Lehmann, A.C. and Myers, J.E. (eds) (1997) *Magic, Witchcraft and Religion: An Anthropological Study of the Supernatural,* 4th edn. Mountain View, CA: Mayfield Publishing.

Leslie, A., Mallon, R. and DiCorcia, J. (2006) 'Transgressors, victims, and cry babies: Is basic moral judgment spared in autism?' *Social Neuroscience, 1,* 270–283.

Lévi-Strauss, C. (1970) *The Raw and the Cooked. Introduction to a Science of Mythology,* vol. 1. London: Jonathan Cape.

Levine, P. and Frederick, A. (1997) *Waking the Tiger: Healing Trauma.* Berkeley, CA: North Atlantic Books.

Lewicki, P., Hill, T. and Czyzewska, M. (1992) 'Nonconscious acquisition of information.' *American Psychologist, 47,* 796–801.

Libet, B. (2002) 'The timing of mental events: Libet's experimental findings and their implications.' *Consciousness and Cognition, 11,* 291–299.

Lindbeck, G. (1984) *The Nature of Doctrine: Religion and Theology in a Post-Liberal Age.* Philadelphia, PA: Westminster Press.

Lo, V. and Schroer, S. (2005) 'Deviant airs in "traditional" Chinese medicine.' In J.S. Alter (ed.) *Asian Medicine and Globalization.* Philadelphia, PA: University of Pennsylvania Press.

Long, D., Elkind, D. and Spilka, B. (1967) 'The child's conception of prayer.' *Journal for the Scientific Study of Religion, 6,* 101–109.

Low, C. and Hsu, E. (2007) *Wind, Life, Health: Anthropological and Historical Perspectives.* Journal of the Royal Anthropological Institute Special Issue Book Series. Oxford: Wiley-Blackwell.

Lukoff, D. and Lu, F. (1988) 'Transpersonal psychology research review: Mystical experience.' *Journal of Transpersonal Psychology, 21,* 1, 161–184.

Lukoff, D., Lu, F. and Turner, R. (1998) 'From spiritual emergency to spiritual problem: The transpersonal roots of the new DSM-IV category.' *Journal of Humanistic Psychology, 38,* 2, 21–50.

Lutz, A., Dunne, J.D. and Davidson, R.J. (2007) 'Meditation and the neuroscience of consciousness: An introduction.' In P.D. Zelazo, M. Moscovitch and E. Thompson (eds) *The Cambridge Handbook of Consciousness.* Cambridge: Cambridge University Press.

Mackey, J.P. (1996) 'Christianity and cultures: Theology, science and the science of religion.' *Studies in World Christianity, 2,* 1, 1–25.

MacKinlay, E. (2008) *Ageing, Disability and Spirituality: Addressing the Challenge of Disability in Later Life.* London: Jessica Kingsley Publishers.

MacKinlay, E. (2010) *Ageing and Spirituality across Faiths and Cultures.* London: Jessica Kingsley Publishers.

Malinowski, B. (1974) *Magic, Science and Religion and Other Essays.* London: Souvenir Press. (Originally published 1948.)

Mandler, J.M. (1992) 'How to build a baby: II. Conceptual primitives.' *Psychological Review, 99,* 587–604.

Markram, H., Rinaldi, T. and Markram, K. (2007) 'The intense world syndrome – an alternative hypothesis for autism.' *Frontiers in Neuroscience, 1,* 77–96.

Marrett, R.R. (1920) *Psychology and Folklore.* London: Methuen.

Marty, M.E. (1985) 'Introduction.' In W. James, *The Variety of Religious Experience.* New York: Penguin Classics.

Maslow, A.H. (1970a) *Religions, Values, and Peak-Experiences.* New York: Penguin.

Maslow, A.H. (1970b) *Motivation and Personality,* 2nd edn. New York: Harper and Bros.

Matte-Blanco, I. (1975) *The Unconscious as Infinite Sets: An Essay in Bi-Logic.* London: Duckworth.

Matte-Blanco, I. (1988) *Thinking, Feeling, and Being: Clinical Reflections on the Fundamental Antinomy of Human Beings and World.* London: Routledge.

Mayer, J.D. (2000) 'Spiritual intelligence or spiritual consciousness?' *International Journal for the Psychology of Religion, 10,* 1, 47–56.

Mayer, J.D., Caruso, D.R. and Salovey, P. (1999) 'Emotional intelligence meets traditional standards for an intelligence.' *Intelligence, 27,* 267–298.

Mayer, J.D. and Salovey, P. (1993) 'The intelligence of emotional intelligence.' *Intelligence, 17,* 433–442.

Mayer, J.D. and Salovey, P. (1997) 'What is emotional intelligence?' In P. Salovey and D. Sluyter (eds) *Emotional Development and Emotional Intelligence: Implications for Educators.* New York: Basic Books.

Mayer, J.D., Salovey, P. and Caruso, D.R. (2002) *MSCEIT.* Toronto, Ontario: Multi-Health Systems.

McCreery, E. (1996) 'Talking to children about things spiritual.' In R. Best (ed.) *Education, Spirituality and the Whole Child.* London: Cassell.

McGaugh, J.L. (2004) 'The amygdala modulates the consolidation of memories of emotionally arousing experiences.' *Annual Review of Neuroscience, 27,* 1–28.

McGrady, E. (1994) 'Metaphorical and operational aspects of religious thinking: Research with Irish Catholic pupils.' *British Journal of Religious Education, 16,* 148–163.

McKean, T. (1999) 'Sensory anomalies.' Accessed at www.geocities.com/~soonlight/SWCTL/ARTICLES/sensanom.htm on 23 October 2002.

McWilliams, N. (1994) *Psychoanalytic Diagnosis: Understanding Personality Structure in the Clinical Process.* New York: Guilford.

McWilliams, N. (2011) 'Some thoughts about schizoid dynamics.' *International Psychoanalysis net.* Available at http://internationalpsychoanalysis.net/wp-content/uploads/2011/07/McWilliamsschizoid_dynamics.pdf, accessed 28 February 2013.

Meehan, C. (2002) 'Confusion and competing claims in spiritual development debate.' *International Journal of Children's Spirituality, 7,* 3, 291–308.

Menzel, E.W. (1970) 'Cognitive mapping in chimpanzees.' In S.H. Hulse, H. Fowler and W.F. Honig (eds) *Cognitive Processes in Animal Behavior.* Hillsdale, NJ: Erlbaum.

Merabet, L.B., Maguire, D., Warde, A., Altertescu, K., Stickgold, R. and Pascal-Leone, A. (2004) 'Visual hallucinations during prolonged blindfolding in sighted subjects.' *Journal of Neuro-Ophthalmology, 24,* 2, 109–113.

Merton, T. (1958) *Thoughts in Solitude.* Boston, MA: Shambhala Publications.

Merton, T. (1968) *Zen and the Birds of Appetite.* New York: New Directions.

Moffett, J. (1994) *The Universal Schoolhouse: Spiritual Awakening through Education.* San Francisco, CA: Jossey-Bass.

Montagu, A. (1978) *Touching: The Human Significance of the Skin,* 2nd edn. New York: Harper and Row.

Morgan, H. (2004) 'Spiritual healing.' *Learning Disability Practice, 7,* 5, 8–9.

Mosse, H.L. (1958) 'The misuse of the diagnosis childhood schizophrenia.' *American Journal of Psychiatry,* 114, 9, 791–794.

Muir, E. (1964) *An Autobiography.* London: Methuen.

Mukhopadhyay, T. (2000) *Beyond the Silence: My Life, the World and Autism.* London: National Autistic Society.

Mukhopadhyay, T. (2008) *How Can I Talk If My Lips Don't Move?: Inside My Autistic Mind.* New York: Arcade Publishing.

Mullan, S. and Penfield, W. (1959) 'Illusions of comparative interpretation and emotion.' *Archives of Neurology and Psychology, 81,* 269–285.

Murchie, G. (1978) *The Seven Mysteries of Life.* Boston, MA: Houghton Mifflin.

Nagel, T. (1974) 'What is it like to be a bat?' *Philosophical Review, 83,* 435–450.

Nagel, T. (1986) *The View from Nowhere.* New York: Oxford University Press.

Nagy, J. and Szatmari, P. (1986) 'A chart review of schizotypical personality disorders in children.' *Journal of Autism and Developmental Disorders, 16,* 351–367.

Neumann, E. (1964) 'Mystical man.' In J. Campbell (ed.), *The Mystic Vision,* Princeton, NJ: Princeton University Press.

Newberg, A., d'Aquili, E. and Rause, V. (2001) *Why God Won't Go Away: Brain Science and the Biology of Belief.* New York: Ballantine.

Newberg, A. and Waldman, M.R. (2010) *How God Changes Your Brain: Breakthrough Findings from a Leading Neuroscientist.* New York: Ballantine.

Nye, R. (2009) *Children's Spirituality.* London: Church House Publishing.

Nye, R. and Hay, D. (1996) 'Identifying children's spirituality: How do you start without a starting point?' *British Journal of Religious Education, 18,* 3, 144–154.

Obeyesekere, G. (1981) *Medusa's Hair: An Essay of Personal Symbols and Religious Experience.* Chicago, IL: University of Chicago Press.

Olson, E.T. (1998) 'There is no problem of the self.' *Journal of Consciousness Studies, 5,* 5–6, 645–657.

O'Murchu, D. (1997) *Reclaiming Spirituality: A New Spiritual Framework for Today's World.* Dublin: Gateway.

O'Neill, J. (1999) *Through the Eyes of Aliens: A Book about Autistic People.* London: Jessica Kingsley Publishers.

O'Neill, J. (2000) 'I live in a home within myself.' *The NAS on-line article* (no longer available).

O'Neill, J. (2003) 'My experiences being autistic.' Accessed at www.bluepsy.com/jasmine.html on 5 April 2001.

Osborn, J. and Derbyshire, S.W.G. (2010) 'Pain sensation evoked by observing injury in others.' *Pain, 148,* 2, 268–274.

Otto, R. (1950) *The Idea of the Holy.* Oxford: Oxford University Press.

Oyebode, F. (2008) *Sims' Symptoms in the Mind: An Introduction to Descriptive Psychopathology,* 4th edn. Philadelphia, PA: Elsevier.

Palmer, J. (1979) 'A community mail survey of psychic experiences.' *Journal of the American Society for Psychic Research, 73,* 3, 221–251.

Paloutzin, R., Emmons, R. and Keortge, S. (2003) 'Spiritual well-being, spiritual intelligence, and healthy workplace policy.' In R. Giacalone and C. Jurkiewicz (eds) *Handbook of Workplace Spirituality and Organizational Performance.* New York: M.E. Sharpe.

Panksepp, J. (1994) 'The basics of basic emotions.' In P. Ekman and R.J. Davidson (eds) *The Nature of Emotion: Fundamental Questions.* New York: Oxford University Press.

Patterson, F. (1980) 'Innovative uses of language by a gorilla: A case study.' In K. Nelson (ed.) *Children's Language,* vol. 2. New York: Gardener.

Paul, K. (1975) *Revelation and Divination in Ndembu Ritual.* Ithaca, NY: Cornell University Press.

Pearsall, P. (1998) *The Heart's Code: Tapping the Wisdom and Power of Our Heart Energy.* New York: Broadway Books.

Peck, M.S. (1978) *The Road Less Traveled: A New Psychology of Love, Traditional Values and Spiritual Growth.* New York: Simon & Schuster.

Peck, M.S. (1987) *A Different Drum: Community Making Peace.* New York: Simon & Schuster.

Penfield, W. and Perrot, P. (1963) 'The brain's record of auditory and visual experience.' *Brain, 86,* 595–596.

Persinger, M. (1977) *Space-Time Transients and Unusual Events.* Chicago, IL: Nelson-Hall.

Persinger, M. (1987) *Neuropsychological Bases of God Beliefs.* Westport, CT: Praeger.

Persinger, M. (1988) 'Increased geomagnetic activity and the occurrence of bereavement hallucinations: Evidence for melatonin-mediated microseizuring in the temporal lobe?' *Neuroscience Letters, 88,* 271–274.

Persinger, M.A (1989) 'Geophysical variables and behavior: LV. Predicting the details of visitor experiences and the personality of experients: the temporal lobe factor.' *Perceptual and Motor Skills, 68,* 1, 55–65.

Persinger, M.A. (1992) 'Enhanced incidence of "the sensed presence" in people who have learned to meditate: Support for the right hemispheric intrusion hypothesis.' *Perceptual and Motor Skills, 75,* 3, 1308–1310.

Persinger, M.A. (1993a) 'Paranormal and religious beliefs may be mediated differentially by subcortical and cortical phenomenological processes of the temporal (limbic) lobes.' *Perceptual and Motor Skills, 76,* 1, 247–251.

Persinger, M.A. (1993b) 'Vectorial cerebral hemisphericity as differential sources for the sensed presence, mystical experiences and religious conversions.' *Perceptual and Motor Skills, 76,* 3, 915–930.

Persinger, M.A. (1996) 'Feelings of past lives as expected perturbations within the neurocognitive processes that generate the sense of self: Contributions from limbic lability and vectorial hemisphericity.' *Perceptual and Motor Skills, 83,* 3, 1107–1121.

Persinger, M.A., Bureau, Y.R., Peredery, O.P. and Richards, P.M. (1994) 'The sensed presence within experimental settings: Implications for the male and female concept of self.' *Journal of Psychology, 78,* 3, 999–1009.

Persinger, M.A. and Healey, F. (2002) 'Experimental facilitation of the sensed presence: Possible intercalation between the hemispheres induced by complex magnetic fields.' *Journal of Nervous and Mental Disease, 190,* 8: 533–541.

Persinger, M. and Koren, S. (2005) 'A response to Granqvist *et al.* 'Sensed presence and mystical experiences are predicted by suggestibility, not by the application of transcranial weak magnetic fields.' *Neuroscience Letters, 380,* 3, 346–347.

Persinger, M.A. and Makarec, K. (1992) 'The feeling of a presence and verbal meaningfulness in context of temporal lobe function: Factor analytic verification of the muses?' *Brain and Cognition, 20,* 2, 217–226.

Persinger, M.A, Saroka, K., Koren, S.A. and St-Pierre, L.S. (2010) 'The electromagnetic induction of mystical and altered states within the laboratory.' *Journal of Consciousness Exploration and Research, 1,* 7, 808–830.

Persinger, M.A., Tiller, S.G. and Koren, S.A. (2000) 'Experimental simulation of a haunt experience and elicitation of paroxysmal electroencephalographic activity by transcerebral complex magnetic fields: Induction of a synthetic "ghost"?' *Perceptual and Motor Skills, 90,* 2, 659–674.

Pert, C.B. (1997) *Molecules of Emotion: Why You Feel the Way You Feel.* New York: Scribner.

Piechowski, M.M. (1999) 'Overexcitabilities.' In M.A. Runco and S.R. Pritzker (eds) *Encyclopedia of Creativity.* Burlington, MA: Academic Press.

Piedmont, R. (1999) 'Does spirituality represent the sixth factor of personality: Spiritual transcendence and the five-factor model?' *Journal of Personality, 67,* 6, 985–1013.

Pierce, K., Muller, R.A., Ambrose, J., Allen, G. and Courchesne, E. (2001) 'Face processing outside the fusiform "face area" in autism: Evidence from functional MRI.' *Brain, 124,* 2059–2073.

Pillsbury, W.B. (1908) *Attention.* North Stratford, NH: Ayer.

Piper, E. (2002) 'Faith development: A critique of Fowler's model and a proposed alternative.' *Journal of Liberal Religion, 3,* 1–16.

Pöppel, E., Held, R. and Frost, D. (1974) 'Residual visual function after brain wounds involving the central visual pathways in man.' *Nature, 243,* 295–296.

Powell, S.D. and Jordan, R.R. (1993) 'Being subjective about autistic thinking and learning to learn.' *Educational Psychology, 13,* 359–370.

Preston, S.D. and de Waal, F.B.M. (2002) 'Empathy: Each is in the right – hopefully, not all in the wrong.' *Behavioral and Brain Science, 25,* 1–71.

Provine, R.R. (2000) *Laughter: A Scientific Investigation.* London: Faber & Faber.

Provine, R.R. (2006) In J. Brockman (ed.) *What We Believe But Cannot Prove: Today's Leading Thinkers on Science in the Age of Creativity.* London: Pocket Books.

Radin, D. (1998) *The Conscious Universe: The Scientific Truth of Psychic Phenomena.* London: HarperCollins.

Rahner, K. (1974) 'The experience of God today.' In *Theological Investigations,* 11 (trans. D. Bourke). London: Darton, Longman and Todd.

Ramachandran, V. (2003) *The Emerging Mind: The BBC Reith Lectures 2003.* London: Profile Books.

Ramachandran, V.S. (2011) *The Tell-Tale Brain.* New York: Norton.

Ranson, D. (2002) *Across the Great Divide: Bridging Spirituality and Religion Today.* Strathfield, NSW: St Paul's.

Reber, A.S. (1993) *Implicit Learning and Tacit Knowledge: An Essay on the Cognitive Unconscious.* New York: Oxford University Press.

Reichel-Dolmatoff, G. (1997) *Rainforest Shamans.* Totnes: Themis Books.

Rensink, R.A. (2000) 'The dynamic representation of scenes.' *Visual Cognition, 7,* 17–42.

Rentenbach, B. (2009) *Synergy.* Bloomington, IN: AuthorHouse.

Ristau, C. (ed.) (1991) *Cognitive Ethology: The Mind of Other Animals.* Hillsdale, NJ: Erlbaum.

Robbins, I. (2008) 'Total Isolation.' BBC documentary. 22 January.

Roberts, R.D., Zeidner, M. and Matthew, G. (2001) 'Does emotional intelligence meet traditional standards for an intelligence: Some data and new conclusions.' *Emotion, 1,* 196–231.

Robinson, E. (1983) *The Original Vision.* New York: Seabury Press.

Rogers, K., Dziobek, I., Hassenstab, J., Wolf, O.T. and Convit, A. (2006) 'Who cares? Revisiting empathy in Asperger syndrome.' *Journal of Autism and Developmental Disorders, 37,* 4, 709–715.

Ross, C.A. and Joshi, S. (1992) 'Paranormal experiences in general population.' *Journal of Nervous and Mental Disease, 180,* 6, 357–361.

Rossiter, G. (2005) 'From St Ignatius to Obe-Wan Kenobi: An evaluative perspective on spirituality for school education.' *Journal of Religious Education, 53*, 1, 3–22.

Rubenstein, J.L.R. and Merzenich, M.M. (2003) 'Model of autism: Increased ratio of excitation/ inhibition in key neural systems.' *Genes, Brain and Behavior, 2*, 255–267.

Russell, J. (1994) Agency and early mental development. In J. Bermudez, A.J. Marcel and N. Eilan (eds.) *The Body and the Self.* Cambridge, MA: MIT Press.

Russell, J. (1996) *Agency and Its Role in Development.* London: Erlbaum.

Russell, P. (2002) *From Science to God.* Novato, CA: New World Library.

Ruttan, L.A., Persinger, M.A. and Koren, S. (1990) 'Enhancement of temporal lobe-related experiences during brief exposures to milligauss intensity extremely low frequency magnetic fields.' *Journal of Bioelectricity, 9*, 1, 33–54.

Sacks, O. (2012) *Hallucinations.* London: Picador.

Samuel, G. (1990) *Mind, Body and Culture: Anthropology and the Biological Interface.* Cambridge and New York: Cambridge University Press.

Samuel, G. (2005) 'Subtle bodies in Indian and Tibetan yoga: Scientific and spiritual meanings.' Paper for the panel 'Rethinking Subtle Bodies in Indian and Tibetan Yoga', Second International Conference on Religion and Cultures in the Indic Civilisation, Delhi, India, 17–20 December.

Samuel, G. (2007) 'Autistic spectrum conditions and religion: Some anthropological notes.' Paper presented at the Autism and Religion Symposium, University of Aberdeen, Aberdeen, 15–16 December.

Samuel, G. (2008) 'Tibetan longevity practices: The body in the "chi med srog thig" tradition.' Paper for the panel 'Theory and Practice of Healing, Medicine and Longevity in Buddhism', 15th Conference of the International Association of Buddhist Studies (IABS), Atlanta, Georgia, 23–28 June.

Samuel, G. (2009) 'Autism and meditation.' *Journal of Religion, Disability and Health, 13*, 1–9.

Samuel, G. (2010) 'Healing, Efficacy and the Spirits.' *Journal of Ritual Studies, 24*, 2, 7–20.

Sapir, E. (1949) *Selected Writing in Language, Culture, and Personality,* ed. D.G. Mandelbaum. Berkeley, CA: University of California Press. (Originally published 1929.)

Sapontzis, S.F. (1980) 'Are animals moral beings?' *American Philosophical Quarterly, 17*, 1, 45–52.

Scharfetter, C. (1981) 'Ego-psychopathology: The concept and its empirical evaluation.' *Psychological Medicine, 11*, 273–280.

Scharfetter, C. (1995) *The Self-experience of Schizophrenics: Empirical Studies of the Ego/Self in Schizophrenia, Borderline Disorders and Depression.* Zurich: Private publication.

Scharfetter, C. (2003) 'The self-experience of schizophrenics.' In T. Kircher and A. David (eds) *The Self in Neuroscience and Psychiatry.* Cambridge: Cambridge University Press.

Scharfstein, B. (1973) *Mystical Experience.* New York: Bobbs-Merrill.

Scherer, K.R. (1994) 'Toward a concept of "modal emotions".' In P. Ekman and R.J. Davidson (eds) *The Nature of Emotion: Fundamental Questions.* New York: Oxford University Press.

Schleiermacher, F. (1928) *The Christian Faith.* Edinburgh: T. & T. Clark.

Schleiermacher, F. (1958) *On Religion: Speeches to its Cultural Despisers.* New York: Harper and Row.

Schneider, E. (1999) *Discovering My Autism: Apologia Pro Vita Sua (with Apologies to Cardinal Newman).* London: Jessica Kingsley Publishers.

Schoonmaker, S. (2008) 'Predicting human behavior.' Accessed at www.sheilaschoonmaker.com on 3 October 2008 (no longer available).

Schultz, R.T. (2005) 'Developmental deficits in social perception in autism: The role of the amygdala and fusiform face area.' *International Journal of Developmental Neuroscience, 23*, 125–141.

Schulz, M.L. (1998) *Awakening Intuition.* New York: Harmony Books.

Scott, D. (2006) 'Spirituality and identity within/without religion.' In M. de Souza, K. Engebretson, G. Durka, R. Jackson and A. McGrady (eds) *International Handbook of the Religious, Moral and Spiritual Dimensions in Education.* Dordrecht: Springer.

Selznick, P. (1992) *The Moral Commonwealth: Social Theory and the Promise of Community.* Berkeley, CA: University of California Press.

Sensky, T. and Fenwick, P. (1982) 'Religiosity, mystical experience and epilepsy.' In F. Clifford Rose (ed.) *Progress in Epilepsy.* London: Pitman.

Shafranske, E. and Maloney, H. (1990) 'Clinical psychologists' religious and spiritual orientations and their practice of psychotherapy.' *Psychotherapy, 27,* 72–78.

Shamy, E. (2003) *A Guide to the Spiritual Dimension of Care for Alzheimer's Disease and Related Dementia.* London: Jessica Kingsley Publishers.

Shiffrin, R.M. (1988) 'Attention.' In R.C. Atkinson, R.J. Herrnstein, G. Lnidzey and R.D. Luce (eds) *Steven's Handbook of Experimental Psychology: Vol. 2: Learning and Cognition.* New York: Wiley.

Shore, S. (n.d.) 'My life with autism: Implications for educators.' Accessed at www.behaviorstore. com/behavior/default.asp?pgC=article2 (no longer available).

Shweder, R.A. (1994) ''You're not sick, you're just in love': Emotion as an interpretive system.' In P. Ekman and R.J. Davidson (eds) *The Nature of Emotion: Fundamental Questions.* New York: Oxford University Press.

Sinclair, J. (1992) 'Bridging the gaps: An inside-out view of autism.' In E. Schopler and G. B. Mesibov (eds) *High-Functioning Individuals with Autism.* New York: Plenum Press, pp.294–302.

Sinclair, J. (1993) 'Don't mourn for us.' *Our Voice, 1,* 3, 3–6.

Sinetar, M. (2000) *Spiritual Intelligence: What We Can Learn from the Early Awakening Child.* New York: Orbis.

Sireteanu, R., Oertel, V., Mohr, H., Linden, D. and Singer, W. (2008) 'Graphical illustration and functional neuroimaging of visual hallucinations during prolonged blindfolding: A comparison to visual imagery.' *Perception, 37,* 1805–1821.

Smart, N. (1996) *Dimensions of the Sacred: An Anatomy of the World's Beliefs.* London: HarperCollins.

Smith, W.C. (1979) *Faith and Belief: The Difference between Them.* Princeton, NJ: Princeton University Press.

Snyder, A.W. (1997) 'Autistic artists give clues to cognition.' *Perception, 26,* 93–96.

Snyder, A.W., Bossomaier, T. and Mitchell, J.D. (2004) 'Concept formation: "Object" attributes dynamically inhibited from conscious awareness.' *Journal of Integrative Neuroscience, 3,* 1, 31–46.

Snyder, A.W. and Mitchell, J.D. (1999) 'Is integer arithmetic fundamental to mental processing?: The mind's secret arithmetic.' *Proceedings of the Royal Society of London, 266,* 587–592.

Snyder, A.W., Mulcahy, E., Taylor, J.L., Mitchell, D.J., Sachdev, P. and Gandevia, S.C. (2003) 'Savant-like skills exposed in normal people by suppressing the left front-temporal lobe.' *Journal of Integrative Neuroscience, 2,* 149–158.

Sobrino, J. (1993) 'Spirituality and the following of Jesus.' In I. Ellacuria and J. Sobrino (eds) *Mysterium Liberationis: Fundamental Concepts of Liberation Theology.* New York: SCM Press.

Solomon, R. (1988) *Continental Philosophy since 1750: The Rise and Fall of the Self.* Oxford: Oxford University Press.

Sonnby-Borgström, M. (2002) 'The facial expression says more than words. Is emotional contagion via facial expression the first step toward empathy?' *Lakartidningen, 99,* 1438–1442.

Spencer, H. (1876) *The Principles of Sociology.* London: Williams and Norgate.

Speraw, S. (2006) 'Spiritual experiences of parents and caregivers who have children with disabilities or special needs.' *Issues in Mental Health Nursing, 27,* 213–230.

Sperber, D. (1975) *Rethinking Symbolism.* Cambridge: Cambridge University Press.

Spiro, M.E. (1973) 'Religion: Problems of definition and explanation.' In M. Banton (ed.) *Anthropological Approaches to the Study of Religion.* ASA Monographs 3. London: Tavistock.

Ssuchareva, G.E. (1926) 'Die Schizoiden Psychopathien im Kindesalter.' *Monatschrift für Psychiatrie und Neurologie, 60,* 235–261.

Stern, D.N. (1994) 'One way to build a clinically relevant baby.' *Infant Mental Health Journal, 15,* 9–25.

Stevenson, I. (1997) *Reincarnation and Biology.* Western, CT: Praeger.

Stillman, W. (2006) *Autism and the God Connection.* Naperville, IL: Sourcebooks.

Stillman, W. (2008) *The Soul of Autism: Looking beyond Labels to Unveil Spiritual Secrets of the Heart Savants.* Franklin Lakes, NJ: New Page Books.

Stillman, W. (2010) *The Autism Prophecies.* Franklin Lakes, NJ: New Page Books.

Strawson, G. (1997) 'The self.' *Journal of Consciousness Studies, 4,* 5–6, 405–428.

Surakka, V. and Hietanen, J.K. (1998) 'Facial and emotional reactions to Duchenne and non-Duchenne smiles.' *International Journal of Psychophysiology, 29,* 23–33.

Suzuki, D.T. (1957) *Mysticism Christian and Buddhist.* London: George Allen and Unwin.

Sweeten, T.L., Posey, D.J., Shekhar, A. and McDougle, C.J. (2002) 'The amygdala and related structures in the pathophysiology of autism.' *Pharmacology, Biochemistry and Behavior, 71,* 449–455.

Swinton, J. (2001) *Spirituality and Mental Health Care: Rediscovering a 'Forgotten' Dimension.* London: Jessica Kingsley Publishers.

Szatmari, P., Bartolucci, G. and Bremner, R. (1989) 'Asperger syndrome and autism: Comparisons on early history and outcome.' *Developmental Medicine and Child Neurology, 31,* 709–720.

Tacey, D. (2000) *ReEnchantement, the New Australian Spirituality.* Sydney: HarperCollins.

Tacey, D. (2003) *The Spirituality Revolution. The Emergence of Contemporary Spirituality.* Sidney: HarperCollins.

Talbot, M. (1996) *The Holographic Universe.* London: HarperCollins.

Tammet, D. (2006) *Born on a Blue Day: A Memoir of Asperger's and an Extraordinary Mind.* London: Hodder & Stoughton.

Tammet, D. (2009) *Embracing the Wide Sky.* London: Hodder & Stoughton.

Tamminen, R. (1991) *Religious Development in Childhood and Youth.* Helsinki: Suomalainen Tiedeakatemia.

Tamminen, R. (1994) 'Religious experiences in childhood and adolescence: A viewpoint of religious development between the ages of 7 and 20.' *International Journal for the Psychology of Religion, 4,* 61–85.

Tandy, V. (2001) 'Ghost sounds: A review and discussion of the infrasound theory of apparitions.' *International Journal of Parapsychology, 12,* 2, 131–151.

Tanquerey, A. (1923) *The Spiritual Life: A Treatise on Ascetical and Mystical Theology.* New York: Desclee.

Tantam, D. (2009) *Can the World Afford Autistic Spectrum Disorders?: Nonverbal Communication, Asperger Syndrome and the Interbrain.* London: Jessica Kingsley Publishers.

Tart, C. (1997) *Body, Mind, Spirit.* Charlottesville, VA: Hampton Roads Publishing.

Tart, C. (2009) *The End of Materialism: How the Evidence of the Paranormal is Bringing Science and Spirit Together.* Oakland, CA: Noetic Books/New Harbinger.

Taylor, J. (1989) *Innocent Wisdom: Children as Spiritual Guides.* New York: Pilgrim Press.

Thalbourne, M.A. and Maltby, J. (2008) 'Transliminality, thin boundaries, unusual experiences, and temporal lobe lability.' *Personality and Individual Differences, 44,* 1617–1623.

Thatcher, A. (1999) 'Theology, spirituality and the curriculum: An overview.' In A. Thatcher (ed.) *Spirituality and the Curriculum.* London: Cassell.

Thomas, P. (1997) *The Dialectics of Schizophrenia.* London: Free Association Books.

Thompson, D. (ed.) (1995) *The Concise Oxford Dictionary of Current English.* Oxford: Clarendon Press.

Thompson, I. (2002) 'Mental health and spiritual care.' *Nursing Standard, 17,* 9, 33–38.

Thun, T. (1963) *Die religiöse Entscheidung der Jugend.* Stuttgart: Ernst Klett.

Thun, T. (1964) *Die Religion des Kindes,* 2nd edn. Stuttgart: Ernst Klett.

Tobert, N. (2010) 'The polarities of consciousness.' In I. Clarke (ed.) *Psychosis and Spirituality,* 2nd edn. Oxford: Wiley-Blackwell.

Tolle, E. (2005) *A New Earth.* New York: Penguin Books.

Toulmin, S.E. (1977) 'Self-knowledge and knowledge of the "self".' In T. Mischel (ed.) *The Self: The Psychological and Philosophical Perspectives.* Oxford: Blackwell.

Tranel, D. and Damasio, A. (1993) 'The covert learning of affective valence does not require structures in hippocampal system or amygdala.' *Journal of Cognitive Neuroscience, 5,* 79–88.

Turner, E. (1992) *Experiencing Ritual.* Philadelphia, PA: University of Pennsylvania.

Turner, V.W. (1969) *The Ritual Process.* London: Routledge.

Tustin, F. (1974) *Autism and Childhood Psychosis.* London: Hogarth Press.

Tylor, E.B. (1958[1871]) *Religion in Primitive Culture,* Vol. 2. New York: Harper & Row.

van Krevelen, D.A. (1971) 'Early infantile autism and autistic psychopathy.' *Journal of Autism and Childhood Schizophrenia, 1,* 1, 82–86.

Varela, F. and Depraz, N. (2003) 'Imagining, embodiment, phenomenology, and transformation.' In B.A. Wallace (ed.) *Buddhism and Science: Breaking New Ground.* New York: Columbia University Press.

Velmans, M. (1991) 'Is human information processing conscious?' *Behavioral and Brain Sciences, 14,* 651–726.

Verny, T. with Kelly, J. (1981) *The Secret Life of the Unborn Child.* New York: Dell Publishing.

Vygotsky, L. (1962) *Thought and Language.* Cambridge, MA: MIT Press.

Wach, J. (1958) *The Comparative Study of Religions.* New York: Columbia University Press.

Walsch, N.D. (2005) *What God Wants: A Compelling Answer to Humanity's Biggest Question.* London: Hodder Mobius.

Walsh, R. and Roche, L. (1979) 'Precipitation of acute psychotic episodes by intensive meditation in individuals with a history of schizophrenia.' *American Journal of Psychiatry, 136,* 1085–1086.

Wapnick, K. (1981) 'Mysticism and schizophrenia.' In R. Woods (ed.) *Understanding Mysticism.* London: Athlone Press.

Warneken, F. and Tomasello, M. (2006) 'Altruistic helping in human infants and young chimpanzees.' *Science, 311,* 5765, 1301–1303.

Watson, L. (1974) *Supernature: A Natural History of Supernatural.* London: Coronet Books.

Webb, J.T., Amend, E.R., Webb, N.E., Coerss, J., Beljan, P. and Olenchak, F.R. (2005) *Misdiagnosis and Dual Diagnoses of Gifted Children and Adults.* Scottsdale, AZ: Great Potential Press.

Weiskrantz, L. (1986) *Blindsight: A Case Study and Implications.* Oxford: Oxford University Press.

Weiskrantz, L. (1996) 'Blindsight revisited.' *Current Opinion in Experimental Psychology, 6,* 215–220.

Weiskrantz, L., Warrington, E.K., Sanders, M.D. and Marshall, J. (1974) 'Visual capacity in the hemianopic field following a restricted occipital ablation.' *Brain, 97,* 709–728.

Wertham, F. (1950) 'The Mosaic Test.' In L. Abt and L. Bellak (eds) *Projective Psychology.* New York: Alfred A. Knopf.

West, T. (1991) *In the Mind's Eye.* New York: Prometheus Press.

Whorf, B.L. (1956) *Language, Thought and Reality. Selected Writings.* Cambridge, MA: MIT Press.

Wickramasekera, I. (1998) 'Secrets kept from the mind but not the body of behaviour: The unsolved problems of identifying and treating somatization and psychological disease.' *Advances in Mind-Body Medicine, 14,* 81–132.

Williams, D. (1996) *Autism: An Inside-Out Approach.* London: Jessica Kingsley Publishers.

Williams, D. (1998) *Autism and Sensing: The Unlost Instinct.* London: Jessica Kingsley Publishers.

Williams, D. (1999a) *Like Colour to the Blind: Soul Searching and Soul Finding.* London: Jessica Kingsley Publishers.

Williams, D. (1999b) *Nobody Nowhere: The Remarkable Autobiography of an Autistic Girl.* London: Jessica Kingsley Publishers.

Williams, D. (1999c) *Somebody Somewhere: Breaking Free from the World of Autism.* London: Jessica Kingsley Publishers.

Wilson, S.C. and Barber, N.X. (1983) 'The fantasy-prone personality: Implications for understanding imagery, hypnosis, and parapsychological phenomena.' In A.A. Sheik (ed.) *Imagery: Current Theory, Research and Application.* New York: John Wiley & Sons.

Wing, L. (1996) *The Autistic Spectrum: A Guide for Parents and Professionals.* London: Constable and Company.

Winnicott, D.W. (1960) 'Ego distortion in terms of true and false self.' In M.R. Khan (ed.) *The Maturational Processes and the Facilitating Environment: Studies in the Theory of Emotional Development.* New York: International Universities Press.

Winnicott, D.W. (1963) 'Communicating and not communicating leading to a study of certain opposites.' In M.R. Khan (ed.) *The Maturational Processes and the Facilitating Environment: Studies in the Theory of Emotional Development.* New York: International Universities Press.

Wolff, S. (1995) *Loners: The Life Path of Unusual Children.* London: Routledge.

Wolff, S. and Chess, S. (1964) 'A behavioural study of schizophrenic children.' *Acta Psychiatrca Scandinavica, 40,* 438–466.

Wolman, R. (2001) *Thinking With Your Soul.* New York: Harmony Books.

Wolski Conn, J. (ed.) (1986) *Women's Spirituality: Resources for Christian Development.* New York: Paulist Press.

Wulff, D. (1996) *Psychology of Religion: Classic and Contemporary Views,* 2nd edn. New York: John Wiley.

Zahavi, D. (2003) 'Phenomenology of self.' In T. Kircher and A. David (eds) *The Self in Neuroscience and Psychiatry.* Cambridge: Cambridge University Press.

Zald, D.H. (2003) 'The human amygdala and the emotional evaluation of sensory stimuli.' *Brain Research Review, 41,* 88–123.

Zohar, D. and Marshall, I. (2000) *SQ: Spiritual Intelligence: The Ultimate Intelligence.* London: Bloomsbury.

Zubek, J.P., Pushkar, D., Sansom, W. and Gowing, J. (1961) 'Perceptual changes after prolonged sensory isolation (darkness and silence).' *Canadian Journal of Psychology, 15,* 83–101.

Subject Index

Author Index